CONDUCT UNBECOMING

A Memoir

CONDUCT UNBECOMING

A Memoir

DESMOND O'MALLEY ∿

Gill & Macmillan

Gill & Macmillan
Hume Avenue, Park West, Dublin 12
www.gillmacmillanbooks.ie

© Desmond O'Malley 2014
978 07171 6226 0

Index compiled by Eileen O'Neill
Typography design by Make Communication
Print origination by Carole Lynch
Printed and bound by CPI Group (UK) Ltd,
Croydon, CR0 4YY

This book is typeset in Linotype Minion and
Neue Helvetica.

The paper used in this book comes from the
wood pulp of managed forests. For every tree
felled, at least one tree is planted, thereby
renewing natural resources.

A CIP catalogue record for this book is available
from the British Library.

5 4 3 2 1

Patris ad memoriam

CONTENTS

PREFACE

In writing this memoir I have ventured to set out my strongest recollections of what has been a fairly long and varied career in public life.

Before doing so, however, I must emphasise that these are mere impressions, not history. The events described herein have, for one reason or another, stayed with me over the decades, but I'd be naïve were I to pretend they constituted more than the written testimony of one man. My perspective, in other words, is not to be mistaken for that of the archivist or historian.

I was variously a participant in and observer of important events, often in difficult times and during periods of great change. As such, I feel I am obliged to comment on them and, in commenting, attempt to give some insight into the political events that have shaped Ireland's recent past. I also feel a duty of sorts to demonstrate the extent to which consensus views of Irish political and cultural life are open to challenge.

Because this is more an impressionistic rendering of a particular time and place than it is a photo-realistic record, I do not go into the lengthy detail that history requires. I can only recall my own experiences of events such as the Arms Crisis and the Beef Tribunal, describing the taste each episode left in my mouth.

This book concentrates on what happened during my various periods as a minister. I have largely avoided more recent events in which I was not directly involved. I have tried to confine myself to occurrences of which I had first-hand knowledge.

During my time in politics I have seen Ireland go through many upheavals, but none so fraught or on so public a scale as the troubles in Northern Ireland. The Republic has been very fortunate that, the Dublin and Monaghan bombings apart, we suffered no major loss of life due to terrorism or subversion. Northern Ireland, by contrast, witnessed countless tragedies and suffered thousands of casualties during four immensely painful decades. People do not fully realise today how easily we might have been dragged into that same maelstrom.

Knowing how narrowly we avoided catastrophe, in the early 1970s in particular, I make no apology for apportioning blame, both for what happened and for what might have been. I am also painfully conscious of the enormous damage done to the economy of this island by the activity of various terrorist and criminal organisations.

A great deal has changed, and changed fundamentally, since I began my political career in the late 1960s. I think it no harm to draw attention to some of these changes, both for better and for worse.

DESMOND O'MALLEY
JULY 2014

ACKNOWLEDGEMENTS

There are several people to whom I am grateful for assistance with this book.

Dr Kevin Rafter helped me greatly, and I am very thankful to him. I am grateful also to Dr Mary Browne, Michael O'Mahony, John McCarthy and Catherine Dardis for their help. I am indebted to my cousin Ruth Murphy, for allowing me to draw heavily on unpublished research by her late husband, Paul Murphy, into the killing of our grandfather, Denis O'Donovan, and its aftermath.

I appreciate the encouragement and support I received from Conor Nagle, commissioning editor at Gill & Macmillan, to see this through. My son Eoin and my brother Joe wanted me to write an academic book. I failed them. Sorry.

PROLOGUE: A JOB OFFER

Can you imagine what it is like to be barely thirty-one years of age, a member of Dáil Éireann for less than two years, and to get a phone call from the Taoiseach offering you the position of Minister for Justice?

That was me on 4 May 1970. The country was about to be convulsed by the series of events known ever after as the Arms Crisis—the gravest moment in the history of the state—and a political novice was now being offered the hottest seat in the Government.

There was nothing quite like it before, nor has there been since. Two Government ministers were fired, on suspicion of illegally importing arms for the IRA; a third resigned in sympathy. These were big beasts in Fianna Fáil, all of them feeling more worthy of the leadership than the man who actually held it, Jack Lynch. It was Lynch who was offering me the job.

The vacancy arose because the incumbent minister—who was not a big beast—was fond of drink, and derelict in his duty. Justice is a crucial portfolio at any time; in May 1970 it was the place where a safe, calculating man wouldn't want to be. It was the centre of the most violent political storm in the short history of independent Ireland.

I was at home in Limerick, relaxing in the bath. My wife, Pat, answered the phone and called out to me that the Taoiseach was on the line and needed to talk to me. These days you might have your mobile beside the bath; in those days it was land lines only, and you had to go to the phone. So, dripping wet and shrouded in a bath towel, I went to the phone to hear that I was needed in Lynch's office in Dublin within three hours. Thus began my career as a Government minister.

So I towelled myself down, got dressed, jumped into the whip's car and was driven to Dublin.

When I reached Lynch's office he was looking pretty grave. He said to me that some major events had happened. He started off by telling me that the Minister for Justice, Mícheál Ó Móráin, had left the Government, although the way he put it was that he had fired Ó Móráin that morning. The resignation statement simply said that the minister had resigned because of ill-health, which was not untrue. Ó Móráin was indeed unwell, and Lynch's conversation with him had taken place at about 8:30 that morning in Mount Carmel Hospital in Rathgar, where Ó Móráin was a patient. Lynch didn't specify what was the matter with him, although it seems that his general poor health was not helped by his fondness for alcohol. At any rate, he was gone, and I was to replace him.

I asked Lynch why he had fired Ó Móráin, and he said that the minister 'had not told me what was going on.' What was going on was the scarcely credible series of events known as the Arms Crisis.

What struck me most about Lynch was how calm he was. There was no sense of panic. The situation was such that most people, myself included, might well have panicked in the circumstances. It was pretty drastic. It was the first time that two senior ministers were about to be fired for what the Taoiseach considered highly improper activities contrary to Government policy.

Subversion has been a fact of life in Ireland. But this was subversion from within the Government, involving powerful and influential ministers, and that was the seriousness of it.

Lynch had had difficulty in interviewing Charles Haughey in particular. Like Ó Móráin, but for a quite different reason, Haughey was also in hospital, having sustained serious injuries. The doctors at the Mater Private Hospital had prevented Lynch from seeing his Minister for Finance on a previous occasion. When he did finally get to see him, Haughey asked for more time, but Lynch felt that the matter had now come to a head and he was not minded to give anyone more time.

In fact he gave both Charles Haughey and Neil Blaney about twenty-four hours but then asked for their resignations. They refused, whereupon he fired them. So Lynch, whom many characterised as weak and indecisive, showed his mettle and his steel. It needs to be remembered that in those days the Taoiseach—any Taoiseach—was not the dominant figure within the Government that he has since become, because there wasn't the same concentration on the Taoiseach by the media that you get nowadays. Taoisigh did not involve themselves to any great degree in the working of individual departments. Ministers had much greater autonomy, so that big beasts like Haughey and Blaney were hugely influential in the party and in the Government. It took a lot of guts to fire them, and of course it caused a political earthquake.

Lynch's version of events has been challenged from time to time, but I have always believed that what he told me was the truth. He had not learnt about the plot to import arms until he was informed by Peter Berry, the long-serving Secretary of the Department of Justice, a few days earlier.

He was also believed by the surviving senior members of the Government, people like Paddy Hillery and George Colley. They had sat at the Government table; they knew what official policy was on the North and knew that this plot to import arms had nothing to do with it; they had been informed of what had happened, knew the danger of it and realised the horror of it. It was, after all, a fundamental challenge to the most important institution within the state. It frightened them, I think, that such a thing could have happened, and they fully approved of Lynch's way of dealing with it. I think they were also impressed that he didn't panic and that he did things in a measured way.

Some people were surprised that Fianna Fáil was so vigorous in defending the institutions of the state, given the party's background and history. But it is worth recalling that this was not something that the party suddenly discovered in 1970. Éamon de Valera had done so during the Second World War with extraordinary vigour; it was one of the reasons that Peter Berry thought so highly of Dev. Indeed what Lynch and the others remaining in Government were doing was following in the footsteps of Dev.

While there was no unanimity in the wider Fianna Fáil party in the country about Lynch's line, it is worth remarking that there was no major split, despite the likes of Kevin Boland (who was still in the party, having resigned from the Government in sympathy with

Haughey and Blaney) stirring up dissent. There were a few others of a similar kidney: Blaney, of course, who was still in the party for a while, and the likes of Des Foley, the former Dublin footballer. But there was no serious split. The only major blow-up came at the 1971 ard-fheis, when a short television clip showed Hillery making an impassioned attack on Boland.

I reckon that at that ard-fheis the Blaney-Boland faction amounted to no more than 8 to 10 per cent of people in the hall. Haughey meanwhile was conspicuous by his silence. He may have been making mischief privately, but he wasn't stirring up the crowd. His greatest desire was to remain in Fianna Fáil (the other two didn't care), because he saw it as the only vehicle for his own ambition, and he was going to do whatever it took to achieve his goal, even accepting a few years of humiliation as the price to be paid.

At any rate, the party didn't split, despite the unprecedented pressures it was placed under. Blaney, Boland and Haughey clearly regarded the outbreak of the Northern 'troubles' as a heaven-sent opportunity to get rid of Lynch, who they wanted shut of anyway. It was a battleground of their own choosing. They were very surprised—to put it no stronger than that—that Lynch was able to resist them with such relative ease and to stop them taking over the party, for that was their game.

They lost the game and found themselves in the political wilderness. Blaney remained in the Dáil for years, now an impotent independent backbencher and no longer anywhere near the levers of power. Boland founded a party of his own, which never went anywhere. He was the least substantial of the trio, and he later made a modest second career out of suing any media outlet that stated that he had been sacked along with the other two, whereas he had in fact resigned in sympathy, claiming defamation of character (and damages).

Haughey, of course, as the world knows, played the long game that had been forced upon him, and in the end, alas, he won it.

But that was in the future. In May 1970 all was still flux and uncertainty as I settled down to work as Minister for Justice.

Chapter 1 ⌒

| INTRODUCTION

Denis O'Donovan, my maternal grandfather, was shot dead during the War of Independence by the Black and Tans in very questionable circumstances. The family owned the Shannon Hotel in Castleconnell, Co. Limerick. My mother, Una O'Donovan, was a young girl of seven at the time. Fortunately, she was not at home, but other family members witnessed the attack.

My grandfather's death, on the evening of Sunday 17 April 1921—and that of a member of the Royal Irish Constabulary and of an Auxiliary—was raised on several occasions in the House of Commons and in the House of Lords and was the subject of a British military court of inquiry.

The success of republican military activity during the War of Independence had convinced the British to recruit auxiliary forces to serve in Ireland, many of whom were former soldiers. The deployment of the temporary RIC constables called the 'Black and Tans' began in March 1920, followed in July by the Auxiliary Division of the RIC, made up of former British officers; and they proceeded to wage a campaign of terror throughout the country. Ill-disciplined and ruthless, they became associated with reprisals against the local population.

Black and Tans and Auxiliaries stationed in nearby Killaloe were responsible for the death of my grandfather in April 1921. The attack may have passed as just another incident in this bloody period in Anglo-Irish history but for the presence in the Shannon Hotel of a guest who was a brother of Lord Parmoor, a Conservative Party politician, the father of Sir Stafford Cripps, who would be Chancellor of the Exchequer in the Attlee government after the Second World War.

This man, William Cripps, a retired surgeon in his mid-seventies, was a regular visitor to the Castleconnell area. On the evening of the attack he had only returned to the hotel from a day's fishing. Castleconnell was a small village, and it was then very well known for salmon fishing. On that evening in 1921 Cripps looked into the hotel bar, where he saw three men in civilian clothes enjoying a drink and talking to Denis O'Donovan, who was working behind the bar. He greeted them before proceeding with his wife to the adjacent dining-room.

Not long afterwards the couple heard a sudden crash, and shooting began. As Cripps dramatically recalled,

> there was a regular roar of shots, 'pip, pip, pip,' far too rapid to be counted; some hundreds anyway. In the middle of the firing there came a deadly rattle of louder sound. This was from a machine gun . . . fired at point blank range, smashing the bar room door to splinters.

The shooting lasted for several minutes amid considerable mayhem.

The initial police report claimed that a party of Black and Tans in plain clothes had entered the Shannon Hotel, searching for republican suspects. When the men standing at the bar, who were talking to my grandfather, produced weapons, both groups opened fire. By the time the shooting stopped, three men were dead, including Denis O'Donovan.

There were very differing interpretations of what had happened. Cripps wrote to his brother about what he had witnessed, and some days later Lord Parmoor felt compelled to read the contents of the correspondence into the record of the House of Lords.

> I much want to tell you about a terrible affair that took place at our little hotel at Castleconnell last Sunday evening. Our landlord, a perfectly innocent, honourable and much-beloved man, was killed almost before our eyes . . . Besides O'Donovan, the proprietor, two others were shot dead in the hotel, and the whole place was shot to pieces by a machine-gun placed inside the hotel. It was the most wicked attack you can imagine, and, to my horror, perpetrated by the Black and Tans Auxiliary Forces, some sixty in number.

The dramatic contents of Cripps's letter was also read into the record of the House of Commons by H. H. Asquith, the former Prime Minister, who was at the time championing a compromise over the violence in Ireland. In one section of the letter, Cripps observed that 'Mr. O'Donovan, the proprietor, I had known well. He was a quiet, lovable man, devoted to his wife and children, and respected by all his neighbours.'

It turned out that the three men at the bar were in fact members of the RIC. These policemen were enjoying a day's leave from their station in Newport, Co. Tipperary, from where they had cycled that day. They were in plain clothes. My grandfather was working behind the bar when the Black and Tans entered the premises. They had observed the bicycles outside the hotel and, having entered the premises, ordered those at the bar to hold up their hands. They believed the men inside were members of the IRA. There was obviously great confusion.

The three policemen thought the IRA was attacking them, having discovered they were RIC men. The fact that the Black and Tans were not wearing uniforms contributed to the confusion. The policemen drew their revolvers, and opened fire. Both groups continued firing until one of the policemen was killed and another wounded. A Black and Tan was also shot dead. The third RIC man made a rush for the door, accompanied by my grandfather. At this point he was captured, and Denis O'Donovan was shot dead.

The attack was widely reported in the newspapers, including the *Freeman's Journal* and the *Irish Times*. A journalist working with the *Cork Examiner* arrived in Castleconnell the day after the attack. He wrote that 'bullet marks on the wood work and panelling show how furious it was for the comparatively brief time that it [the attack] lasted.'

My grandfather was forty-six at the time of his death. He had been born between Clonakilty and Skibbereen, the youngest son of a well-known family in West Cork and a neighbour of Michael Collins. He had worked in London before returning to Ireland to become an agent for a Cork brewery. In 1905 he married Agnes McNamara from

Co. Limerick. Twelve years later the couple—by now joined by four children, including my mother, Una—bought the Shannon Hotel at Castleconnell. Their politics were described as those of constitutional nationalists; but nobody was immune from the turmoil of those years.

A military court of inquiry opened in the New Barracks in Limerick four days after the attack. The newspapers reported the proceedings, although, because of censorship, the published articles were limited in what they recorded of the inquiry. In all, eight Black and Tans and the two RIC men who survived the attack gave evidence, as did my grandmother, her daughter Mary, her niece, and a hotel maidservant, Margaret Wade. Cripps—who had offered to return from London—was not called to give evidence.

The military inquiry was a whitewash. No civilian witnesses of the incident were called except family and the hotel maid—and their evidence was discounted. In a remarkable coincidence, however, the first witness was my paternal grandfather, Joseph O'Malley, an architect, who had been requested by the tribunal to provide a drawing of the floor plan of the hotel.

There were widely differing accounts of what had happened during the attack. One of the RIC men said O'Donovan emerged from the bar with his hands up and was standing straight, but he did not see what happened to him after they entered the outside yard.

Margaret Wade stated that O'Donovan was taken out into the yard and shot in cold blood. She told the inquiry that she saw O'Donovan and another man captured but unwounded in the yard behind the hotel.

The next thing I heard was shots and cries from Mr O'Donovan. I then ran back to the kitchen and through the window saw Mr O'Donovan lying on the ground. I saw a man in a black mackintosh . . . with a rifle in his hands. I said, 'My God, what are you after doing, shooting an innocent man.' The man replied, 'It was good enough for him. He was harbouring rebels.'

The Black and Tans denied this version of events. The inquiry supported their explanation that O'Donovan fled towards safety outside but in the crossfire was struck by six bullets, three of which entered from the front, one from the right side, and two from the back. The death certificates of the three men gave their cause of death as 'shock and haemorrhage due to gunshot wounds. Instantaneous.'

Not only had the British side failed to adequately explain what had happened in the Shannon Hotel but they also failed to deal with a further piece of evidence provided by Lord Parmoor's brother in his correspondence, which was also read into the record of the House of Lords.

I have a bullet in its cartridge case picked up by me on Sunday the 17th, the cap dented by the striker but unexploded. The bullet has been reversed, thus converting it into an expanding bullet of the most deadly character. Such bullets inflict the most terrible wounds, and were prohibited in the late war.

In what must have been a dramatic sight even by the standards of this period of continuing violence in Ireland, Lord Parmoor produced the bullet in the chamber of the House of Lords. The revelation that outlawed 'dum-dum' bullets, which inflicted terrible pain on their targets, were being used by Crown forces in Ireland was a serious matter. Interestingly, however, in the official British inquiry this issue was not pursued, despite the testimony of Cripps and the evidence produced in Parliament.

Cripps was a very credible eyewitness. A distinguished surgeon at St Bartholomew's Hospital, London, he could be described as a member of the British establishment. The weight of his testimony had convinced senior political figures, such as Lord Parmoor and Asquith, to call for an independent inquiry. The Lloyd George government, however, was unwilling to go beyond allowing the military court of inquiry to determine what had happened.

The unsatisfactory report of this inquiry was the subject of further comment in Parliament, including that of Captain William Wedgwood Benn MP (father of the future British Labour minister and author Tony Benn), who questioned the fact that Cripps had not been allowed to give evidence, though willing to do so.

The official files on the attack were not released for almost half a century. One item of correspondence is highly revealing. General Nevil Macready, commander-in-chief of Crown forces in Ireland, commented on the inquiry in a letter to the Under-Secretary of State at Dublin Castle:

Instead of going into the bar and satisfying themselves, after seeking a drink, as to whether suspicious characters were there, the plain clothes men shouted 'Hands Up' the moment they opened the door, without apparently having any good grounds for thinking that the persons inside were suspicious characters . . . As soon as firing began, there is no doubt that [the Black and Tans] became very excited.

Denis O'Donovan's funeral cortège was said to have been a mile long. Prominent business and political figures attended, including the Mayor of Limerick and local religious leaders. The size of the attendance was a show of solidarity with the family. Limerick Corporation (as the city council was then called) held a special meeting to pass a motion of sympathy.

Within weeks of my grandfather's tragic death a truce was agreed between the two warring sides. In the months from January 1921 to the ceasefire of July the same year more than a thousand people were killed, 70 per cent of the total deaths in the three-year conflict that ultimately led to the Anglo-Irish Treaty.

The Shannon Hotel remained in family ownership for some years. The door to the passageway outside the bar still has its bullet holes.

I was born in February 1939, the eldest in a family of four, but my mother never talked about what had happened to her father. I heard about the attack only from her brothers. Remarkably, however, I don't think the O'Donovan family harboured lasting bitterness, despite the terrible events in their home and the death of their father. Like so many others who were caught up in the birth of the Irish Free State, they looked to the future rather than dwelling on the unhappy events of the past.

Many years later, in April 1997, I unveiled a plaque to commemorate her father's death at my mother's home in Castleconnell.

The significance of that killing in 1921 was referred to a couple of years later by W. T. Cosgrave, President of the Executive Council (head of the Irish Free State government). He was attending a prize-giving day in Castleknock College, Co. Dublin, where my mother's two brothers were at school. He told them that their father's death had greatly influenced the subsequent truce agreed in July 1921. It had had an effect on British political opinion after it was described in the two houses of Parliament there and after the dum-dum bullet was produced. Five days after the Castleconnell affair, Lord Derby set off for Dublin, with Lloyd George's approval, to start the talks that eventually led to the truce.

There were two local men in the second or public bar in the hotel when the Black and Tans raided. They were lucky that the Tans made for the residents' or hotel bar, where O'Donovan was. When the first shooting died down the two men made a dash for the yard, just as O'Donovan was being brought out. They climbed up a wall to escape. The Tans fired and hit one of them in the foot, and he fell off the wall on the far side. The Tans apparently thought they had killed him. The two of them got away.

Another of the strange coincidences with the Collins family was that Father Peter Hill PP, a first cousin of my grandfather and who married him and my grandmother, baptised Michael Collins in Ross Carbery church. After Collins was killed, one of his brothers, Seán, recently widowed, proposed to my grandmother. She turned him down—not surprisingly, as he was a widower with eight children and she was a widow with four of her own.

In the House of Lords the Lloyd George government, which fully supported the Auxiliaries and the Tans, was represented by Lord Birkenhead, the Lord Chancellor, who subsequently signed the Treaty, and by Lord Crawford. In the House of Commons the Crown forces were defended by the Attorney-General for Ireland, Denis Henry MP.

Another curious coincidence that arose later was that Lord Parmoor's second wife, Marian Emily Ellis, was a descendent of a family of English

Quakers named Priestman, as also was Phyllis Gill, whom Donogh (or D. K.) O'Donovan, a son of Denis O'Donovan, married in 1938. Lady Parmoor and Dr Gill were, it seems, third cousins.

———

Violence in Ireland should ideally have ended when the truce between Irish republicans and the British was called in July 1921. Unfortunately, even after the Civil War, a small minority throughout twentieth-century Ireland continued to see conflict as the way to achieve their political aims. These people caused terrible pain and hardship. I saw the impact of their activities at first hand when I was appointed Minister for Justice during the Arms Crisis in May 1970. These terror-ist groups, who styled themselves 'republican'—with no legitimate lineage from the past—took it upon themselves to act on behalf of the Irish people. They had no mandate. They killed, maimed and caused terrible destruction.

Throughout my thirty-four years as a member of Dáil Éireann I remained firmly of the view that only a peaceful, political approach would deliver a solution to the Northern Ireland problem. Division over Northern Ireland policy was one of the issues that led to my expulsion from Fianna Fáil, and by the time the Progressive Democrats were founded, in December 1985, the so-called troubles had entered their eighteenth year. The continued violence could not have been envisaged at the outset of the conflict in 1969, and that the conflict went on so long was a tragedy. The continued Provo activity was indefensible. Much of the contrary violence tended to be reactive, in the early days particularly.

At the outset of my political career I strongly believed in Irish unity. But as the years progressed, while I still saw unity as the preferred outcome of a political and constitutional agreement between all sides, I came to the conclusion that this situation could not be achieved. The unity of the people on the island superseded any territorial claim. I found the federal solution as outlined in the report of the New Ireland

Forum in 1984 satisfactory. The unitary-state model, as favoured by Haughey's Fianna Fáil, as well as by the Provos, was simply not workable.

The Progressive Democrats were very conscious that the text of articles 2 and 3 of the Constitution of Ireland, when taken together, was a remarkable example of the gulf that separated Irish minds and of the unreality with which we often convinced ourselves. The original article 3 asserted that it was the right of the parliament established in Dublin to govern the whole of Ireland. This was no mere denial of legitimacy to the Union, no mere objection to partition: it was an unequivocal claim of right on the part of the people south of the border to impose their parliament, their constitution, their laws and their values on the entire population of the island.

Looking back now, it is clear that the Progressive Democrats were hardly saying anything revolutionary, despite the hostility we faced. It was, moreover, a statement of reality. The all-party Oireachtas Committee on the Constitution had agreed in 1967 that such ambitions were inappropriate. There were a significant number of people who joined the PDS because they believed that it was time to abandon that claim. We wanted a different formulation about unity in the Constitution. We proposed substituting an aspiration for unity by consent and by peaceful means. In this respect we were advocating ideas that would eventually appear in the Good Friday Agreement in 1998.

When the IRA ceasefire was announced in August 1994 I doubted that it would last, and, in fact, it didn't. I never believed or trusted the words of people like Gerry Adams and Martin McGuinness. The original ceasefire broke down several times, including, most dramatically, with the Canary Wharf bombing in London in January 1996 but also six months later with the murder of my friend Garda Jerry McCabe.

There is no denying that Northern Ireland is a better place today than at any time since 1969. The Provos claim credit, but the real architect of the peace process was John Hume, although at a terrible price to his own party, the SDLP. Nothing achieved in this era of the peace process, however, justified the preceding violence. Welcoming the relative stability and comparative peace that exist today should not be taken as excusing three decades of terrible deeds carried out by Adams and his supporters. A 'peace process' would not have been necessary but for the Provos.

Sinn Féin has been the big loser from the peace process. The Provos have ended up doing all the things they said they would never do. They canvassed for the Good Friday Agreement and the principle of consent. They accepted the revised articles 2 and 3—the very proposal they would have excoriated the PDs for if it had been agreed a decade earlier. They even took their seats in Leinster House, the parliament they had previously described as a sham assembly. They recognised the courts, south and north, and they agreed to work in a power-sharing Executive at Stormont.

But no credit should be given for these decisions. We should not forget so quickly that they failed to achieve any of their aims, notwithstanding all the death and destruction they inflicted.

After all the years I spent in national politics, watching terrorism so deeply hurt the people on the island of Ireland, I genuinely hope that Adams and co. will transform themselves into genuine democrats. But people would be well advised not to treat them as normal democrats. The IRA continued to engage in serious organised crime until very recently. It controlled a large part of the drug scene in Dublin, and it murdered anyone who attempted to muscle in on its patch. When Martin Cahill, the criminal known to the press as 'the General', crossed the Provos on the drug trade, they killed him.

The IRA's involvement in serious crime did not end with the ceasefire in August 1994. One Sinn Féin TD who was elected in 2011, Martin Ferris, was closely connected with and supportive of the individuals who carried out the post office robbery in June 1996 in Adare, Co. Limerick, that led to the murder of Garda Jerry McCabe and the attempted murder of his colleague Garda Ben O'Sullivan. That murder happened during the 'peace process' period. It must never be forgotten.

I had known these two men since the early 1970s. They had driven me when Garda intelligence judged that I was a security risk. The IRA had failed once to shoot me when I was Minister for Justice. The advice was that I needed round-the-clock protection. One garda would drive me while the other sat in the back seat with an Uzi sub-machine gun on his lap. I last saw them together at a meeting of the British-Irish Parliamentary Body in Adare in March 1996. A number of prominent Conservative Party politicians were in attendance, including Tom King. 'Nothing ever happens in Adare,' I recall joking with Ben O'Sullivan and Jerry McCabe, who were among the strong Garda presence in Adare Manor. 'It's the boys down the road in Patrickswell we have to watch,' Jerry replied. Little did we know that within a matter of weeks those 'boys' would act in such a deadly fashion and murder Jerry himself right there in Adare.

I disagreed fundamentally with the favourable treatment given to the killers of Jerry McCabe. It was made abundantly clear before and at the signing of the Good Friday Agreement in 1998 that the benefits of that agreement would not extend to his four killers. But then other convicted terrorist criminals in Sinn Féin lobbied on their behalf, and they were granted temporary release on several occasions. Notwithstanding that, their temporary release in 2000 was described in some quarters as 'confidence-building measures in the peace process.' I would have thought we needed to build confidence in the legal system, particularly the criminal justice system, and not confidence among the members of an organisation that had spent several decades murdering, maiming and robbing people.

Why were these four murderers not kept in Port Laoise Prison? That was the appropriate place, rather than enjoying themselves in Castlerea Prison in an individual bungalow of their own, with telephones paid for by the taxpayer and the IRA sending into the town for a Chinese takeaway whenever the prison diet was not to their liking.

I discussed this situation on several occasions with Mary Harney. We both took the same view, as did Michael McDowell, who in fact expressed opposition to appeasement of the Provos more forcefully and more articulately than I could ever have done. But others were more concerned about keeping Adams and his cohorts happy. When moderate democrats who seek to abide by and uphold the rule of law come a bad second to these kinds of people, it is surely time to ask ourselves some fundamental questions about how we order our affairs. When the lives of our policemen, and the welfare of their widows, come second to the creature comforts of these sorts of people, we may find ourselves eventually in a position where the thin blue line disappears and our society and its institutions are put at grave risk.

I have watched over the last few years how the so-called republican movement has sought to reinvent itself, moving from support for murder and mayhem to occupying the anti-establishment space. I have found it hard to take the public posturing of the likes of Adams, McGuinness and other Sinn Féin/IRA figures, given their lengthy record of murder, mutilation and torture. They abused the term 'republican'. In Provo terms, it was equated with 'Brit-bashing' or 'Prod-bashing' and nothing more.

In reality they are the worst type of populists. In Leinster House today they practise blanket opposition. They are against everything and have nothing serious to contribute. There's real hypocrisy in how they criticise policies in the Republic while the same policies are implemented by the power-sharing Executive, of which they are part, in Northern Ireland. Time may have passed, and relative peace has delivered great progress, but before giving their support to Mr Adams and his friends people would be well advised to remember their background and the terrible things they have done that sullied the name of Ireland. The virtue of tolerance can sometimes go too far here.

Fintan O'Toole has described apparent tolerance in Ireland as often mere indifference. I think he is right. It is dangerous not to care.

Chapter 2 ⌒

| ORIGINS

My father, Desmond O'Malley, was born in 1908, the eldest son in his family. He went into the law and had a busy legal practice in Limerick. He was well known in the city, and not just in legal circles, largely on account of his sporting exploits. He was a keen sportsman, a good rower; but his greatest sporting success was on the rugby field. He played for UCD and for Bohemians in Limerick, was capped for Munster and got two final trials for Ireland, although he was unfortunate in having to mark an outstanding Ulster centre, George Stevenson, which didn't help his cause. He later became president of Bohemians and was also president of the Munster Branch of the IRFU.

I played rugby myself, and was on a team that got to a Munster Schools Senior Cup final. But I was very light, and I kept picking up injuries. Anyway, I was no good.

My father's sporting profile and professional reputation attracted interest from Fianna Fáil. The party had entered government for the first time in 1932 and in 1934 was seeking candidates for the local elections. He was asked to stand. He was duly elected and served as Mayor of Limerick in 1942 and again in 1943. It was an office later held by two of his younger brothers: Michael, who was also a solicitor, was elected Mayor in 1947, and Donogh held the position in 1961. In fact when Donogh followed his two brothers in wearing the mayoral chain the *Limerick Leader* reported that the situation was an 'epoch in mayoral history.'

Donogh held the office for only a short period. It was the era before the so-called dual mandate was outlawed. He was a backbench TD when he was elected mayor but he had to resign when he was appointed a parliamentary secretary in November 1961.

My father had actually been approached about moving from local to national politics in 1952. One of the sitting Fianna Fáil TDs in Limerick, Dan Burke—a republican veteran who had held the seat at every election since September 1927—had passed away. Given his profile in Limerick, my father was an ideal choice for the by-election, and he was interested in the offer. But I have a very clear memory of my mother's opposition. She was concerned for my father's health. He had had a heart scare a few years earlier, and the politician's life-style was also a worry for her. If you go into Leinster House today, most deputies you find in the Dáil bar will be drinking coffee; but in the 1950s, and for several subsequent decades, politics was associated with alcohol. My mother wanted my father kept well away from that environment.

Nevertheless, Fianna Fáil was very keen on his candidacy and kept up the pressure. Before the selection convention had been organised, I remember we were on our way to Spanish Point, Co. Clare, one Saturday afternoon. Some Limerick Fianna Fáilers had actually blocked the road outside Milltown Malbay on the way to Spanish Point. My father had already turned down the invitation to run, but these party supporters wanted to talk him into changing his mind. But my mother was still having none of it. She was frantic in the car. When my father got out he said to the Fianna Fáil men, 'I won't be running.' And, pointing back at my mother, he said: 'You can hear my problem.' Fianna Fáil ended up selecting Tom Clarke, son of the famous 1916 leader. He topped the poll but got caught on transfers, which allowed Fine Gael to win the seat fairly easily.

In the general election two years later the local Fianna Fáil organisation was unhappy with Clarke and so returned to the idea of having an O'Malley on the ticket. But this time it was my father's younger brother, Donogh, who was selected. I think my father pushed Donogh's candidacy, although Éamon de Valera wasn't keen, given what he had heard about his reputation. My father assured de Valera that he would do his best to make sure his brother behaved himself. His best was not good enough.

Donogh's reputation as a hell-raiser was well established. One story will suffice. He and one of his boon companions, a tiny man with large jug ears, went off to Shannon Airport on one occasion. Shannon was a 24-hour airport and therefore had a 24-hour bar licence. An American woman in the bar appeared to be fascinated by the small man's appearance, which prompted Donogh to approach her and ask her if she would like to buy the little fellow, that he was an authentic leprechaun. The woman declared that she coveted nothing more in the world than her own leprechaun, and the price was struck at $100. Jug Ears was half way to the plane before he realised what was afoot and began to protest. The $100 was restored to the woman and the little fellow was restored to the bar.

My father got on well with de Valera but he was closer to Seán Lemass. He considered Lemass as being more in tune with the real world. I remember at this time, during the 1950s, when I was a teenager, that Lemass would ring our house, usually at night, to talk to my father. The phone was in a small downstairs cloakroom, and I'd be sent out to answer it. The first time Lemass rang I thought it was a joke. I came back into the living-room. 'There's a fellow on the phone who says he's Seán Lemass,' I said. 'And that would be right,' my father replied as he went to take the call. When he returned after about twenty minutes I asked what Lemass had wanted. 'He had some idea he wanted my opinion on,' my father explained. It was Lemass's style to take soundings from a handful of trusted people around the country.

It would be fair to describe my family as part of the establishment in Limerick. We lived comfortably in Corbally, which was in the city but was then in a rural setting, to all intents and purposes a small village. Virtually everyone knew everyone else.

I would cycle to and from school. When I was about nine I saw a commotion on a small quay while crossing a bridge over the Abbey River. Gardaí and firemen were dredging the river beside the quay, using strands of barbed wire weighed down with stones. A small boy had toppled into the water following his ball, which had bounced into the river. After a while the men shouted to one another. Slowly the wire came up. The body of the boy was attached to the wire by his blue home-knitted pullover. I was wearing one exactly the same. The boy's face was ashen-grey, turning blue and swollen. He was streaked with mud from the bed of the river. I had never seen a dead body before. This boy was about my age, also about my size. I raced all the way home, my heart pounding. That night I asked my father to leave the light on in the landing. I kept asking myself, 'What if that had been my ball that had bounced into the river?'

There was far less class distinction in Limerick than in Dublin or Cork. The atmosphere was different. I would attribute this fact to sport, and rugby in particular. Rugby in Limerick was open to all: nobody was excluded. My father had had a good career on the playing-field. I remember men coming into his solicitor's office, some of them labourers working on the docks in the city, and many would have been tough fellows. 'Is Dessie here?' they'd ask. They had either played rugby with him or against him, but either way they regarded him as a friend. And he'd never say 'no' to them. I couldn't imagine that happening in some of the legal firms in Dublin or Cork; in fact I would guess that men like those dockers would have been run off the premises.

It was a tough era, and there was very real poverty in Limerick. At school I was a member of the Society of St Vincent de Paul. We would visit the houses of the needy to deliver vouchers for food and clothes. But even still the general atmosphere in the city was good, and much better than in more recent—and more affluent—times. There was also less crime. Peer pressure helped in getting young fellows to behave themselves. The breakdown in social structures came with the fragmentation of the population, with new housing estates built in the 1960s and 70s.

In reviewing my political career I think my greatest failure was not working harder to win arguments I had with local government officials about urban house-building policies. I recall in the mid-1970s discussing with officials in Limerick Corporation their plan to con-tinue building large new housing estates on the outskirts of the city rather than on sites closer to the city centre and to existing services. This was a more expensive option than the large-scale house-building plans pursued by local planners to meet national housing targets, but we've been reaping the social costs of those decisions for several decades now.

———

When I was growing up in the 1950s the Catholic Church had a big influence on life in Limerick. The clergy probably had a stronger grip in the city than in other places. The local bishops were milder men than their counterparts in Dublin or in Galway or in Cork. But the real religious influence in Limerick was not in the bishop's palace: power resided with the Redemptorist Order, which was very much in its fire-and-brimstone phase.

The Redemptorists had an excessive degree of control. Their zeal drove many people away from Limerick, including the local novelist Kate O'Brien, whose books were banned. I remember being in a cinema in the city when there was a commotion in the back seats. A Redemptorist priest was stalking the aisles with an umbrella in his hand. He had spied some poor fellow who had his arm around a girl. For this indiscretion this fellow had been poked in the back with the point of the umbrella. It was common practice for cinema-owners to allow the Redemptorists into films to make sure there was no hanky-panky when the lights went down.

My parents were religious, but not in the Redemptorist way. They ensured that I went to school at the other centre of religious power in Limerick, the Jesuits at the Crescent College. The Jesuits had a very different outlook, even in the prevailing conservative ethos of Ireland in the 1950s. They were more compassionate people, and they avoided the fire and brimstone of the Redemptorists. Nearly all my teachers were Jesuits, with only a handful of lay teachers. The era of blind obedience was slowly coming to an end. There was greater questioning among my generation—those who reached adulthood from the 1960s onwards—but still for many years large numbers of people still took their lead from the bishops.

Rugby was important in the school, but Latin and Greek were the intellectual interests of the Jesuits. Subjects like science were deemed to be inferior and less important. I started in the Crescent in September 1946 and left eleven years later for University College, Dublin. The one lesson I took from my schooling was that if you believed something to be correct, then stick by it and don't be deflected, even if I have not always been correct in my judgement of what was the right course of action.

As a family—I had two younger brothers and a younger sister—we used to go to Kilkee on holidays. But it wasn't really a break for my father. The Co. Clare seaside town was a favourite with many people from Limerick. Clients of my father would constantly approach him to ask about their cases. As a result we ended up taking a house in Spanish Point.

Two classes of people holidayed in Spanish Point in the 1950s: nuns and retired British army officers. Neither the nuns—and there were hundreds of them there in their sweeping habits—nor the retired soldiers had any interest in my father. The peace was more to his liking. The nuns swam in outfits that would have won the approval of the Taliban.

We'd go down most weekends, and it was in Spanish Point that I learnt to play golf. I started on the small links course before progressing to the course in Lahinch. One of my tutors was the local GP, Paddy Hillery, who some years later would be a ministerial colleague. Hillery would arrive at the course when his work finished at the local dispensary at about 5:30 p.m. I'd often have been out playing most of the day, but I learnt a great deal about the game from Hillery and his regular partner, Paddy Leyden, who owned a garage in nearby Milltown Malbay. Leyden was capped for Ireland many times as an amateur golf international and was a South of Ireland champion at Lahinch.

Leyden had a plus handicap, but Hillery, who was minus three or four, was nearly as good. They would play nine holes with five balls each. Golf was not as popular in the 1950s as it would become in later years, and the course was never busy. I would play the eleventh ball to each hole, and my tutors would tell me what I was doing wrong. I eventually got my handicap down to seven. I was still playing when I went to university in Dublin. The UCD Golf Society had a great arrangement with the course in Portmarnock, Co. Dublin. Unfortunately, few of us students had cars in those days. I cycled a few times from the city centre to the course in north Co. Dublin; but not being a member of the club meant it was not possible to have a locker. Cycling with a golf bag was a major chore, and although I made the trip a few times I eventually gave up playing regularly.

_____

By the time I was in my mid-teens it was almost taken for granted that I would pursue a legal career in the family practice. My father was not in good health, and I think even at that stage he was already looking forward to having me involved so as to ease the responsibility on his shoulders.

Arriving at UCD was a big change from living at home with my parents. I lodged with the Jesuits at their university residence, University Hall, in Lower Hatch Street. The situation was very convenient for UCD, which at that time was in nearby Earlsfort Terrace. The move to Belfield got under way in the 1960s, but my university days were associated with the space that is now home to the National Concert Hall.

There was no points system governing admission to university. I arrived on my first day to be met by three registration desks: one for arts, a second for law and a third for medicine. I was obviously already decided on studying law. The fee for all courses was the same: £50 for the year. I soon got talking to another new student. He had also signed up for law but was having second thoughts and decided he was going to change to medicine. 'But will they allow you?' I asked. He explained that changing courses was no problem. I watched him get back his law application, and his £50 cheque, as the registration staff directed him to the medicine table.

UCD was home to about five thousand students, but I remember Earlsfort Terrace as a relatively small place. The academic work wasn't too severe. I took two courses simultaneously, going each day between classes in Earlsfort Terrace and the Four Courts. I wasn't qualified to practise, but I recall, while a student and solicitor's apprentice, accompanying a barrister to two consultations with two clients of my uncle, who practised in Limerick. We visited the two men—each of whom had been convicted of the murder of his wife—in the condemned cell in Mountjoy. Each was subsequently reprieved.

I enjoyed university life. I was involved in UCD Law Society, where I found the quality of the debate much stronger than a lot of the prancing around at the Literary and Historical Society. I also organised debates at University Hall.

I had a dispute with the Jesuits over my inaugural debate, at which Mr Justice Seán Kenny and the former Taoiseach John A. Costello had agreed to speak. The difficulty was with the third speaker I had invited, Owen Sheehy Skeffington, a member of Seanad Éireann. Sheehy Skeffington represented Trinity College, still a no-go institution for Catholics at that time. He had had a row with the Jesuits, and his presence in the Hall was vetoed. 'That man isn't suitable,' I was told. I argued with the Superior, Father Roland Burke-Savage, but they had made their decision. On the night of the debate I ensured that an empty seat was placed prominently on the platform. Twenty years later Burke-Savage wrote me a letter from Clongowes Wood College, out of the blue, apologising for what he did about Sheehy Skeffington. Not many would have done that.

———

I met my future wife, Pat McAleer, at UCD. Pat was from Omagh, Co. Tyrone, and she was studying French and history. She later worked in England and in Strabane before moving to Limerick after we married in February 1965. Our wedding reception was held in the Glencormac House Hotel in Kilmacanogue, Co. Wicklow. The Cold War thriller *The Spy Who Came In from the Cold,* based on a John Le Carré novel, was being shot at the nearby Ardmore Studios in Bray. The leading role was played by Richard Burton, who was married to Elizabeth Taylor. Burton and his entourage were staying in the Gresham Hotel, but on the Saturday afternoon they finished filming. Taylor went back to the Gresham, but Burton headed for the Glencormac, where he obviously sensed some activity. So, with the prospect of a few drinks and company, the Hollywood star joined our party. He insisted on kissing the bride. We still have a photograph of Burton planting a kiss on Pat's cheek while I look on slightly apprehensively. I think the bride enjoyed it!

With Pat's family from Co. Tyrone I got a good understanding of the situation in Northern Ireland and the grievances of the Catholic nationalist community. Our own family eventually increased to six children. Pat was a constant presence throughout my political career, and when the journalist Raymond Smith wrote a book about the heaves in Fianna Fáil in the 1980s he quite correctly identified Pat as an important influence on me. I could never have done what I did in politics without her wholehearted support. She put up with the absences and the threats.

When I came back to Limerick from UCD my father insisted that I practise criminal law. So every week I would spend a couple of days in court. Few of the cases were very serious. After a while I said to my father: 'It's an awful waste of time going down there. And a lot of the time we don't get paid, and when we do it's a pittance.' But my father saw otherwise. 'Don't worry about the payment,' he replied. 'Stay with it. You're learning how to think on your feet.' He was correct. And I have to say that the experience in the courthouses of Limerick city and county did benefit me later when I was elected to the Dáil, and most definitely in my period as Minister for Justice.

Watching my father and several other solicitors in Limerick, I saw what practising a profession consisted of. The same care had to be taken of the small and routine matters as of the larger. The client's welfare was paramount; remuneration was secondary. Poverty was no bar to legal representation. There were many barristers who took a similar view. Particularly outstanding and memorable was William Binchy (father of the novelist Maeve), an amazingly brilliant man, equally in litigation, conveyancing and crime, who refused to become a senior counsel because he was not interested in money and preferred to travel regularly to the south-west.

I notice that nowadays legal services by leading firms are paid for in advance, and per hour—the same system as that used in calculating remuneration for a profession even older than the law! Increasingly, serious litigation is so expensive that it can now be undertaken only by the mega-rich, or by the state or a quango. Somebody of limited means or limited assets often fails to vindicate their rights because they cannot take the risk of being wiped out. A man of straw has nothing to lose and so can litigate if he can get someone to act for him. Personal litigants do not get much encouragement.

The whole notion of justice has become so uncertain that many will not even seek it, because they regard it as a pretty pointless pursuit. I find it bitterly disappointing that in the space of a generation or so not just the practice of law but its very ethos has profoundly changed, and not for the better. The same sad story could be told of banks and bankers.

One of my most vivid memories of these court cases is of a time when the president of the Circuit Court, Mr Justice Barra Ó Briain, came to Limerick. He was on the circuit that included Cos. Clare, Kerry and Limerick, and he'd take cases in Limerick four times a year. At the start of proceedings the County Registrar would frequently stand up to announce: 'Judge, I am happy to tell you that there are no criminal indictments for you to try, and so I haven't had to summon a jury.' Precedent meant that such an occasion was marked by the presentation of a pair of white gloves to the judge, symbolising a clean pair of hands.

The absence of serious crime in Limerick meant that this was a regular event. But Mr Justice Ó Briain was obviously tiring of this legal pageantry, inherited from British times. I recall when it was discontinued. Addressing the registrar, the judge said: 'I have a wife and seven daughters. And my wife has told me that they all already have plenty of white gloves, so I think we can bring this practice to an end.'

———

When I came back to Limerick from UCD I threw myself into amateur dramatics with the College Players and the Old Crescent Players. I particularly remember a production of Oscar Wilde's *The Importance of Being Earnest* and a comedy, *My Three Angels* by Samuel and Bella Spewack, that was a commercial success. I entered the Féile Luimnigh drama competition, performing a number of extracts from Shakespeare plays, including *Richard III*. The adjudicator was Ria Mooney, artistic director of the Abbey Theatre. She was staying with an aunt of mine during the week of the festival, and I think she felt the need to repay the favour, as I got through to the Munster final in Charleville, Co. Cork. This time the adjudicator, who was from Wales, brought me down to earth.

Worse was to follow. The drama critic of the *Limerick Leader*—who wrote anonymously, but everyone knew he was the army chaplain at Sarsfield Barracks—delivered a withering review of my performance. 'Des O'Malley's Richard the Third might more accurately have been called Richard the one-third because that was about all he got out of it.'

I wasn't planning on having a political career—maybe at the local level in Limerick as a councillor at a later stage; but with my uncle Donogh in Leinster House there was no room for another O'Malley in the constituency. I expected Donogh to be in the Dáil for another twenty years. He was, after all, still only in his mid-forties. I canvassed at elections, but I did not anticipate being a Dáil candidate myself. Instead I concentrated on building my legal career.

My father's continuing poor health meant that I had responsibilities with the practice right from my return from university. His wish was that I would look after the practice. He was still involved but was pulling back. He had also been city coroner over the previous eight years.

While my father's health had never been great, his death was a shock. He passed away unexpectedly in December 1965, only fifty-seven years of age. After his death my mother offered to sell the family house to me, but after talking over the idea with Pat we declined. It was sold the following year, and my mother decided to move to Dublin.

The family was to suffer another unexpected loss in 1968 when Donogh, my father's youngest brother, also died prematurely.

Donogh was in Sixmilebridge, Co. Clare, for a by-election meeting. He had just come down from the platform when he suffered a very bad heart attack. I was visiting my grandmother, who lived in O'Connell Avenue in Limerick, when the phone in the hall rang. I answered to hear that Donogh was very ill. He had been taken to St John's Hospital. I had to tell my grandmother, who was insistent on coming with me to the hospital.

When we arrived I got somebody to look after her in the reception area. I went upstairs, where Donogh was lying on the floor, in the same room in which my father had died two years earlier. The scene was an awful shock. Three doctors were working on him, thumping his chest. The sweat was pouring off them; but their efforts were in vain. His death came as a huge shock to the public. In some quarters he was a kind of folk hero—partly because he was colourful (if at times too much so) and partly because of having been the one to announce the free secondary education scheme.

Donogh's funeral was an elaborate affair. It was a state funeral, with morning dress and the like. The protocol section in the Department of the Taoiseach had taken over the seating arrangements. Two front rows in St John's Cathedral were reserved for 'family'. I told them that a large number of family members would be attending and they could not fit in two benches. Then I made the first serious mistake of my political career. I was asked by one of the officials from Dublin to go outside and identify those who were claiming to be relations. There were more than two hundred people trying to get inside—none of them close relations as far as I could see—and I had no idea where they would all fit. A proper politician would have let them all in and let the protocol people sort it out. That's what Donogh would have done.

Donogh had won a Dáil seat at the 1954 general election and the following year became a member of Limerick Corporation. He benefited from the generational change in Fianna Fáil when Lemass, after succeeding de Valera, promoted new, younger TDs. Donogh's first position was as Parliamentary Secretary to the Minister for Finance with responsibility for the Office of Public Works. After the 1965 general election he was appointed Minister for Health, and fifteen months later he was moved to the Department of Education, where he is remembered for the decision to introduce free post-primary education.

Although Donogh got the credit for the free scheme, it was not as if he had pulled a rabbit out of the hat. His predecessor in Education, Paddy Hillery, had overseen a lot of the preparatory work and deserved much of the credit. Lemass, in his closing days as Taoiseach, must have been complicit in the whole thing, because by some miracle they all managed to keep the Department of Finance in the dark. Finance would have found dozens of reasons for objecting to a scheme that amounted to the writing of a blank cheque, arguing that the cost was bound to increase far beyond anything budgeted or contemplated—as indeed it did. Lynch, the Minister for Finance, was abroad when the announcement was made and returned to learn of the scheme for the first time. At any rate, fair or not, it is Donogh's name that has been indelibly associated with what some people regard as one of the more important initiatives in the history of the state.

I have to be honest in saying that my father had a lot of trouble with Donogh. When my father was ill, and I was studying in Dublin, he asked me to meet Donogh to talk about a matter in which my father was helping him. He was difficult. I didn't get any co-operation. My father was considerably more tolerant than I was.

The real shame of Donogh's premature death was that by this time he had quietened down a good deal and was becoming more effective in using his talents to good effect as a Government minister. That final stage of his life was tragically short. I think that if he had lived he would have been at the height of his powers in the 1970s. As against that, his mother told me in 1970, when she was over ninety, that she now understood why God had taken Donogh when he did. 'If Donogh was still alive he would have been involved with his pals Haughey and Blaney in whatever they were up to.'

The phone calls came from Dublin almost immediately after the funeral. There were also approaches from members of the local Fianna Fáil organisation. The belief was that I had a better chance of winning than anyone else.

I wasn't willing to be the candidate. My father had died only two years earlier, and taking over responsibility for the legal practice hadn't been an easy task. I had spent a lot of time sorting out the finances, and politics had not been on my agenda at all. There were also life-style issues. I was the father of three young children and was conscious that leaving the law for a career in politics would reduce my earning capacity greatly. But Pat was supportive of the idea, and she would later canvass and speak at meetings in support of my election. I couldn't have allowed my name to go forward without her support.

Before confirming anything with Fianna Fáil I went to see Donogh's widow, Hilda. Her name had been mentioned as a possible candidate, but she wasn't interested in contesting and had a poor view of the political life. She was very critical of Haughey and Blaney for their negative influence on her late husband. In fact she very strongly advised me not to run, for my own sake. But I was coming round to the idea.

When I finally decided that I would stand I got an agreement from the hierarchy in Fianna Fáil that, if elected, I could withdraw at the following general election. I was only twenty-nine. I never envisaged a lifetime in politics and was already keeping open the option of making an early exit.

By the time the Fianna Fáil convention was held it was clear that I would not face any serious opposition for the nomination. Still, several hundred people packed into the George Hotel in Limerick. Jack Lynch and Brian Lenihan were seated at the top table. I had met Lynch for the first time at Donogh's funeral; in fact the only senior Fianna Fáil people I had met previously were my old golf tutor, Paddy Hillery, and George Colley, who I knew from holidays in Ballybunion.

There was a by-election culture in the 1960s. Since the beginning of the decade there had already been fourteen by-elections, and in the three years since the 1965 general election six vacancies had arisen through the death of sitting TDs. As a result the main parties were well prepared for another contest when Donogh's death caused the Limerick East vacancy. Paudge Brennan from Co. Wicklow was appointed Fianna Fáil's director of elections. He had himself stood unsuccessfully in a by-election caused by the death of his father in 1953, only to take a seat at the following year's general election. By 1968 he was a parliamentary secretary to Kevin Boland. Brennan was a quiet man with a calm, steadying influence. Under his stewardship the campaign was going well. Then, with about two weeks to go to polling day, Neil Blaney took over.

Blaney was the party's self-declared champion of by-elections. He arrived with a team of workers from his Donegal bailiwick, the 'Donegal mafia'. They were tough boys, ready for a fight. In the 1960s they were by-election aficionados who travelled around the country to organise local campaigns.

Brennan was duly sidelined when Blaney decided, without consultation with the local party organisation, or myself as the candidate, to take over and to liven up the campaign. There were internal rows, mainly over Blaney's autocratic style. But he was a Government minister and a senior party figure, so he was hard to talk down.

He saw an opportunity for mischief when Fine Gael supporters wrote the name of their candidate, *O'Higgins*, in white paint many times on footpaths around the city. This unsightly action led to a certain amount of annoyance among citizens; but it drove Blaney into a fury. His response was immediate. His imported election workers were sent out the next night with tins of red paint. Their instructions were to paint the figures *77* after *O'Higgins* on every footpath where the word appeared.

The figure referred to the seventy-seven anti-treaty prisoners executed during the Civil War by the pro-treaty party, from which Fine Gael was born. My Fine Gael opponent in the by-election was a nephew of Kevin O'Higgins, who was Minister for Justice in that first government and who was later murdered. Blaney's action was a deliberate attempt to fan the Civil War flames and to resurrect past passions. There was widespread anger at the move.

I was furious when I discovered the following morning what had occurred. I realised that I would now lose quite a lot of number 1 votes from traditional Fine Gael supporters who were considering backing a new young Fianna Fáil candidate. I was even more concerned about lower preferences from the other candidates, especially as it was increasingly clear that the Labour Party candidate might come second on the first count. If this happened the seat would be determined by transfers from supporters of the eliminated Fine Gael candidate, whom Blaney had just seriously antagonised. In all six by-elections during the 18th Dáil the Labour candidate had finished in third place on the first count; but the prediction for Limerick East was that Mick Lipper would poll strongly. I began to panic over the possibility that Lipper would push O'Higgins into third place. I was fearful that the '77' slur would cost me victory, with Fine Gael transfers favouring Lipper, allowing him to win the seat.

There were no opinion polls in those days, so the outcome was still a concern on the day the votes were counted. My minder for the day was Don Davern from South Tipperary. He was only a few years older than me and had been appointed a parliamentary secretary in 1966 after just over a year in the Dáil. He would die suddenly in November 1968. Seeing my nervousness, Don brought me to a bar. He encouraged me to drink my first brandy. In his words, which I remember vividly, 'the situation calls for a brandy.'

I was ahead on the first count, receiving 16,638 first-preference votes. As forecast, Lipper had polled strongly, with 10,151 first preferences, slightly more than O'Higgins, who had 10,039. The Fianna Fáil tallymen were just hopeful of victory. But I got more of O'Higgins's transfers than expected and took the seat with a margin of more than 900 votes. I was now a politician, a public representative.

I got my first real taste of what this meant to some people a little over a week later. A woman approached me and put her television licence in front of me. 'It's up,' she said. 'Donogh always paid it for me.' 'Oh, did he?' I replied, wondering whether having been elected was such a good idea after all.

I was not really a typical Dáil deputy. My main interest was always in national issues. One of the defects of the political system is that few Dáil deputies get to focus on national issues. In my first year I had clinics regularly, but as I became more established I reduced them to one day a week, generally a Saturday. I never held 'mega-clinics', like some TDs, who travelled around their constituencies over several days with fixed hours to hear the concerns of the public. For many TDs these clinics are the most important part of their working week. Attendance in Leinster House from Tuesday to Thursday is almost a rest break.

I would have found that interpretation of the public representative's role to be soul-destroying. Thankfully, my constituents in Limerick East recognised and supported my role as someone whose work was primarily in the Dáil. I also had great party back-up in Limerick from scores of loyal and hard-working people.

I was fortunate in having a relatively high profile from the start of my political career, and within a year of my by-election success I was appointed Government Chief Whip, and ten months after that was appointed Minister for Justice.

Most issues raised at clinics are local or personal, and I found this aspect of the job unrewarding. But over the years I had constituency colleagues who revelled in this type of political work. After one general election in the 1980s, on the morning after a late-night con-clusion to the count, a PD member rang me in disbelief. 'You won't believe this,' he said, 'but I've just seen Willie O'Dea and two of his supporters canvassing in a local housing estate.' It was barely twelve hours since O'Dea, a Fianna Fáil candidate, had been re-elected to Dáil Éireann. The unfortunate man seemed to have nothing else to do and no other interests.

Most TDs will tell you that they get no thanks in the ballot box for working as legislators. That sort of work is largely ignored by the media, whose coverage of the Dáil is frequently dominated by rows and person-ality clashes. Serious coverage is the exception rather than the rule. Up to very recently, committees were largely ignored. Multi-seat constituencies encourage parochial and personality approaches to politics.

In my thirty-four years as a member of Dáil Éireann I worked with some fine parliamentarians. Despite our considerable differences, I don't mind admitting that Charles Haughey had an excellent grasp of parliamentary politics. When the PDs returned with fourteen seats after the 1987 general election the party had within its ranks many serious legislators. Michael McDowell was one of the most outstanding parliamentarians during all my time in Leinster House. He was actually much more effective in opposition, where he had far more scope to range over issues and display his tremendous intellectual abilities. Others, like Anne Colley and Geraldine Kennedy, were also extremely able individuals. It was a terrible pity that so many of these people served for such a short period. Others, like Liz O'Donnell, later gave terrific dedication to the public interest.

What is incredibly frustrating is that while the voters have rejected many excellent people—as is their right—there has repeatedly been in recent elections a toleration at the ballot box both of incompetence and of outright corruption. Many others do not even get as far as being rejected. Public cynicism towards politics and the constant negativity from the media have meant that many fine people would not now countenance a political career.

Shortly after the 1987 general election John McCoy from Limerick West, one of the new PD deputies, came to see me. I got a terrible fright at the conversation. He wanted to resign his seat. It was only three months since the election but he was already disillusioned with political and parliamentary life and a sense of not having the ability or the opportunity to achieve anything worthwhile. I talked him out of resignation but I perfectly understood the frustration.

We need to rethink how politics works in Ireland. The Oireachtas undoubtedly needs a champion. Unfortunately, the role of Ceann Comhairle is too weak for taking on this task. Several of the deputies who have been Ceann Comhairle have been weak and essentially held the role on the sufferance of the Government of the day. When I was first elected, the role had greater independence and authority. Deputies like Paddy Hogan and Cormac Breslin gave the position some stature; but since then it has been a home for those who don't make the Government or those who don't upset the Government of the day. The outcome is that the Dáil suffers.

We need to rethink how the Oireachtas works. For example, it is true that supporting a Government is the worst place to be, especially as a backbencher. The whip system is highly restrictive of parliamentary freedom, and it is most restrictive on government TDs. They become pure lobby fodder, and lack a real role in parliamentary work. That is pretty soul-destroying.

There was a tradition, long since gone, that when a male politician died in office his widow would be approached to stand in the ensuing by-election. There were plenty of widows elected during the 1930s, 40s and 50s. Unfortunately, few of them were really interested in politics and they had little to say in the Dáil. I remember being told the story about the funeral of one of our Fianna Fáil TDs in the 1950s. The mourners were around the graveside, and included among them was Martin Corry, a bachelor farmer from Co. Cork, a veteran of the War of Independence and boastful of his part in the Civil War. Corry was a founding member of Fianna Fáil who had held his seat in every election since 1926. He was still in the Dáil when I was elected in the 1968 by-election, although he stood down the following year at the age of seventy-nine. At this other TD's funeral, as the coffin was being lowered in silence into the grave, Corry was overheard saying, 'Move the writ on the 29th and put up the bloody widow.'

Nowadays, happily, women are elected in their own right. One way to increase the pool from which candidates are chosen would be to introduce a list system. But the disadvantage then is that the party apparatchiks are given an even greater say in who gets into Leinster House. Ultimately, the Irish people like to know who their public representatives are, and they want a direct say over who sits in Dáil Éireann. So it may be that the present system, imperfect as it is, actually works better than the alternatives. Democracy never achieves perfection, but it generally prevents tyranny.

I had no expectation that any of my children would seek a political career. Growing up they would have been aware of the long hours, the absences and, to a degree, the tough times during the leadership battles in Fianna Fáil. Even at the best of times politics is not an easy career. My six children were always involved at elections, helping out with canvassing and the like. It seemed that the closest any of them would come to a political career was when my son Eoin studied political science and went on to establish a career as a university lecturer. I was therefore surprised when my daughter Fiona first expressed an interest in becoming more involved in politics with the Progressive Democrats. She had been working in arts management in London before coming back to Dublin in the late 1990s to work with Liz O'Donnell as her parliamentary assistant. She won a seat—to my great surprise—in the 1999 local elections in Dún Laoghaire-Rathdown and used that experience to win a Dáil seat three years later. She enjoyed nine years in the Oireachtas—as a TD from 2002 to 2007 in Dún Laoghaire and, having lost her seat in 2007, as a Taoiseach's nominee to the Seanad from 2007 to 2011. Our Leinster House careers did not cross, because, when she was arriving as a new TD in 2002 I had finally brought the curtain down on my own time in politics.

Chapter 3 ❧

| 'THE MAN FROM UNCLE'

first entered Leinster House as a Dáil deputy on 22 May 1968. The
by-election was my first electoral contest. Over the following years
I was a candidate in ten general elections—six as a Fianna Fáil
candidate and another four for the Progressive Democrats.

I had never envisaged staying so long. I eventually retired from
politics in 2002, some thirty-four years after my first election.
Following tradition, on my first day in the Dáil Michael Carty, the
Government Chief Whip, introduced me to the Ceann Comhairle.
We walked down the steps into the chamber to applause from the
Fianna Fáil deputies. This positive welcome was matched on the other
side of the house by jeering and booing from the Fine Gael and
Labour Party TDs.

The Labour deputies in particular were intent on revisiting the
recent by-election. One Dublin TD, Seán Dunne, is captured in the
Dáil record as shouting, 'Lipper is the word and Lipper is the man.'
From the Government side Neil Blaney couldn't resist responding:
'Another moral victory,' he replied.

I was introduced to Cormac Breslin, a Fianna Fáil deputy from
Co. Donegal, who had been elected Ceann Comhairle the previous
year. As we briefly shook hands a distinctive Dublin voice rose above
the other interruptions. 'Here comes the man from Uncle,' Paddy
Belton of Fine Gael roared out. His reference to the popular American
television series raised laughter around the chamber, and the mood
immediately became more light-hearted on both sides.

Donnchadh Ó Briain, a veteran Fianna Fáil TD for Limerick West,
adopted me from my first day in Dáil Éireann. He was an Irish-
speaking stalwart of the old revolutionary brigade and he was at that

time in his early seventies. He had spent the 1920s cycling around Co. Limerick teaching Irish. Having been first elected to the Dáil in 1933, he certainly knew his way around Leinster House. 'Be warned, you're on your own now,' were his first words of advice.

Ó Briain offered to take me up to my new office accommodation. 'We've a great girl working for us,' he said. 'She's the only one in Leinster House who can take shorthand in Irish.' My 'office' was a small shared room on the top floor in Leinster House. Six deputies and a secretary worked from this tiny space, sharing two desks and a table.

I was informed that, as I was the most junior TD, I would receive the least amount of the secretary's time. I discovered that this allocation amounted to two hours a week. The absence of minimum administrative support came as a shock. From my legal practice I was used to a normal office environment. Leinster House was not the modern parliamentary complex it would later become. The facilities were poor and in many areas simply non-existent. I had to write everything out in longhand and frequently couldn't even find some place to sit down. I often worked from the Leinster House library.

Telephones were in short supply, and you could only dial Dublin numbers. The practice in Leinster House meant that each non-Dublin TD had to provide a single phone number to the exchange, and we were only allowed to ask the exchange to call that number. So, if I needed to phone anyone in Limerick in relation to constituency work or the legal practice I had to ring Pat at home to get her to ring whoever I needed and to ask them to phone me in Dublin.

Despite all these limitations, everyone just got on with the work. I was a new TD in my late twenties. I was hardly going to 'rock the boat' with men who had fought in the War of Independence.

Nevertheless, it was a difficult transition from my previous career to the world of politics. I was still involved in the legal practice, spending two days in Limerick and three days in Dublin. The salary of a TD in the 1960s was £850—a lot less than what I had been earning as a solicitor—so that politics amounted to practising a profession for the public good. There was no personal enrichment, least of all when you consider that the purchasing power of £850 in 1968 was equivalent to about €16,000 in 2014. The present-day TD's salary is €87,258.

As I was able to keep on some legal work, the drop in salary was not as sharp, and when I was made a minister a couple of years later the ministerial allowance eased the impact of the lower income. I thought there was a public-duty element to being a TD. I never saw the position as a long-term career, although I was fortunate in that the voters in Limerick East returned me to the Dáil over many elections.

In all the progress made in more recent years, with deputies better resourced, I believe the public-service aspect of being a TD has been lost to a degree. The pay is now high enough for many to see politics as a fairly lucrative career, if they can get re-elected. On the other hand, the uncertainty would not be tolerated in any other job. In effect, you are fired every few years.

I made my maiden speech on 18 June 1968, during a debate on that year's Finance Bill. Charles Haughey was Minister for Finance, and he listened to my speech. When I concluded, James Dillon, the former Fine Gael leader, was the first to acknowledge my contribution. 'It gives me great pleasure to compliment him upon it,' he said. Haughey is recorded as saying 'Hear, hear' to Dillon's remarks. Shortly after I sat down one of the ushers passed a sheet of paper to me. It was a note of congratulation from Haughey. He was already actively cultivating backbenchers, with the leadership of the party in his sights.

The group of ministers with which Donogh had been associated assumed I would be 'part of their gang.' I was an obvious disappointment to them. I was unimpressed with some of the new generation who viewed politics through the prism of money and business. They were also enthusiastic about the semi-secretive fund-raising organisation Taca. Kevin Boland, who would feature noisily in Government meetings as events in the North worsened in 1969, was a prominent backer of Taca, which was dominated by builders and property developers as well as ambitious ancillaries of that industry, such as architects, solicitors, quantity surveyors, and engineers. Jack Lynch and George Colley were not enthusiastic about how this aspect of Fianna Fáil was evolving, and this did not endear them to Haughey,

Boland or Blaney. The close relationship this latter trio had with the building industry was undoubtedly the motivation for Boland's attack on those who wanted to preserve Ireland's architectural heritage. He dismissed some such opponents as 'belted earls' and 'so-called clerics' (a reference to Prof. F. X. Martin, a less than austere Augustinian friar and a champion of the architectural conservation movement).

Haughey and others in the 'men in mohair suits' grouping stood in stark contrast to the older generation, who, while declining in number, still had a presence in Leinster House. It was hard not to be impressed by people like Frank Aiken, Seán MacEntee, Paddy Smith and Dr Jim Ryan. They understood the meaning of public duty and public service. Seán Lemass was still in the Dáil when I won the by-election. I didn't speak with him at any length but I noticed that on the days he was in Leinster House he always arrived early.

My favourite moment in his company was shortly after I was appointed Minister for Justice in 1970. We met at a sports award dinner in the Gresham Hotel. Lemass had breathing difficulties and for that reason was sitting on a chair in the reception area. He called me over. After offering me congratulations on my appointment he asked me a direct question. 'I want you to tell me exactly what age you are—exactly, in years, months, weeks and days.' I began to work it out as he watched me mentally calculate the total. 'Well, blast you!' he replied. 'You're exactly two weeks younger than I was when I was appointed a minister, and up to now I was still the youngest ever.'

This conversation took place while the revelations about the Arms Crisis were still emerging. Naturally, I never discussed Haughey with Lemass, but it was well known that he did not have a high opinion of his son-in-law, and that view remained until his death.

Lemass was arguably the most successful politician in Ireland since independence—not just because he was intellectually very striking but he simply had a feel for what made things work. Few politicians have that innate quality. I think if he had got his way in the 1930s Ireland would have become a very different country. De Valera had a vision that was romantic but unrealistic. In economic terms at least, it is one of the tragedies of this period that Lemass did not succeed De Valera earlier.

I entered politics having completed eight years' experience as a solicitor in Limerick. Not surprisingly, I had specific interests in the area of law reform, alongside economic policy, which was the focus of my first Dáil speech. The legal professions, and barristers in particular, were—and remain—one of the most powerful interest groups in Ireland. We hear regularly about the need to eliminate restrictive practices in various industries, but when it comes to the law the practitioners' bodies, and frequently the bench, have long seen themselves as immune from reform. Throughout my political career, and during my various times as a minister, I tried to promote greater competition, but when it came to getting reforms in the legal profession I regret to say the pace of change was always painfully slow, to our cost as a country.

At a meeting with the Benchers of King's Inns in 1971 about legal education I was informed: 'Our motto since Queen Anne is *Nolumus mutari*. 'Mutari' is both a transitive and an intransitive verb. You can take it either way, minister: we will neither change, nor be changed!'

Despite my initial reluctance to contest the Limerick East by-election in 1968, a year later I was a general election candidate. I was shocked when Hilda O'Malley, Donogh's widow, announced that she would contest the constituency as an independent. This decision was all the more surprising given her refusal to stand in the by-election. She had strongly urged me not to run in the by-election because of her negative view of political life. Some disaffected local party members and other elements in Dáil Éireann—unhappy that I wasn't another Donogh—encouraged her. All in all, it was a difficult situation, portrayed in the newspapers as a family rift.

The 1969 contest was significant in being Lynch's first contest as party leader. Fianna Fáil was seeking to extend its period in power, having won successive elections since 1957. There was a section in Fianna Fáil who were not convinced that Lynch would win, and they were already preparing for a leadership contest. But Lynch had an excellent campaign. He toured the country in what was the first truly professional election campaign in Irish politics. The slogan '*Let's back Jack*' connected with voters. Fianna Fáil won three extra seats, and the party was returned to office. Despite the local difficulty of having two O'Malleys on the ballot paper in Limerick East, I was happy to be successfully returned as a TD.

Once the fourteen Government appointments were announced, Lynch left a gap of a week before confirming who would get the five junior posts of parliamentary secretary (today called minister of state).

During the week in which the Dáil returned after the election and the new Government had been appointed, David Andrews from Dún Laoghaire asked me if I would like a trip to Germany. With the election over, I decided I would accept. Tom O'Higgins, the Fine Gael deputy who had narrowly lost out in the 1966 presidential election, was on the visit to Bonn as chairman of the Irish Council of the European Movement, with Denis Corboy, the secretary. There was a day of meetings at several state offices, but afterwards we enjoyed a very pleasant dinner in a restaurant overlooking the Rhine.

After dinner O'Higgins said to me, 'Aren't you a foolish, innocent young fellow?' I was puzzled by his question. 'Well, your friend Mr Andrews wasn't the only one we invited. We originally had Michael O'Kennedy on the list, but he passed the invitation on to Andrews, who passed it on to you. And of course the reason neither of them wanted to be away from home this weekend was that both wanted to be near a phone in Dublin. You see, they're expecting a call. I thought for that reason you might stay at home.'

I replied that I wasn't expecting any phone call. And I was genuine in my lack of expectation of elevation.

I enjoyed my weekend in Bonn. But when I arrived back at Dublin Airport on Tuesday morning a member of the Aer Rianta staff was waiting for me with a message asking me to contact the Taoiseach's office. Lynch was offering me the position of Government Chief Whip and parliamentary secretary to himself.

I was surprised but delighted at the unexpected promotion from the back benches after such a short period in the Dáil. It was a big promotion for someone who had just turned thirty and who had a bare twelve months' experience in the Dáil. As Government Chief Whip I was now spending much more time in Dublin. I started the process of disengaging from the legal practice. I brought in solicitors to cover my work, but in truth my legal career effectually came to an end with this first step on the ministerial ladder. When Fianna Fáil returned to opposition after the 1973 general election I did some work in the practice; but with the unpredictable demands of politics—and with Lynch often ringing and asking me to meet him in Dublin—it was impossible to commit myself to any substantial work. I ended up doing probate cases only. This was straightforward, predictable work but terribly boring. After a couple of years in opposition it was clear that combining even this small volume of legal work with the demands of being a frontbench spokesperson was unsustainable.

The Government Chief Whip is responsible for the business of the Dáil. One of the main tasks is ensuring that government TDs turn up when there is a vote. At the 1969 general election Fianna Fáil got a narrow majority. In truth there was very little indiscipline in the parliamentary party. The private secretary to the Chief Whip was a woman called Hettie Behan, who had been *in situ* since the 1930s. As far as she was concerned, I was just another politician passing through the office who'd be gone again in a short period. My predecessor, Michael Carty, had let her run the office without much interference.

Irish politics was in a period of transition. The older generation was gradually being replaced through retirement and death. As Chief Whip I was very conscious that suddenly I was 'in charge' of these fellows. I had to be very careful not to be seen to be giving orders to the greats of the independence struggle. Many of these older TDs had been first elected years before I was even born.

The new generation was a more mixed collection. Erskine Childers constantly complained about the quality of the more recent arrivals. There were very few women. It was hardly a family-friendly job. The Dáil rarely sat in the morning; there was lots of waiting around until late into the evening, and sittings to midnight were the norm. In this environment many politicians gravitated towards the bar. As I mentioned previously, there was undoubtedly a lot more drinking than there is today.

The Chief Whip gets to attend the weekly Government meeting. From my point of view it was probably the most interesting part of the job. I received all the Government papers circulated on the Friday before the meeting, and then I got to listen to the discussions when the Government met. The Chief Whip sat in a fixed seat at every meeting, two chairs down from the Taoiseach, who chaired the meetings. The convention at that time was that the Chief Whip did not speak, and I made a contribution only when I was asked. This convention was dispensed with later. Aside from the fifteen members of the Government—the Taoiseach and his fourteen ministers—three other office-holders attended meetings: the Attorney-General, the Secretary to the Government, and the Whip.

Jack Lynch was an effective chairman, and he got through the weekly agenda very efficiently. We usually began at 11 a.m., and it would be unusual if the meeting had not concluded by 1 p.m. It was only when there was a crisis—as later with the situation in Northern Ireland—that the Government met more than once a week, or for more than two hours. The hostile attitude held towards Lynch by some ministers had not come to the fore at that stage. As a new deputy, and as a new presence at the Government table, I detected little personal antagonism towards him. I saw a lot of Lynch in this period, although most of our discussions were about procedural matters in organising Dáil business. I found him straight, honest and decent. His style was to remain relatively detached; ministers and parliamentary secretaries were allowed to get on with their jobs with little interference. In later years the office of Taoiseach would become more presidential, with a greater concentration of power and authority in the individual who was head of government. This centralisation began under Haughey but was continued by Garret FitzGerald, although these two had very different reasons for this approach.

Throughout my career, from my first appearance in 1969 as Chief Whip, I was fortunate to serve in several different Governments: as Minister for Justice (May 1970 to March 1973), Minister for Industry, Commerce and Energy (July 1977 to December 1979), Minister for Industry, Commerce and Tourism (December 1979 to June 1981), Minister for Trade, Commerce and Tourism (March to October 1982) and Minister for Industry and Commerce (July 1989 to November 1992).

I served under three Taoisigh—Jack Lynch, Charles Haughey and Albert Reynolds—and as a representative of two political parties. The context was very different. In the 1989–92 Government, not only was it a coalition but I was no longer a Fianna Fáil member but rather leader of the Progressive Democrats.

As well as the differences in style and approach of different Taoisigh, I came to see the qualities of a variety of figures who were fortunate enough to serve as ministers. I came to the view that at any given time about 20 per cent of ministers were essentially passengers. They simply turned up for Government meetings and then got on with their respective ministerial responsibilities, but without any individual spark or initiative. They were simply glad to be in the Government. They went for the easy life, avoiding conflict with their senior civil servants. As I discovered over the years, officials are very good at placating their ministers. And to stay out of difficulty, not a few ministers failed to assert the authority of their office.

There is much talk of the civil service as the 'permanent government'. But in my opinion, inaction is generally due to the failure of ministers to be active in delivering on their political responsibilities. I saw some unsuitable people securing ministerial rank, people with no ideology and no feel for policy. Charles Haughey placed a few second-team players in the Government. He had, of course, huge debts to repay after the leadership contest in 1979. People who would never have had any expectation of ministerial rank began to appear at the Government table. In his quest for the Fianna Fáil leadership Haughey had promised jobs to so many TDs that he could not give them all a Government post. His response was to increase the number of ministers of state; but there was no quality control over who was promoted. Haughey's single-party Governments were weak, and (as I will discuss later) his 1987–9 Government had an aura of corruption about it.

In more recent years the number of ministerial passengers has decreased. Part of the reason is that ministers are now more exposed. They can't get away so easily with coasting on the job. This is one of the benefits of more vigilant media. Newspaper and television reporters are far more vigilant today than in an earlier era. They are frequently unfair to politicians; but at the same time all this attention tends to weed out the weak in a parliamentary party from which those of ministerial rank are drawn. No Taoiseach today could afford to have too many ministers who are essentially passengers.

The prerogative of appointing members of the Seanad to the Government has only twice been exercised. Taoisigh are afraid to disgruntle ambitious backbenchers. Nearly every foot-soldier now sees himself as a potential general.

Lynch and Haughey were effective in chairing Government meetings. Reynolds had little interest in detailed discussions and, as Taoiseach in a coalition Government, was reckless in his treatment of his unhappy partners. I also worked with some excellent Government colleagues. In fairness to Haughey I must say he was one of the better ministers under Lynch. He had a view on policy and he knew what he wanted to achieve, and he was well able to take on his departmental officials. But with Haughey it was always necessary to consider the motives behind his decision-making.

Paddy Hillery was another effective minister. He was a quiet and decent man. He was also honourable and helpful, and an acute observer of what went on around him. I'm sure when I was appointed Chief Whip in 1969 and Minister for Justice a year later Hillery would have been amused that the callow youth whom he had instructed on the golf course fifteen years earlier was now his Government colleague. I came to appreciate his qualities, which did a great deal to sustain Lynch at a dangerous time during the Arms Crisis. As Hillery saw it, he was not just sustaining the leader of Fianna Fáil but was also protecting the representative democracy that Lynch personified and that was under threat.

Hillery was a constant source of encouragement to me when I was often beleaguered in the Department of Justice because of my opposition to terrorism. He kept a close eye on events at home while spending an increasing amount of time in Brussels, leading the Irish negotiations for membership of the EEC. Apart from difficulties with fisheries, the negotiations were largely concluded by the end of 1971.

The existing six member-states were adamant on access to our fishing waters, and Hillery could not prevail. It was the only disadvantage in the successful entry terms, and Ireland reaped the benefits of the work of Hillery and his team for several decades afterwards. His appointment as Ireland's first member of the European Commission was a great loss to national politics. Things might have been different in and after 1979 if he had stayed in Irish politics.

Chapter 4 ∾

'‎EQUAL MEASURES OF TENACITY AND CALMNESS'

I was at home in Limerick when Jack Lynch rang early on Monday 4 May 1970. Pat took the call. I was in the bath when she announced, 'The Taoiseach is on the phone.' I was intrigued about why the Taoiseach was ringing me on a Monday morning. 'Something serious has happened,' Lynch said. He then asked, 'Can you be in my office by 12 noon?' The roads were not as good as they are today, but I was in Dublin within three hours.

When we met, Lynch explained that earlier that morning he had visited the Minister for Justice, Mícheál Ó Móráin, in Mount Carmel Hospital. Ó Móráin had not been well and he was now likely to be laid up for several more weeks. Lynch said he needed a Minister for Justice working to full capacity and with his full faculties. He had just become aware of a range of activities being pursued by some of his ministers, and that Ó Móráin had not passed on important security information over recent weeks and months. Ó Móráin's blatant failure to report on certain activities had put the Taoiseach in an extremely difficult position. When Lynch asked him why he had not passed on certain security reports, Ó Móráin replied that his inaction was because he could not believe that his ministerial colleagues could be engaged in illegal activities. He thought the reports were far-fetched.

Lynch was left with little choice, and that morning he requested Ó Móráin's resignation. It was announced that he had resigned on health grounds, which was true.

'I propose to appoint you Minister for Justice,' Lynch explained. As I was taking in this dramatic news he delivered the even more startling announcement that he was about to sack Charles Haughey and Neil

Blaney. Haughey was Minister for Finance, Blaney was Minister for Agriculture, and they were two of the biggest beasts in the Government. As Lynch explained in detail what had led him to these dramatic actions, my first words were 'Oh, my God!'

Lynch had become aware on Monday 20 April of a plot to illegally import arms for use in Northern Ireland. His source was Peter Berry, Secretary of the Department of Justice. The security information available to Berry directly implicated Blaney and Haughey. With Ó Móráin not passing on this information, Berry—having consulted President de Valera—bypassed his minister to contact the Taoiseach. Lynch wanted to substantiate the allegations and asked Berry to get more Garda information. Steps were immediately taken to ensure that no arms importation would take place.

Lynch then sought to interview both ministers on Wednesday 22 April. It was Budget Day, but Haughey was seriously indisposed and under medical care in hospital. The official story stated that he was the victim of a horse-riding accident that morning at Kinsealy, which had rendered him unconscious. However, doubt was immediately cast upon that version of events; rumours began to circulate that Haughey had actually been the victim of a violent assault, carried out by persons unknown upon the discovery of a personal indiscretion. Indeed, this was the story related to me by Peter Berry some weeks after I was appointed Minister for Justice. He, in turn, had been informed by the Gardaí. Despite its widespread circulation, no evidence was ever produced to substantiate that version of events.

Lynch contacted Haughey's doctor on a number of occasions, seeking permission to meet Haughey, but was prevented from doing so for roughly a week. He was told it would not be appropriate to ask questions about anything serious. The Taoiseach ended up delivering Haughey's budget speech.

When Haughey had sufficiently recovered, Lynch went to see him in hospital, after first interviewing Blaney. Haughey had a fractured skull and other injuries. Lynch spoke to him for only a few minutes; it was not possible to question him in any detail. Nevertheless, on the substantive issue Haughey, like Blaney, denied any involvement in an illegal arms plot. But the evidence against them was substantial. Lynch requested their resignations but agreed to their separate requests for more time to consider their positions.

When the Government met on Tuesday 5 May, Lynch revealed that serious allegations had been made against Haughey and Blaney. He informed the Government that both ministers had denied any involvement in a plot to illegally import arms. Blaney was at the meeting; Haughey was still in hospital. Having received more Garda information, Lynch again requested their resignations, and when these were not forthcoming he duly sacked Blaney and Haughey.

News of their dismissal was released in the early hours of Wednesday 6 May. Much was later made of the fact that the Fine Gael leader, Liam Cosgrave, had gone to Lynch earlier that evening with information on an arms plot; but Cosgrave's intervention was immaterial. Lynch had already decided on a course of action. In any event, with so many people having some knowledge of the plot it would have been impossible—even if he had wanted to, which he did not—to ignore the serious information now available.

The facts that had come to light presented a threat of unparalleled gravity to the Irish state. I wasn't sure that the Government could survive this turmoil. We were vulnerable to either political defeat in the Dáil or—such were the uncertain times—extreme civil unrest.

Ó Móráin's resignation was confirmed to the Dáil on Tuesday 5 May. My appointment was to be debated the following day, but it was caught up in the dramatic news about the sacking of Haughey and Blaney.

There was real crisis in Leinster House throughout the Wednesday. The sitting was adjourned until 10 p.m. In moving the motion on my nomination as Minister for Justice, Lynch also confirmed that Blaney and Haughey had refused to resign and so both had been dismissed from the Government. Another minister, Kevin Boland, resigned in sympathy with his two dismissed colleagues.

The broad outline of what had taken place was now known. An illegal consignment of arms was meant to land at Dublin Airport from the Continent, ostensibly for use in Northern Ireland. Those involved had planned to bring the arms through Customs without the consignment being examined; but the Gardaí had received a tip-off about the plot, as well as intelligence that Haughey, as Minister for Finance, had authorised passage through Customs. According to Garda sources, others involved included Blaney, Captain James Kelly (an army intelligence officer), John Kelly (a Belfast IRA man), and Albert Luykx (a former Nazi from Belgium who owned a hotel in Sutton, Co. Dublin).

The Dáil debate on my appointment continued until 2:50 a.m. on what was now the Thursday. All sorts of wild rumours were in circulation in Leinster House. Talk of a general election was everywhere. It wasn't clear whether the Government could muster a majority in the Dáil; but there were ultimately no defections on the Fianna Fáil side. Blaney and Boland voted with the Government, which had a majority of seven, to approve my appointment.

After a few hours' sleep I accompanied Jack Lynch to Áras an Uachtaráin to receive my seal of office at 9 a.m. Éamon de Valera was into his second term as President of Ireland. He was an old man and his health was failing, but he was abreast of the dramatic developments of the previous twenty-four hours. 'These are terrible times,' he said. He told us that he had been keeping in touch with the overnight drama in Leinster House. With my nomination having only been approved by the Dáil in the small hours of the morning, it was considered too late to hold the ceremony of receiving my ministerial seal; but the President had been waiting for us. 'I stayed up until 4 a.m. I thought you'd come up,' he said.

Because of the gravity of the situation, de Valera did not want to detain us too long that morning. Before the end of the year I was to have two interesting discussions with him about the continuing crisis.

I knew that being Minister for Justice was going to be difficult, given the worsening situation in Northern Ireland; but with the revelations about the attempted illegal importing of arms the job was made all the more difficult. Nevertheless I was happy to accept the position. You don't turn down an opportunity to become a Government minister, particularly when you're young and presumably full of confidence.

Looking back now I can see that I was spectacularly inexperienced for the job, and most egregiously so in the context of the events that emerged in May 1970. I'm not sure why Lynch turned to me. We had developed a good relationship since I had been appointed Chief Whip a year previously, although we were not particularly close. I think he knew he could trust me. Part of the difficulty in May 1970 was that he had not been told about events to which he should have been alerted, and he didn't want to be put in that position again.

I should make it clear from the outset: there was never a Government proposal or any intention to buy arms or to supply arms to people in the North. I sat at the Government table as Chief Whip for almost a year. It was not Government policy. And it couldn't have been Government policy unless it was decided at the Government table. It was, of course, possible legally to import arms for that purpose had the Government been so minded, but it was not.

The Arms Crisis was the greatest internal crisis to hit the state since the Civil War in the aftermath of the treaty debates in 1921. As we took stock after the dramatic few days in early May 1970, which had seen four ministers and a parliamentary secretary replaced, it was possible not just that the Government might collapse but that the state itself might be engulfed in violent turmoil.

As I got to grips with my new role as Minister for Justice I was amazed at what was emerging. I'd go so far as to say I was speechless. The atmosphere at party meetings was very strange. In the immediate aftermath of the revelations there was a lot of roaring and shouting at parliamentary party meetings. But as the weeks went by some of this crowd stopped coming to meetings. I suspect they realised that Lynch's authority had grown and that their desired leadership change was not going to happen.

While some people, with the benefit of hindsight, now criticise Lynch for not moving as rapidly as present-day pundits think he should, the fact of the matter is that the truth prevailed. As we now look back we know that the conflict in the North left almost 3,500 people dead and many thousands more injured. I think the number could have multiplied tenfold if Lynch and others had not nipped in the bud some of the things that might have been caused by the events of 1970. In the southern part of the island, at least, peace prevailed, and the conflict in Northern Ireland, bad and all as it was, did not get as bad as it would have been if there had been outright civil war.

'Treason' is a term that has a precise legal definition, namely levying war against the state; so in a strict definitional sense the actions of those involved did not qualify as treason. But I believe that encouraging people who later showed themselves well capable of levying war against the state qualifies as an act of treason in a moral sense. If Jack Lynch had caved in in May 1970, God only knows what would have happened.

———

To understand the Arms Crisis it is necessary to understand what had been happening from July 1969 onwards in Northern Ireland. There was an emerging crisis in the North, and in this increasingly complex situation the Arms Crisis was one frightening aspect. My wife's family was from Co. Tyrone, so we were regular visitors to Northern Ireland. But Omagh was a relatively quiet place; there was no great tension. The situation was obviously very different in Derry and Belfast, where tensions were running much higher. The nationalist community were treated as second-class citizens. The Unionist government at Stormont pursued a policy of deliberate discrimination, and it was understandable that nationalist frustration at their treatment would increase.

The arrival of television in the 1960s made a huge difference. People saw the injustices at all levels of society in the North and they were no longer prepared to tolerate such behaviour. There was huge sympathy for the civil rights campaigners. The Unionist regime responded badly, and its actions—and inactions—created the space for those who favoured violence to exploit. Emotions were running high, and the Government had legitimate concerns for stability on the entire island. It met to discuss the heavy-handed and brutal police response to civil rights marchers in Derry in August 1969 and the ensuing escalation of violence throughout the North.

I had only just been appointed Chief Whip the previous month and, in keeping with protocol, I did not contribute at Government meetings, but I listened carefully to discussions on the unfolding crisis. A number of actions were agreed, including setting up field hospitals and emergency accommodation centres along the border for those fleeing from the North. The possibility of some form of humanitarian incursion into the North was contemplated if needed; but it was a discussion in the context of a possible serious attack on nationalists close to the border and consequent loss of life. In fact the British would have driven out our troops in a very short space of time. The Government never seriously contemplated military intervention in the sense of marching across the border or anything like that; the only policy contemplated was the possibility of putting troops on the border for the humanitarian purpose of getting people out of the North.

The Minister for Finance, Charles Haughey, and the Minister for Defence, Jim Gibbons, were asked to liaise to ensure that the army was prepared for a worsening of the situation. The contingency plan was essentially for a Doomsday situation if the British did not defend nationalists from attack and if there were large numbers of casualties and a significant loss of life. In such an extreme eventuality Irish troops would have sought to extricate those under attack, as best they could. Their sole role would have been a purely humanitarian one, to facilitate the evacuation of wounded and frightened people and to get them to safety before there was further loss of life. In this context the field hospitals set up along the border would have treated the injured before moving them to hospital where necessary.

We asked the relevant authorities to prepare for the possibility that such an extreme situation might arise. The Government was discussing what would happen if Armageddon arose. And even if that scenario had come to pass it would not have been an 'invasion': it would have been a purely humanitarian response. The way this plan was later represented by Blaney and others was very different from how it was discussed within the Government. Lynch and the great majority of the Government weren't naïve enough to think that the Irish army could take on the British army and air force.

Neil Blaney and Kevin Boland spoke forcefully about the possibility of the army going across the border. In particular I recall these discussions to be in respect of events in Derry but also in respect of attacks on Catholics in west Belfast, although I think even Blaney and Boland admitted that that would be hopeless and counter-productive. Most of their urgings related to people living close to the border, because they realised that these were the only people who could be saved in the event of an Armageddon type of situation. I especially remember Derry being talked about in this regard.

It is difficult at this remove to realise that some of what was going on in Derry was diversionary. The most serious violence was certainly in Belfast. The Government was very concerned about the situation there. There was more information about what was happening in Derry, but it was recognised that Catholics in west Belfast and in one part of east Belfast were especially vulnerable. These people were hostages to a great extent, while many of those in Derry could have got out fairly quickly in an extreme situation.

There were many outbursts at Government meetings during these months. Blaney and Boland tended to be the loudest voices. My main memory from this period, when trouble began to break out in the North, was how vociferous they were, frequently roaring and shouting. Boland in particular was a bag of noise. There was never any mention of the party leadership, but they were clearly preparing the ground for a challenge. They had never accepted Lynch as leader when he replaced Lemass in 1966; in their view he was not green enough and was a temporary occupant of the position. They thought the trouble in the North gave them an opportunity to shaft Lynch.

I actually thought Lynch had good control over the Government throughout this period. The great majority of ministers backed him and, like myself, found the behaviour of the others very hard to take. Most ministers avoided an ultra-nationalist stance. People like George Colley, Erskine Childers, Paddy Hillery, Pádraig Faulkner and Joe Brennan were horrified and disgusted at the behaviour and demeanour of Boland and Blaney.

We eventually got used to Boland sounding off. He wasn't taken too seriously; and I would include Blaney and Haughey as sharing that view. I don't think they ever fully trusted Boland; he'd be attacking everyone and everything. For his part, Blaney would go on about the Drumboe incident. During the Civil War in 1923 Free State soldiers executed without trial four anti-treaty soldiers at Drumboe Castle, near Stranorlar; but the way Blaney kept mentioning Drumboe you'd think it was something that happened the previous week.

I also remember how quiet Charles Haughey was at these Government meetings when the North was discussed. He didn't play any part in these rows. I think that was why we were all astounded the following May to learn that he was a prime mover in the whole arms affair. Through these months, whenever Haughey did make a contribution it was always in a calm, logical manner; but he was playing both sides. It was revealed many years later that in October 1969 he had met the British ambassador to discuss terms for a united Ireland. He was also secretly meeting senior IRA members. He was clearly keen to outflank his more vocal Fianna Fáil rivals in the republican stakes.

Given the direction in which events were moving, I was half-expecting Boland and Blaney to leave the Government. Boland did walk out, but unfortunately he came back without much of a delay. He became very agitated at one meeting about whether the FCA should be called up for full-time service. The question was discussed in detail, and a consensus was reached that there was no point in involving part-time reservists who were not trained for this type of conflict. Boland was furious with the decision. He packed up his papers and stamped out of the room, muttering threats to resign as he left. There were two big oak doors in the Government room, to prevent anyone in the corridor hearing a discussion at Government meetings. On his way out Boland slammed the first door, but his momentum was stopped when he had to open the second door. My abiding memory is of waiting two or three painful seconds for the second door to be slammed. It was, but the reverberation was not quite as bad, because the inner door had closed.

President de Valera became aware of the walk-out. He contacted Boland and talked him out of resigning. He probably thought he was doing the right thing by the Government and by Fianna Fáil in persuading him to stay; but with hindsight I'm not sure it was such a good intervention. I don't think Lynch would have been at all displeased if Boland's resignation had been forthcoming.

Boland was a complex character who by this stage in his career had come full circle. His father, Gerry Boland, as Minister for Justice during the war years had ratified the execution of several IRA members for the murder of gardaí. As Minister for Defence in the early 1960s Kevin Boland had approved the internment of IRA men in the Curragh in military custody, who were thus legally under his care as minister. There is no evidence that he dissented from the Government decision to introduce internment, nor did he offer to resign. Yet a few years later he was waving the green flag. Boland's new-found 'republicanism' was probably as much due to his dislike of Lynch— and resentment at Lynch's success as Taoiseach—as any other factor.

For three people who apparently had a similar objective they didn't get on very well, a fact borne out by events. After the firing of Haughey and Blaney, and Boland's resignation, they never came together as a cohesive force. They were deeply suspicious of one another. In the subsequent court case Blaney and Haughey adopted fundamentally different approaches: Blaney took the line that 'we were entitled to do this,' whereas as far as Haughey was concerned it never happened at all. Haughey wanted to remain in Fianna Fáil at all costs, no matter how demeaning, including having to vote confidence in his enemies. Blaney left the party and remained in splendid isolation with his Donegal organisation for the remainder of his political career.

After Boland resigned from Fianna Fáil later in 1970 he formed a new political party, Aontacht Éireann. Along with twelve other candidates he contested the 1973 general election, but the party won less than 1 per cent of the national vote, and all failed to be elected. Shortly beforehand one wit set up a limited company called Aontacht Éireann Teoranta. In its memorandum and articles of association this company listed its principal objective as the sport of hot-air ballooning!

In later years, long after his political career had finished, Boland received several handsome sums from libel actions against newspapers and other publishers. The alleged libel arose from articles that said Lynch had fired three ministers in May 1970 for complicity in the illegal importing of arms, whereas the truth was that Lynch fired two ministers but Boland resigned on the same day, in solidarity with Blaney and Haughey. Boland claimed he had been libelled, as he had never tried to import arms, although I always thought he would have been happier if he had. I think he was annoyed that Blaney and Haughey had never told him what they were up to, because they regarded him as a bit of a loose cannon.

The Government was getting conflicting stories about what was happening in the North, and that is why a number of initiatives were taken. Of course there were no Provos in 1969. There was a Sinn Féin, which was very left-wing, and an almost non-existent IRA. Some of the Southern leaders, especially those in Dublin, were Marxists. This radical politics gave people like Blaney and Boland certain qualms. They would have wanted nothing to do with a Marxist-oriented organisation. And that political leaning was in part responsible in early 1970 for the split and for allegations that individuals in Fianna Fáil facilitated the setting up of the Provos. The formal split in the IRA came in December 1969 and in Sinn Féin in January 1970, although it had been brewing in the latter months of 1969. My recollection is that the Northern leaders were not being talked about very much, largely because little was known about them. The Dublin leadership was known, and they were mentioned in intelligence circles.

I know nothing about any directive being issued to the army in January 1970 that, as was claimed, ordered it to be ready to intervene across the border in a Doomsday situation. Any discussion I heard in this regard was purely in the context of the army seeking to facilitate the departure of threatened or wounded nationalists. This is why the emphasis was on medical posts, to enable people to be treated, recognising that some of the people would probably be injured, perhaps seriously. In such a Doomsday situation these people could not walk out, or even be taken out on the backs of lorries: they were going to have to be removed by ambulance. In such an eventuality 'Doomsday' never went beyond getting people out or saving as many people as possible.

————

Among the measures agreed by the Government in August 1969 was the allocation of money for assisting victims of the unrest in the North. Haughey, as Minister for Finance, was to ensure that the money was made available. It was clearly intended to support humanitarian measures, and it was to be administered by the Red Cross.

A Government sub-committee to organise measures for relieving distress in the North met only once. I think only two attended, Pádraig Faulkner and Joe Brennan. As a result, Haughey alone oversaw the allocation of the £100,000 in the emergency fund.

There was no major debate in the Government about this money. It was approved by the Government and was intended for 'the relief of distress in Northern Ireland' and to provide shelter, food and clothing to those in need. It was never intended for buying arms. Mystery remains about what all the money was spent on. It does seem that some of it was used for humanitarian purposes; but I have no doubt that part of it was used illegally and for violent purposes.

When the IRA and Sinn Féin split in late 1969 and early 1970 they emerged as two separate movements: the traditionalists on the Provisional side, who were happy to use violence to achieve a united Ireland, and the left-leaning Officials, who had dreams of a socialist republic. The outlook of the Provos was more in keeping with the views of the Fianna Fáil republican dissidents.

The ability of the Public Accounts Committee to inquire into what had happened to the money was stopped by a High Court action brought by Pádraig (Jock) Haughey, a brother of Charles Haughey, and the committee was unable to complete its inquiries. From the initial inquiries we can account for part of the money, but not for the bulk of it, and that question remains unanswered to this day.

That was only a small part of the money provided to assist the Provos at that time. They were heavily supported by private donations, mainly from the United States and, I would think, money from Colonel Gaddafi. He later gave them free arms and explosives, given his twisted logic in wanting to support 'anti-imperialist freedom-fighters'. He was always keen to arm anti-Western groups, and he saw the Provisional IRA/Sinn Féin in that guise.

The arms plotters knew they were acting without Government sanction. Blaney had recruited the assistance of a junior army intelligence officer, Captain James Kelly, in an operation to import arms from the Continent for use in the North. In October 1969 Kelly met senior IRA figures at a meeting in Bailieborough, Co. Cavan, and pledged £50,000 for the purchase of weapons.

Kelly always claimed he was working with official approval; but there was something highly unusual in an army intelligence officer reporting to the Minister for Agriculture. If the Government had wanted to import arms the correct procedure would have been followed and the Minister for Defence or the Minister for Justice would have signed the relevant purchase and import documents at the request of the Quartermaster-General. That process was not followed, and the reason was that those involved did not have official sanction for their illegal activities, and they knew it.

While Haughey was relatively silent during Government discussions about the North, reliable informants told the Gardaí that a Government minister met Cathal Goulding, the IRA's Chief of Staff, in August 1969. It was alleged that they discussed a deal whereby, if the IRA agreed to stop the destruction of foreign-owned property in the South, it would be facilitated in moving weapons in the North. The Special Branch learnt the identity of the minister: Charles Haughey. Peter Berry informed his minister, Mícheál Ó Móráin, who subsequently dismissed the meeting when accepting Haughey's explanation that he had been asked to meet an individual whom he didn't know, and that it had not been an important encounter.

In the autumn of 1969 the Special Branch received further information that small consignments of arms were being imported through Dublin Airport at times when a sympathetic Customs officer was on duty. The belief in Garda circles was that Haughey was involved; there were also suspicions that Blaney was active in this.

We now know that Haughey not only made available public money for clandestine arms purchases but sought to secure Customs clearance for their safe arrival in the state. He rang Peter Berry at his home in Dartry, Dublin, at 6:25 p.m. on Saturday 18 April 1970. Berry recognised the minister's distinctive voice. There was no small talk. Haughey immediately asked Berry if he was aware of a certain cargo that was due to arrive at Dublin Airport the following day. Berry (who had already received information about the plan) confirmed that he knew by replying, 'Yes, minister.' Haughey asked if the cargo would be allowed through Customs if a guarantee were given that it would go directly to the North. Berry—fully aware of Government policy, and that such an importation was illegal—replied with a single word, 'No.' Haughey responded: 'I think that is a bad decision.' When Berry did not reply, the minister asked, 'Does the man from Mayo know about this?' He was told that Ó Móráin was aware of the arms plot. 'What will happen when it arrives?' Haughey asked. 'It will be grabbed,' Berry replied, to which Haughey responded, 'I had better have it called off.'

Berry had a contemporaneous note of this conversation, written in the back of his diary, which he later showed me. It was a bit jumbled and messy, as one might expect, but it was legible, and I am perfectly certain that it was authentic.

This telephone call is crucial in confirming Haughey's involvement in the plot to import arms, regardless of his subsequent denials. If it had had legal approval—that is, had been officially authorised by the Government—Ó Móráin would surely have known. Why did Haughey then go on to enquire whether there was any possibility of it getting in—'it' being a consignment of arms? He was told by Berry that there was no possibility, because there was a 'ring of steel around the airport,' placed there at his direction.

Charges were brought in late May 1970 against Haughey, Blaney, Kelly and two other men: John Kelly of Belfast and Albert Luykx. These five men stood accused of a conspiracy to import arms. Informations against Blaney were refused in the District Court; then, dramatically, following accusations of bias against the judge, Mr Justice Aindrias Ó Caoimh (a son-in-law of President de Valera), the first trial in the Central Criminal Court collapsed on 29 September 1970. A second trial of the four remaining defendants before a new judge lasted from 6 to 23 October.

Throughout this period there was never any certainty that the Government would survive. There was constant pressure, and an air of crisis engulfed Leinster House. Hardly a day passed without some development, and there were constant newspaper reports and specu-lation about what might happen next. Fianna Fáil was on the verge of rupturing. There was a venomous attitude towards Lynch on the part of a small but vocal section of the party, and there was a share of 'mutterers' in the parliamentary party.

Some people were sitting on the fence to see how the crisis would play out. They were half with us and half against us: with us when talking to Lynch-loyalists but against us when talking to the other side. Recriminations abounded. I was told by Treas Honan, a promin-ent Fianna Fáil member, subsequently a senator, that Lynch and I were 'felon-setters' (an expression that meant putting patriots in harm's way with the law—a hangover from Fenian days, when the law, of course, was English law) and that we had the blood of innocent Irishmen on our hands.

I had arrived in the Department of Justice at the beginning of all this political confusion. I didn't really know what I was letting myself in for. While I had been at Government meetings as Chief Whip, I had no departmental experience.

After receiving my seal of office from President de Valera I immedi-ately returned to Government Buildings. Peter Berry and Hettie Behan, my private secretary in the Parliamentary Secretary or Chief Whip's Office, were waiting for me. Hettie introduced me to the most senior civil servant in my new department, which was now at the centre of a political crisis.

Berry had served in the Department of Justice without a break since 1927. By the time I arrived as minister in May 1970 he was nearing the end of his career, and he wasn't in the best of health. He had also endured a challenging period with Ó Móráin as minister over the previous two years. I think from the outset he found it difficult to come to terms with the fact that political authority was being handed to a youthful 'whippersnapper'.

He looked at me and said, 'Well, minister, I was expecting to meet someone who was young enough to be my son, but I now see someone who looks young enough to be my grandson.'

I did not react. There was a short pause.

'You're my thirteenth minister,' Berry said.

'My goodness, you've been here a long time,' I replied. I was intent on not being cowed by his longevity in the department.

'Yes, I have,' he said, before adding, 'My first minister was Kevin O'Higgins—and he was shot, you know.'

'I know that,' I replied.

I decided that this introduction was to put me in my place; my instinct was not to be put in my place. I was unwilling to kowtow, so there was some tension between us. I had all the ambition of a young lawyer: I had practised law for eight or nine years and had a reform agenda. Indeed what needed doing was staring me in the face, but I joined Justice at a time when the security situation was the only game in town, so I never got to initiate most of the things I had identified. It was a constant firefight on the security front for all my time there; and security was very much Berry's constant concern.

Berry displayed the siege mentality that afflicted so many of those who worked for prolonged periods in the Department of Justice. The security situation, which had been quiet since the early 1960s, had begun to bubble up again in 1968. He was keen to be informed about every detail of security policy and activity; in fact everything went through him. He had a close relationship with the Gardaí.

We take it for granted now that the Garda Commissioner is a member of the force, but this was not always so. For several decades after the Gardaí were established the Commissioner was either a senior army officer or a senior official from the Department of Justice.

As I quickly discovered, Berry was in contact with everyone who mattered in the Guards and knew practically everything that happened. He was strong-willed; but there were two of us with those qualities. I was young, inexperienced, brash and, if the newspapers were to be believed, arrogant. Berry was easily agitated, and was not shy about raising his voice. It was not a totally happy relationship. But we worked pretty well together, and of all the public servants I worked with in my ministerial career Berry probably was the biggest influence on me. In the eventful seven-and-half-months, up to Berry's de facto retirement shortly before Christmas 1970, we disagreed on a handful of occasions, often not so much about what should be done but rather how it should be done.

I quickly discovered that it was an education working with him. I learnt to respect and admire Berry as a man who was single-minded in pursuit of his duty and also as someone who was honourable in the exercise of his office. I came to regret that he was the author of some of his own misfortunes, in that he took far more public stances on some issues relating to security than was necessary or than his office demanded.

I was in my early weeks as minister, somewhat at sea and assailed by the scale of the issues constantly coming at me. Berry confided in me his view that some of his senior colleagues were rather odd. I thought this was a peculiar thing for the secretary of a department to say to the minister. Some of these senior officials (including Berry himself) had never worked outside the Department of Justice; some had worked only in one specific area within the department. Berry, who had spent most of his career dealing with security policy, was an example of this phenomenon. I thought it was an unhealthy practice, and I recall speaking to Lynch about the desirability of mobility within the civil service.

Berry was unique among civil servants in various respects, but the acid test of his integrity and honour as a civil servant was in his evidence to the Arms Trial in the autumn of 1970. I doubt if any Irish civil servant before him or since was faced with a test like that. He did not fudge the truth. His evidence was brief and to the point. It was totally damning of Haughey and established his guilt beyond any reasonable doubt. The fact that Haughey was eventually acquitted by a jury is by the way. The acquittals were totally illogical, as the defence offered by Haughey was that the whole thing never happened at all (this despite the phone call with Berry), while the other three implicitly admitted that it had happened but allegedly with Government approval, almost suggesting that they should be regarded as patriots of some sort. It is hard to see how a jury could have brought in the same verdict on all four in the face of this blatant contradiction.

Berry had provided Lynch with the startling news about the arms plot in April 1970. A large part of the problem was that Mícheál Ó Móráin had not been a very attentive minister, and Berry had become increasingly frustrated with him. Ó Móráin had been in the Dáil since 1938 and had served in Government since 1957, being appointed Minister for Justice in 1968. Unfortunately, he was not a great attender at the department.

I later discovered that he had a solicitor's practising certificate for the period in which he was Minister for Justice. He may have just about got away with this work when he was in lesser departments, but it really was an outrageous situation once he became Minister for Justice. So, as events unfolded, the problem was not only that Ó Móráin had been a weak minister but also his absences from his department.

Berry increasingly found himself operating without political supervision; in this situation the Secretary—already a formidable presence—had become the de facto minister. He knew from security briefings that certain ministers were operating independently of Government policy on Northern Ireland. Reliable Garda sources claimed that Haughey had met the Chief of Staff of the IRA. There were also suspicions that small quantities of arms were being illegally imported without Customs examination at Dublin Airport, and that Haughey was aware of these activities.

After his phone call from Haughey, Berry realised the enormity of the arms plot. He attempted to contact Ó Móráin but without any success. He knew the minister had not been well, and he had even discussed his situation with a doctor who was friendly with him. Berry was concerned that important security information was not being passed on to Lynch. At that time it would have been regarded as unthinkable for the secretary of a department to bypass his own minister and go directly to the Taoiseach. Berry described himself to me as being in a quandary over what to do about Ó Móráin.

He eventually decided that the best thing he could do was talk to the President. Berry greatly admired de Valera and valued his experience. His respect was probably substantially founded on how de Valera had dealt with the IRA during the war years and again just before his retirement with the border campaign in the late 1950s.

Berry phoned the Áras and told the President that information of a very serious nature had come into his possession, information perhaps of national significance. He did not reveal specific details, nor did the President ask any question about the nature of the information. Berry asked for advice on whether his loyalty ended with informing the minister or whether he was justified in speaking directly to the Taoiseach.

The President asked if he was certain of his facts. When Berry said he was absolutely sure, de Valera told him that he owed his duty to the Government as a whole and not just to his own minister and that he should talk to the Taoiseach, which he duly did on 20 April, returning some time later with further security information on the arms plot.

Berry thought the ultimate treachery was that of Haughey. He felt it so keenly, as he repeatedly told me, because, of his thirteen ministers, Haughey was the most able. Subversion, in one form or another, was and is always going to be a fact of life in Ireland, given our history and our gullibility to 'flag-wavers' and tribal instincts. But subversion by members of the Government was, for Berry, the ultimate act of betrayal and treachery. He had thought highly of Haughey and was shocked at his disloyalty to the state.

In my view, Peter Berry gave the most crucial piece of evidence in the Arms Trial. This evidence was not disproved or even contradicted. I venture to think that if the non-jury Special Criminal Court had been in operation in 1970 the judges involved would have convicted in

Haughey's case at least, and very possibly in the cases of some of the other defendants too.

I remained flabbergasted about Haughey's involvement. He had been a regular contributor to general Government discussions. Given the central role of the Minister for Finance in all aspects of governmental activity, this was not unusual. On Northern Ireland he had relatively little to say; but he was obviously shadowing Blaney. They saw the North as Lynch's weak spot, and believed that he would be unable to handle the situation, which meant that a leadership vacancy would arise.

In the weeks after his sacking from the Government and after his return to the Dáil following his release from hospital I saw Haughey in Leinster House, but we never spoke to each other. My first contact with him took place in late August 1970 at the racecourse in Tralee, when he approached me. He said he had a problem of a personal, family nature and would appreciate an opportunity to meet me. I agreed to meet him in Leinster House the following week. I probably shouldn't have done so.

Back in Dublin, I told Peter Berry, who thought it was not a good idea. But I felt that, as the meeting was not being concealed, it was better to find out what Haughey wanted and had to say for himself.

At the meeting Haughey began to talk about a close relation of his who was in some form of trouble. We had a brief discussion, but it quickly became obvious that this was just a ruse for meeting me.

He mentioned Peter Berry by name. 'Will he give evidence?'

'Of course,' I replied.

He then asked, 'Is there anything that can be done?'

I reminded him that material now in the book of evidence—including statements made by Berry—could not and would not be altered. Having listened to him berate Berry, I quickly ended the conversation—the meeting had lasted about fifteen minutes at most—and returned to my department. I immediately told Berry everything that had been discussed.

Later Berry said he felt that my purpose in telling him what happened was to prevail upon him to do as Haughey wanted. That certainly was never my intention: I was simply telling him what had been said. At that time in 1970 and later Berry never gave me the impression that he saw it as an attempt to pressure him. He neither suggested nor implied that; it was only when a so-called diary dossier was published years later in the news magazine *Magill* that this interpretation was made known. Of course the 'Berry diaries' were not contemporaneous diaries at all but were prepared after he had retired.

With hindsight, I fully accept that I should not have met Haughey. But, to be honest, I felt he was still a bit of a mystery man. A lot of people, myself included, found it hard to believe that he could have been silly enough to be involved in the arms affair. I didn't believe he was innocent—far from it—but I was mystified about his role. I did wonder whether there was some strange sort of explanation for his involvement.

With the trial approaching, it was clear that Haughey knew he was in trouble. His demeanour was still his normal self-confident one; but he was clearly worried about the information Peter Berry would give the court. As I mentioned previously, the most important piece of evidence in the Arms Trial was the phone conversation between Haughey and Berry in which Haughey told him that he would have to call it off.

The second Arms Trial took place in the Central Criminal Court in October 1970. Haughey continued to deny any knowledge of the fact that arms were being imported, although he accepted that he arranged Customs clearance for the importing of an unspecified cargo. His evidence was flatly contradicted by Jim Gibbons and Peter Berry as well as by his co-defendants. The others in the dock admitted their involvement in the attempted importation but argued that it had official sanction.

To cloak the plot in some degree of approval they sought to draw the Minister for Defence into the controversy. Jim Gibbons was an honest man. He was junior to the others, and seniority in that Government meant a lot. He was too deferential to Haughey and Blaney, and this left him open to accusations afterwards about his role. He wasn't a great man at defending himself; but the idea that as Minister for Defence he was organising an invasion of the North was totally spurious.

Any arms that the state wished to purchase could have been bought abroad without any difficulty under a certificate issued by the Minister for Defence or the Minister for Justice and duly imported legally and without difficulty. In his position Gibbons had the authority to approve the importing of arms: all he had to do was sign the relevant certificate and give it to the Quartermaster-General to procure whatever arms were listed. But there were no circumstances in which Gibbons would sanction a junior intelligence officer like Captain Kelly to go abroad to buy arms. For one thing, Army Intelligence had nothing to do with purchasing or importing arms. And, along with a junior intelligence officer, it beggars belief that Gibbons would approve the involvement of an IRA member and a Belgian citizen with a dubious Nazi past. The attempted importation was done in secret. It was a freelance operation, regretfully involving members of the Government. And great efforts were made to cover up these activities.

There was evidence against all five, in the view of the Attorney-General. I have no definitive idea about what motivated those involved; I can only speculate that the involvement of some of these individuals was connected with internal Fianna Fáil matters. They thought Lynch was a soft touch and would not withstand the pressure placed upon him. Their response to the situation in Northern Ireland was to wrap themselves in the green flag.

An amount of work went into preparing the Arms Crisis case. The Attorney-General was the prosecuting authority, filling the role that the Director of Public Prosecutions carries out today. The most senior official in the Attorney-General's office, Declan Quigley, went through all the witness statements. He was a marvellous man who worked very hard to carry the Attorney-General's office in this highly pressured period.

It was normal practice to review all statements. Lawyers for the state deleted from the original statements any conversation that took place where the accused had not been present, although the fact that the conversation took place was acknowledged. They also removed any expressions of opinion, and any hearsay and allegations not pertinent to the case, in accordance with the law of evidence. Nothing significant was deleted, and the general thrust of a statement was not altered. Nevertheless, all the original statements signed by all witnesses were available at the trial, and it was open to all to inspect them.

Since 1970 a lot of nonsense has been written and spoken about the Arms Crisis and the events that led up to it. We have had to endure the 'sneaking regarder' version of events, whereby every waver of a green flag is sanctified and those who tried to do something as boring as maintaining the integrity and stability of the state and the rule of law are vilified. It was the most fraught and difficult period of my career, even though there would be times of intense pressure in the early 1980s during the heaves against Charles Haughey.

In an extraordinarily one-sided 'Prime Time' programme in 2001 I was accused of doctoring statements to benefit the prosecution. I was amazed and horrified at what RTE had broadcast. The station was essentially rewriting history. The programme seriously misrepresented many aspects of what happened in the relevant days of 1969 and 1970, creating the clear impression that changes made to the witness statement provided by the head of Military Intelligence, Colonel Michael Hefferon, corresponded closely to the markings apparently made by Berry on that statement, and that I had been furnished with the Hefferon statement, complete with the Berry markings. The implication was that I had colluded in making deliberate and deceitful changes to the statement.

I did not alter any documents. I had no involvement in changing or editing the witness statements. Neither had Peter Berry. There was no suppression of lawful evidence that I was aware of, and I am confident that there was none. The prosecuting team acted with total propriety in accordance with the accepted practice of the day.

The RTE programme concentrated on one single document and attributed to it all sorts of meanings and significance that the facts and the context did not warrant. But what the 'investigation' undertaken by 'Prime Time' failed to notice was that the changes made to the Hefferon statement were made entirely to comply with the rules of evidence. They were made by the prosecution legal team and typed by the Gardaí. There was no involvement by either me or any member of the Department of Justice in the process. RTE presented a conspiracy when there was none. The programme presented the changes made to the Hefferon statement as if they were exceptional, in that they altered the sense and intent of that statement, and that none of the changes to other witness statements altered the sense and meaning of those statements. This point did not stand up to scrutiny.

In a statement I published on 6 May 2001, and in a speech in the Dáil on 6 July, I was able to show how the changes to the Hefferon statement were made as part of normal practice and that other statements had been changed, and that some of those changes were not helpful to the prosecution side. For example, large sections of Jim Gibbons's statement, containing highly damaging evidence and assertions against the accused, were excised. Answers given by Gibbons that were damaging to Haughey and Blaney were not included in the book of evidence. These deletions clearly altered the thrust of Gibbons's original statement; but this decision was taken— as with the Hefferon statement—by Declan Quigley and prosecution counsel on the grounds that the content contained a mixture of hearsay and opinion.

The 'Prime Time' programme prompted investigations by the Minister for Justice, the Attorney-General and the Garda Commissioner. Their conclusions totally undermined RTE and the contributors to its programme, and were perfectly compatible with my published response to the broadcast. I had no involvement in making those changes, nor had Peter Berry. Ironically, given the thesis RTE was promoting, it was proved that not all the changes to the Hefferon statement favoured the prosecution: many were neutral and, on one view at least, favoured the defence.

The RTE programme also made a fuss about my claim of privilege over certain documents. Peter Berry had recorded details about the Arms Crisis in his personal diary. On the advice of the Attorney-General, I claimed privilege over parts of Berry's statement, specifically the diary sections dealing with his meeting with de Valera. The objective was to ensure that the President was not unnecessarily—and without any benefit to either side—called to give evidence.

The file over which privilege was claimed in October 1970, file S/7/70, was a very different file from that released to the National Archives. In the intervening years this file had become a sort of depository within the Department of Justice for matters relating to the Arms Crisis. It was also highly improbable that the Hefferon statement was contained in this file as it existed in October 1970 or was the subject of a claim of privilege. The original statement was already in court, and in any event the privilege expressly contained a saver for inspection by the trial judge. If the original Hefferon statement had been deliberately suppressed by means of the claim of privilege, any such deception would have been immediately exposed had the trial judge requested to see the documents that were the subject of the privilege claim, as he was entitled to do.

The reports of the official Government inquiry in 2001 accepted that the claims of privilege were made on foot of legal advice and that the certificates of privilege were drafted in the Attorney-General's office. RTE's conspiracy programme was without foundation. It was an attempt to write history from a superficial view of one document. Television is a powerful and potentially lethal weapon. It should be used to crusade only with care, accuracy and genuine fairness.

The allegation that statements used in the Arms Trial were heavily edited on my signed instruction was subsequently published by several national newspapers. I received apologies from these newspapers. In their published apologies they accepted that the statement was without foundation and groundless. I did consider taking the matter further and seeking damages in the courts, but I was ultimately more concerned that the apology appeared as soon as possible.

It took me a month to produce my statement in reply to the RTE obloquy. I had the assistance of two skilled people. It took several letters and the threat of legal action to get any sort of apology from RTE. I wasn't really interested in taking up my retirement years with battling in the courts, but I wanted an apology. RTE eventually grudgingly issued a half-baked apology of sorts.

The Government never made a decision on the lines suggested by RTE and by those who it interviewed. Lynch's Government never provided any arms for any civilians within Northern Ireland or for invading Northern Ireland. If it was official Government policy to import arms, then why did the people concerned go to such elaborate lengths to conceal what they were doing? The lawful obtainer and importer of weapons for the Defence Forces is the Quartermaster-General. He was never involved in this activity. There was no need for anybody to go skulking around Hamburg trying to buy arms from dodgy back-street arms dealers: there was a perfectly legal and regular procedure for the proper acquisition of arms. Only persons involved in an illegal activity, deliberately hidden from most of the Government, would feel the need to behave in this furtive manner.

The defendants in the Arms Trial were charged with conspiring to import weapons, surreptitiously and illegally, into this jurisdiction. The evidence presented in court implicating Haughey and the others was very strong. I was shocked at the verdict; and it was the outcome of trials like this one that convinced me two years later to reintroduce the Special Criminal Court with non-jury trials for cases involving subversive and serious organised criminal activities. There were increasing examples of tampering with juries and pressure being put on individual jurors as well as the intimidation of witnesses. The IRA and its terrorist friends were active in ensuring that cases did not reach their logical conclusion. There were trials that clearly should have led to convictions but, for reasons that were never clearly explained, did not.

In the immediate aftermath of the verdict being announced, Haughey questioned Lynch's leadership. The Taoiseach was returning from the United States when these developments unfolded. He was on a commercial flight that was due to land at Shannon Airport before travelling on to Dublin. It was decided that members of the Government and the parliamentary party would meet him at Dublin Airport in a show of support. I was at home in Limerick, so I joined the flight in Shannon. It gave me an opportunity to brief Lynch on developments while he had been away and also to discuss a strategy for dealing with the fall-out from the trial.

I let Lynch get off the flight first to be greeted by waiting ministers before disembarking myself. We were all surprised at the number of

TDS and senators who arrived at the airport. Any thoughts that
Haughey had about a leadership heave were ended by this show of
support for Lynch. He would spend the 1970s rebuilding his career;
but crucial questions about the Arms Crisis were never answered.
Which politicians conspired to subvert Government policy through
illegally importing arms? Did politicians conspire with members of
illegal organisations? Did some politicians encourage the establishment of the Provisional IRA? What happened to the bulk of the public
money voted for the relief of distress in Northern Ireland?

The answers were unfortunately not always in the written files;
some of what happened in 1969 and 1970 was never put down on
paper. This presents an enormous challenge for historians attempting
to unravel these events.

This can be attributed largely to the fact that a great deal of what
transpired was reported only verbally to the relevant authorities, such
as the presence of a member of the judiciary in Haughey's house on
the morning when gardaí arrived to charge him. I was given information about this event long afterwards, but I never saw it mentioned
in any written report. Furthermore, as far as I can see, quite a number
of files relevant to this period are incomplete or missing.

I had two private meetings with President de Valera in the second
half of 1970. These meetings both began with the same question: 'How
are things in the party?'

Protocol at that time was for the Taoiseach and the Minister for
Justice to accompany a judge of the Supreme or High Court to Áras
an Uachtaráin to receive his seal of office on his appointment. They
were then always male! De Valera invariably held these ceremonies at
nine o'clock on a Monday morning, which was not very convenient
for a minister who was living in Limerick. Two other features of the
ceremony did not appeal to me either. Firstly, it was necessary to wear
morning dress—which de Valera and the judges insisted on—and
secondly, champagne was served, despite the early hour. De Valera had
very strict and undeviating views on protocol, which I believe explains
why he insisted in calling on the German minister in 1945 to sym-
pathise on the death of Adolf Hitler.

When I arrived each time in 1970 Col. Seán Brennan, de Valera's long-standing aide-de-camp, met me at the door of the Áras. He said: 'An tUachtarán would be grateful if an tAire would wait over after an Bhreitheamh has left to have a private conversation.' When Lynch and the judge had departed I was ushered into de Valera's small private office. The conversations were informal, and nobody else was present. He listened carefully as I did my best to describe the political situation that had arisen since the Arms Crisis revelations had been made public.

His replies at these two meetings—one in the summer of 1970, the other in the autumn of the same year—were similar. He clearly expressed the view that Haughey would inflict great damage on the party, and that the bitterness and division would last for years. He had less to say about Blaney or Boland. He was extremely sympathetic to Lynch, whom he thought had been treated very unfairly. With the precarious security situation and violence in the North, de Valera said Lynch was deserving of total support and full loyalty, particularly from his Government. He told me that there had been rows in his own Governments, with ministers arguing with him on matters of policy; but, he said, he had been lucky as Taoiseach in that his ministers had always remained loyal and acted loyally. He said Lynch was the first Fianna Fáil Taoiseach who had to suffer that lack of loyalty, which made his difficult job even harder.

All the older generation—people like Seán Lemass, Frank Aiken, Jim Ryan, Paddy Smith and Seán MacEntee—were supportive of Lynch. These people had experienced bloodletting, they had experienced civil war, and they knew it was their duty to support Lynch. And, to a man, that is what they did. Their support undoubtedly strengthened Lynch. I always thought it remarkable, when there was so much ambivalence about Haughey, that the older generation of deputies who had been involved in the War of Independence and the Civil War were apparently unanimous in their rejection of him. This was in spite of the fact that Haughey sought to cultivate them as and when he could.

When Seán MacEntee was nearing the end of his days in 1984 and was in failing health he had a visit at his home from Haughey, who brought a photographer with him. By all accounts, MacEntee rather abruptly declined the honour of being photographed with Haughey, and the visit ended.

Frank Aiken was so strongly opposed to Haughey after the Arms Crisis that he refused to stand for re-election in 1973, because Haughey was a Fianna Fáil candidate. Aiken had first been elected in 1923. He brought an end to his fifty-year Dáil membership in protest at Haughey's continued involvement with the party. When Aiken died, in 1983, Haughey turned up to pay his respects—accompanied by a photographer. A member of the family had to intervene to prevent a photograph being taken of Haughey beside the coffin. In my opinion, Haughey craved this association with the greats of Fianna Fáil out of insecurity about his credentials as a true republican, in the sense in which that word began to be used from 1970 onwards.

Erskine Childers had similar views about Haughey and was very annoyed that Lynch did not stop him standing for the party in the 1973 general election. Childers had a long-standing aversion to Haughey, and his intuition from a very early stage proved to be correct. His widow, Rita Childers, wrote to me in June 2000 and in that correspondence she recollected a number of episodes when her husband made known his attitude towards Haughey. As far back as 1962, while at a dinner in the Russell Hotel celebrating Rita's birthday, she observed a couple of young men, headed by Haughey, in the main dining-room. 'All those men are the future entrepreneurs of Ireland, and every one of them will be corrupt,' Erskine Childers predicted.

Many years later, while campaigning for the presidency in 1973, Childers told his campaign team that he would not canvass in Haughey's constituency of Dublin North-Central. When it was pointed out that he would potentially lose thousands of votes, he replied, 'I would rather die than be photographed beside him.' At the final rally in the same campaign in College Green, Childers insisted that Haughey not be allowed on the platform.

In dealing with Haughey in the aftermath of the Arms Trial, Lynch was in a difficult position. He was anxious to avoid a row, and probably one that Haughey would have won, as he still controlled his local constituency organisation, and even if he was stopped as a Fianna Fáil candidate it was likely that he would have run as an independent, and won a seat. Lynch opted to keep him near, but ultimately it was at a huge political cost.

———

The events of 1969 and 1970 presented a threat of unparalleled gravity to the Irish state. There was a conspiracy to import arms for use by an illegal organisation in Northern Ireland—and quite possibly in their criminal money-raising activities south of the border. Had Jack Lynch, Peter Berry and others been less than steadfast in their determination to preserve democracy and the rule of law, heaven knows what catastrophe would have befallen the state and the people of the entire island of Ireland. Lynch and those who backed him within the Government—the great majority of ministers—had to stand in the breach with a situation that could have led to an outright sectarian war that would have made the Civil War of 1922–23 look like a relatively minor episode.

Lynch ultimately held the Government together. He had been underestimated, but when tested he displayed equal measures of tenacity and calmness. He had been seriously provoked and for a period was in a very lonely position. Hillery, Colley and Childers provided strong support and worked closely to deal with the crisis. Lynch had great trust in Hillery and came to rely greatly on his judgement. Childers and Colley were equally loyal. But the final decisions rested with Jack Lynch, and in every respect he proved equal to the enormous challenges that came his way.

Chapter 5 ∿

| 'THE ENEMIES OF SOCIETY'

I served as Minister for Justice from 7 May 1970 to 14 March 1973. It was a uniquely difficult time. The situation in Northern Ireland was very dangerous. Three different groups of 'republican' terrorists were threatening the security of our state. The issues raised by the existence and activities of these unlawful organisations were stark. Were we to be ruled by the democratically elected government and parliament or by small unrepresentative and self-appointed groups that, without any semblance of a mandate from the electorate, had arrogated to themselves the right to carry on a campaign of violence and bloodshed and to dictate the policies to be pursued, in the name of the Irish people? As a community we had to decide whether our affairs were to be conducted according to policies decided on by the elected government and parliament or whether we were to succumb to conditions of anarchy in which a minority that had organised itself into private armies could terrorise and impose its will on the law-abiding majority.

As Minister for Justice I had a duty to act. I was aware that people considered me a bit gruff. I never went out of my way to cultivate people. I did not act to court popularity. I wasn't unduly interested in image; in fact the security measures I had to introduce in this period did not win support in many quarters. I was accused of repressing and compromising civil rights. But what I did in my three years as Minister for Justice was motivated by the need to protect democracy and to crush terrorism. The country was hovering on the verge of falling into anarchy. It was necessary to take tough stances, even though there was a good deal of ambivalence at the time towards allegedly political violence. The Department of Justice was under great pressure in the aftermath of the Arms Crisis revelations and the deteriorating situation in Northern Ireland and a real fear that violence would spill over the border.

The IRA had split in late 1969 into two separate organisations, which the press dubbed the 'Officials' and the 'Provisionals'. They were joined by another particularly vicious group of criminal anarchists, Saor Éire. These three violent subversive organisations were hostile to one another and generally operated independently. The Gardaí faced a difficult task in monitoring the activities of members of all three groups.

During the 1970s the Provisional IRA emerged as the largest of these groups. But it was initially the least active in the Republic, which with hindsight is probably why the Haughey wing of Fianna Fáil was believed to favour it, along with its aversion to left-wing politics. The Provos quickly became the dominant republican terror group. Security information that I gave to the Government in November 1970 indicated that they had about 1,300 members throughout the island. Most of their weapons were held by members in the North.

In the aftermath of the split the Officials were intent on shedding the more traditional 'Brit-bashing' image in favour of Marxist stances. They also operated a number of front organisations that protested against policies such as Ireland's membership of the EEC. But, while gradually becoming more politically sophisticated, the Officials were no less criminal. Security information in late 1970 showed that they were responsible for a bank robbery in Derry and for a raid on a security van in Strabane four months previously. My memo to the Government in November 1970 concluded: 'This group envisages the kidnapping of important personages to hold as ransom to secure particular ends. Two of its most active members are in Cuba undergoing training. In general, membership is largely confined to Dublin and Cork.'

In time the Officials graduated from robbing banks to printing their own banknotes as a means of enriching themselves. They maintained close contact with Moscow and with some form of communist trade union school in Prague, where they had quite a number of people trained in labour and social agitation. They had people trained to infiltrate trade unions in Ireland and to achieve positions of leadership and responsibility there and elsewhere.

Saor Éire probably had no more than thirty or thirty-five active members, but it caused huge problems towards the end of 1970 and for some time afterwards. It was a small, ill-disciplined anarchist faction attracted to murder, armed robbery and the use of explosives. The problem with Saor Éire gradually eased as they developed a habit of murdering one another, and the survivors mutated eventually into an organisation called the INLA, which continued the habit of mutual destruction.

Saor Éire had been successful in getting money from bank robberies in the Republic. In one of those robberies at the Allied Irish Bank branch at Arran Quay, Dublin, in April 1970 Garda Richard Fallon was shot dead. He was the first member of the force to be murdered since terrorism had re-emerged, and the first in twenty-eight years to be shot dead in the line of duty.

Peter Berry reminded me of what had happened to those who had murdered Gardaí during the 1940s. They were hanged.

Reliable security information reached us in December 1970 that Saor Éire was plotting to kidnap a foreign diplomat. The Gardaí were convinced that connected with this conspiracy were plans to carry out armed bank robberies, which they believed might well have involved murders or attempted murders. Given the gravity of the threat, I was forced to act. Legislation from the Emergency era, the Offences Against the State Act (1939), gave the Government the option of introducing internment. I had already asked Berry to prepare the necessary paperwork if such a course of action was required. We made it clear to those involved in the kidnap plot that, unless the Government was satisfied that the threat was removed, internment would be introduced. Places of detention were identified. We were determined to act, and those concerned had a final opportunity of drawing back and obviating the need for internment. If we had failed to act on the security information we would have been in dereliction of our duty.

There was considerable criticism when news of the possible introduction of internment was made public. There was noisy debate in
the Dáil, and more than a thousand people protested at the gates of
Leinster House.

Internment never had to be activated. At the time, the Provisional
IRA were confining their activities mainly to the North. They were
afraid, of course, that internment would apply to them, and they
leaned on Saor Éire to desist from certain activities in the South. In
that way the Government's actions worked and it was not necessary to
introduce internment, which would in any event have been confined
to members of Saor Éire.

———

The context of the time is hugely important. At the outset of the
Northern conflict there were many 'fellow-travellers'. A lot of
reasonable people were not entirely unsympathetic to the Provos.
Traditional republican ideas were fresher in people's minds than they
are today. There was a generation of people who were far less removed
from the War of Independence than people are now; when they
thought about the Provos they tended to hark back to a more
romantic republican past. For some, the Provos were national heroes;
some others were prepared to give them the benefit of the doubt,
given the degree of ambivalence about the 'national question' and the
behaviour of the Unionist government at Stormont.

By the end of 1970 there were twenty-five deaths associated with
the conflict; the following year that number increased to 174. The
worst year in the entire conflict was 1972, when 470 people were killed.
The Provos were surviving off bank and post office robberies and the
proceeds of crime. They were bombing and shooting innocent people.
The Government's job was to remind people that the Provos had
nothing in common with the earlier generation of republicans, who
had fought for Irish freedom. Given all the pain and suffering and
turmoil they caused, it was hard to believe that they carried on for all

the years that they did. In all, about 3,500 people lost their lives in the Northern Ireland conflict.

Given my attitude to terrorism, and the policies I pursued to protect the Irish state and its citizens, I was now seen by the Provisional IRA as one of their so-called legitimate targets. For six years from late 1970 I had continuous Garda protection. I carried a gun on Garda advice, and I had a personal weapon for about twelve months after I left ministerial office in 1973. I didn't want a gun, but the Gardaí insisted. I carried it in a holster under my left arm during the day, and at night, as recommended, I put it under my pillow. Every six months or so I had to go to Kilmainham for shooting practice. Thankfully, that was something I never had to do beyond the practice range.

It was an unpleasant time. The closest attempt by the Provos to shoot me came in 1972. At that time I didn't have a house in Dublin. I stayed originally with my mother, who had moved to Dublin after my father died; but when a garda was stationed outside her house she freaked out and asked me to leave. Maternal love has its limits.

In fact the Gardaí didn't want me staying too long in any one place, so I had to move accommodation every week. A few times in early 1972 I stayed with a friend who lived in a flat in Waterloo Road. Early one morning the gardaí arrived at the front door and ordered the two of us to lie down on the floor. We were lying there for about three hours; when finally we could leave it was only with several gardaí surrounding us as we left the house. It emerged that they had dis-covered a rifle and a telescopic sight in a flat directly across from my friend's flat. The landlord told the gardaí that the flat had been rented a few weeks previously. The name given by the person who rented the flat was a false one. He appeared to have been from the North.

These were three tough years for my family. I was working very long hours. There were weekends when I did not return home to Limerick, such was the volume of work or the security developments. We had four young children, but thankfully they were too young to be conscious of the criticism and the danger.

There was Garda protection also at our home in Limerick. On two or three occasions Pat and the children had to be moved from our house in Corbally, as the Gardaí felt they might be harmed if they remained at home. There were Provo protests outside the house. The protesters would throw red paint, and on occasion a coffin, into the front garden. I didn't tell Pat about every death threat that was made or every security alert that was a false alarm. The situation was tough enough. Many spouses would have crumbled, but Pat seemed to take the pressure in her stride.

The Provos also targeted Pat's family in Co. Tyrone. They owned a public house in Omagh, which was blown up in 1970 and again a year later when the premises had been rebuilt. Thankfully, nobody was injured in either attack.

The Unionist government at Stormont made it clear that they were not interested in working with us. Co-operation to find a solution and defeat the IRA was not an option. I never met my counterpart at Stormont. The Unionists were more interested in accusing us of all sorts of things. We were described as an 'alien state'. They rarely talked about the 'border': it was usually the 'frontier', as if there were an army on our side waiting to invade part of Her Majesty's realm. At that time the British still left the internal running of Northern Ireland, including control over security matters, to the Unionist regime at Stormont. They too were unwilling to establish serious ministerial-level contacts. It was only after the suspension of Stormont in 1972 that communication between the Dublin and London governments was strengthened.

What contact there was at any level in this period was arbitrary. The Department of Justice would get reports from a Garda sergeant in Co. Monaghan who had a good relationship with an RUC sergeant just across the border. These men would exchange information about IRA activity. The garda reported the details to his superiors, and it would end up in a security briefing on my desk. It was a terrible pity that this type of co-operation was not more systematic.

When I arrived in the Department of Justice in May 1970 there were approximately 5,500 members of the Garda Síochána. There was no overtime: every garda, in theory at least, was on duty twenty-four hours a day, seven days a week. They were widely spread throughout the country, a great many of them in small rural stations that often had been taken over from the RIC in 1922. The spirit in the force was good, as was discipline. There were a few 'bad apples', but the few that there were tended to get rooted out quickly. Members of the force were known in their localities, and the communities in which they served liked them. Crime tended to be local rather than mobile, and was relatively minor. I knew from my time as a solicitor in Limerick that district courts in the 1960s usually had a good quota of prosecutions of farmers for having noxious weeds on their land and of cyclists for not having a light on their bicycles.

The emergence of the republican terror groups changed the situation dramatically. The shooting dead of Garda Richard Fallon in April 1970 focused minds on the new security threat. The force lost another member to republican terrorist violence during my time as Minister for Justice when a booby-trap killed Inspector Sam Donegan in June 1972 while he was involved in a joint Garda-army search along the border between Cos. Cavan and Fermanagh.

Throughout these years the Gardaí displayed outstanding devotion to duty and performed exceptional police work. A range of measures to assist the force, including increasing the number of gardaí, was introduced. The strength of the force was increased by almost 2,000 to 7,560, which was the highest it had ever been. We also improved terms and conditions in the areas of pay, allowances, overtime and hours of work as a result of the report of the Conroy Commission.

———

In security and subversive matters there was an unexpectedly close relationship between the Gardaí and the Department of Justice. This was principally due to Peter Berry's almost obsessive interest in subversive and security matters. There was also the fact that the then Commissioner, Michael J. Weymes, was the first policeman to become Commissioner of the Garda Síochána. Previously the position had usually been held by an assistant secretary in the Department of Justice or by a retired army officer. This policy was, presumably, a carry-over from the Civil War days and showed an anxiety to maintain tight political control. As between Weymes and Berry, I was left in no doubt about who was the boss in security matters.

In the second half of 1970 Berry came under very considerable public pressure as both wings of the IRA and their political front men in the two Sinn Féins became more strident. Most unusually for a civil servant—and, I thought, most unfairly—he was attacked from various platforms and discussed at various subversive meetings. Fairness was hardly a factor that mattered at that time as the North became increasingly bloody. Subversive organisations held marches to Berry's house. Apart from whatever was said, the marchers carried placards describing Berry in unquestionably defamatory terms. 'Felon-setter' was a popular term of abuse. Newspapers carried photographs of the placards, which were clearly legible.

Berry decided to sue them for libel, and the Department of Justice indemnified him for costs. To my amazement, he lost the case. I think this personal hostility, and the pressure from the Arms Crisis generally, caused a deterioration in Berry's health. He was in hospital at least twice towards the end of 1970. The hospital was only about 150 yards from the Department of Justice. During this period he would send over a series of notes and instructions on his famous 'pink sheets'. (He wrote on pink paper so that officials would know they had received a note from the Secretary, which had to be given the highest priority.)

When Berry became ill again just before Christmas 1970 he informed me that he proposed to retire early in the new year. He had about two years to serve until he reached the compulsory retirement age of sixty-five and had over forty years of service in the Department of Justice. He asked me whether, because of the circumstances of his 'enforced retirement', as he put it, the Government would agree to pay him his full salary up to his sixty-fifth birthday.

I agreed readily to do this, but the Department of Finance was very much against the idea, and George Colley would not agree to the payment for fear of creating a precedent. I thought then, and I think even more strongly since, that the relatively paltry additional payment—half his salary for two years—was not unreasonable. Berry told me that he felt 'let down' by the Government.

It was a difficult time and a difficult situation. While I could not say it to him directly, I shared many of his misgivings and his sense of disappointment. He had gone out on a limb in the course of his duty. He had faced terrible pressures and had faced them down. He could have kept his head below the parapet, but his sense of honour and duty to the country compelled him to act as he did. For his efforts he got very little reward or thanks. In other countries he would certainly have got some form of honour or title in recognition of what he had done, both in 1970 and over many years previously.

Berry subsequently wrote what became known as the 'Berry Diaries', although they were not in fact contemporaneously written. When I studied what was published some years after his death I could see from internal evidence that they were written after his retirement and while he still had an understandable grievance. Although Berry was not an easy man to get on with, and was not popular in many quarters because of his uncompromising attitude to his duty as he saw it—and those quarters included civil servants in other departments— he was nonetheless a major influence on my life and career. That influence was exercised even though we worked together for little more than seven months. He saw his mission in life as the protection of the state and its citizens and institutions against armed subversion. Perhaps he was lucky that he never lived to see the official appeasement of terrorism and terrorists.

Andrew Ward, previously Deputy Secretary of the Department, succeeded Berry in 1971. The contrast was enormous. Ward was calm and extremely private. The day he was appointed he rang the steward of his golf club in Dublin and told him to take down from the wall a photograph in which he appeared. He told me this was the only photograph of him that he knew of on public view. He was afraid some newspaper would get hold of it; his great horror was that he would be recognised and forced to live a semi-public life, like Berry. Amazingly, as I thought at the time, Ward succeeded in maintaining virtually total anonymity. He was hugely able and unflappable.

Ward was only forty-four when we appointed him. During some typical security crisis in 1971, as we both contemplated the dire situation facing the state, I said to him (not very consolingly, I fear): 'At least I will be out of here in a few years at most. I hate to think that you could be stuck here for twenty-one more years.' He just shrugged. 'That's life. We'll survive.' And he did. He quietly and brilliantly carried out a thankless and vital task for another sixteen years. Berry and Ward were totally different personalities, but they are equally deserving of a nation's gratitude.

––––

The situation with Mícheál Ó Móráin as a part-time minister was not the only strange working arrangement at the time. The office of the Director of Public Prosecutions had not yet been established, and the Attorney-General filled this role. Shortly after my appointment in May 1970, to my surprise I discovered that the Attorney-General, Colm Condon, had not given up his private practice; his job was being done on a part-time basis. This emerged in the middle of the Arms Crisis when I was looking for the Attorney-General. It turned out that he was in Cork. He had an arrangement whereby he would go to Cork twice a year to the High Court for three continuous weeks each time.

In those days, contacting somebody quickly was often impossible. It was difficult to get through to the courthouse in Cork. With little luck with the main number, we eventually got a number for the barristers' and solicitors' room. When I rang, a young solicitor answered. 'This is the Minister for Justice,' I said. 'I need to speak urgently to the Attorney-General. Would you go into whatever courtroom he's in and ask him to come to the phone?'

The young man at the other end of the line obviously did not believe at first that I was the minister, but after some persuasion he eventually went off to find the Attorney-General. He returned without success. 'He's on his feet in court. I can't interrupt him.' I eventually ended up contacting the Garda chief superintendent in Cork. He was so taken aback at having the Minister for Justice on the phone that he decided to go down to the courthouse himself rather than send a guard.

In a memorandum prepared for the Government in November 1970 I set out a variety of policy options for dealing with terrorism and with those people who planned 'acts of violence and destruction and plot the overthrow of our system of government.' We were confronted by an intolerable situation. The memo asserted: 'Stern action by Government brought the IRA to a full halt by 1947, and again by 1962, but a softening policy in succeeding years in the hope that reason would prevail allowed extremists to regroup, re-arm and to preach and practise violence.' I argued that by that stage in late 1970 the position had become so serious—especially with the ruthlessness of Saor Éire at that time—that such options as juryless special courts and internment had to be considered.

The Special Criminal Court was ultimately re-established in 1972, although internment was not actively pursued. In the face of the threatened kidnapping of Government ministers, ambassadors and other important figures the Government was faced with contemplating very difficult responses.

There were other measures open to us. I ordered a round-up of privately held weapons other than shotguns. Gun-owners were annoyed with my response, but we had sufficient evidence that the IRA was stealing privately held licensed weapons. The Firearms Act (1971) significantly increased the penalties for illegal possession, from £50 or imprisonment not exceeding three months, or both, to £200 or five years' imprisonment. All sorts of commercial explosives were also withdrawn, although the Provos quickly learnt how to make bombs from fertiliser, and obviously, in an agricultural country, it wasn't possible to withdraw access to fertiliser. We know they eventually got arms from eastern European states and from Libya.

I felt that there should be no room for ambivalence. I was intent on trying to discourage support for republican or any other violence. I was regularly attacked by the likes of Conor Cruise O'Brien and other opposition figures for my actions in dealing with terrorism. Yet when they themselves entered government in 1973, fortunately Fine Gael and the Labour Party were quick to forget their opposition to me and acted in a similarly strong manner.

One fairly innocuous piece of legislation was put through in 1971. Given the grand title of the Prohibition of Forcible Entry and Occupation Bill, this short bill took three months to pass, given the reaction of some Fine Gael and Labour TDs and a collection of members of the Seanad.

A problem had arisen over organised and forcible squatting in local authority housing in Dublin by quasi-political groups, many of which were no more than front organisations for subversive elements, including the Official IRA. It was on a scale that seriously interfered with the fairest possible allocation of available housing by Dublin Corporation among those in need of housing. In many instances, if a resident was away or in hospital the Officials would simply arrive and take possession.

The Gardaí argued that dealing with this activity was really a civil matter. Dublin Corporation was effectively powerless. At best it could take many months to evict the illegal occupiers.

The way the opposition responded to my proposals one would think that what I was proposing was the end of the world. They kept the debate going throughout the summer, and there was a long-drawn-out debate before the legislation was passed by the Dáil on 4 August 1971.

There were then a further six full sitting days in the Seanad. There was a long and sometimes very difficult and acrimonious debate. Senator Mary Robinson was one particular critic throughout the passage of the legislation. For the most part I simply sat through the debate without responding to the opposition's attempts to provoke me. I mentioned that I had heard a lot of law of a kind that I might not have learnt in Pallas Green District Court, but that was not to say that the type of law that I would have learnt in Pallas Green District Court might not have been more useful. In my final contribution before the legislation was eventually passed by the Seanad on 26 August 1971 I mentioned that we were 'at the end of possibly one of the longest debates on any bill in the history of the Oireachtas.' I suggested that a year later the Act would be regarded as unremarkable.

After the legislation was passed, as with so many similar over-the-top predictions, the world did not come to an end. The law served its purpose. Afterwards I wrote to the Leader of the Seanad, Tommy Mullins, the long-time general secretary of Fianna Fáil, to thank him and the Oireachtas staff who had had their summer disrupted by the prolonged debate. He replied that mine was the first letter he had ever received from a Government minister offering thanks about anything.

———

The security situation in Northern Ireland continued to worsen. Stormont introduced internment in August 1971. It was a one-sided and botched policy, and they ended up arresting a lot of the wrong people. Some of those they sought had been dead for twenty years, while many republican terrorists evaded arrest. Unfortunately, some fled south of the border.

Many threats posed never reached public knowledge, thanks to the actions of the Gardaí. For example, reliable information emerged in early 1971 that the Provos were watching the military attaché at the British Embassy in Dublin with the intention of either kidnapping him or blowing up his house. He was given appropriate protection.

The situation reached a new level on 30 January 1972, 'Bloody Sunday', when the British army shot dead thirteen civil rights pro- testers in Derry. There was at first some confusion about what exactly had happened; but the early reports we received from reliable sources said that those shot had been unarmed. Lynch sent a telegram of protest to the British Prime Minister, Ted Heath. The reply was dismissive, Lynch being told not to interfere in internal UK affairs. He then spoke by phone with Heath. He warned that the Stormont government was incapable of governing and that action from London was needed. We had real fears that the situation could now escalate beyond anything we had seen previously. Emotions were running very high. We pressed the British to act on the control of security policy.

The Government met the next day and agreed to a National Day of Mourning and recalled the Irish Ambassador from London. Lynch also addressed the nation in a television broadcast. Once more his calmness under severe provocation was in evidence. My priority as Minister for Justice was to ensure that law and order was maintained. There was strong anti-British feeling in many quarters. There were many peaceful protests, but there were others who wanted to exploit the situation, and we had to try to prevent the IRA taking advantage. In the days after Bloody Sunday, bombs went off at a British-owned travel agency in Grafton Street, Dublin, at a branch of the Royal Liver Friendly Society, a British insurance company, in Dún Laoghaire and at the Royal Air Forces Association club in Earlsfort Terrace. Union Jacks were burnt at otherwise peaceful protests around the country.

Many brought their protest directly to the British Embassy, then at 39 Merrion Square. Letters of condemnation were handed in, while some people held black flags and shouted anti-British slogans; but in general these people obeyed the instructions of gardaí on duty and engaged in peaceful protest. The day after the events in Derry about a thousand UCD students marched from Belfield to the embassy, where they were joined by other students and city-centre workers. The attendance rose to about five thousand. Some IRA figures were identified in the crowd. Stones and bottles were hurled at the building, and some sections of the crowd attempted to rush the gardaí. The student leaders requested the crowd to disperse peacefully.

The situation was even more tense at another protest march to the embassy two days later. The building had been evacuated earlier that day; we had also ordered appropriate protection at the homes of members of the embassy staff. It was estimated that about twenty thousand people attended the protest on 2 February. Emotions were running high. The crowd was made up of a lot of genuine people who were horrified at what had happened in Derry and wanted to register their protest, but there was a sizeable contingent that had been bussed in from the North and were there to cause trouble. I met Jerry Cronin, Minister for Defence, the Chief of Staff of the Defence Forces and the Garda Commissioner in the department. We were receiving reports from the scene. The protest moved beyond chanting slogans. Rocks were thrown at the building; then one of the crowd poured petrol in the windows while petrol bombs were thrown. Some people had come prepared for trouble. The very size of the crowd made it impossible for the gardaí to deal effectively with the element that engaged in criminal acts of arson and violence. As it was, several gardaí were injured and some had to be admitted to hospital.

We could see the flames from my office. The Commissioner urged caution. The Chief of Staff advised that it was not possible to send in army units unless they were armed with live ammunition. 'I can't protect them in the event that the mob turns on them,' he said. As minister, I wasn't prepared to play into the hands of the Provos. Any response that risked the loss of life had to be avoided if at all possible; so we let the mob burn down the empty building. I thought it better to let the tension be released by that action. And in a way, it worked. Once the building was aflame the passions dampened.

Over the following days there was sharp criticism of the Garda response. The opposition accused me of letting the situation get out of control. But any action would only have exacerbated a highly hostile situation. The Ambassador, Sir John Peck, wrote some days later to the Commissioner to express his admiration for the work done by gardaí during the disturbances. They had shown tremendous patience, restraint and discipline in the discharge of their very dangerous duty.

We now had real evidence that the Provos had the ability to cause serious trouble in the Republic too. We had a freely elected parliament and a freely elected Government. Nobody had any right under any pretence to disregard the law as enacted by the Oireachtas. To claim such a right was a challenge not just to the Government but to the basic institutions of the state. A public speaker, a newspaper commentator or somebody being interviewed on radio or television who, in the circumstances of those times, sought to support, excuse or explain away the actions of illegal bodies bore grave responsibility.

The Provos' access to weapons was not my only concern: they were also getting huge donations from the United States. An older generation of Irish-Americans were being spun a version of events in Northern Ireland that was far from the truth. Many were incredibly naïve in their understanding of what was happening in Ireland.

In an attempt to diminish republican fund-raising abilities, I travelled to the United States in 1971 and 1972. Unlike the Provo sympathisers, who were in the United States looking for money to finance their so-called 'struggle', I had a very clear brief. It was important to convince middle-ground Irish-American leaders that the British were not the only cause of trouble in the North. I spoke at a dinner in New York where I sought to undermine the romantic view of the conflict. My speech was blunt in focusing on the reality of what was happening and what I described as the 'horror, bombs and bullets on the streets of Northern Ireland . . . scarring young minds for a generation to come.' I accepted that many Irish-Americans wanted to donate money to help people in the North but asked that, rather than giving to organisations linked to the IRA, they give to the Irish Red Cross or to local churches. I got a poor hearing. The New York police became concerned, and rushed me out of the hotel.

I was strongly of the view that we needed to focus on the support the IRA was getting from some of the Northern Catholic community. Despite their ability to carry on a campaign of violence, the Provos were limited in number. If community support was withdrawn, the significance of the IRA would diminish, and in my opinion the way to do this was to strengthen nationalist politicians such as those in the SDLP. This required the British to make a worthwhile political initiative. The objective had to be to show that political activity was more beneficial than terrorist activity.

I had discussions on these points with Harold Wilson in Dublin in March 1972. Wilson was then in opposition but, as leader of the Labour Party, was keen to know more about the volatile situation in the North. The Taoiseach hosted a lunch in Iveagh House in St Stephen's Green, the head office of the Department of Foreign Affairs. I sat opposite Wilson over lunch, although we spoke as much about reform of the legal professions as we did about the situation in the North. Afterwards there was a private meeting involving Government ministers and Wilson, who spoke about the need to get the IRA to restrain themselves in order to give the SDLP more room to manoeuvre. I was suspicious that he might try to start some dialogue with the Provos, and so I immediately said that none of us—and I included British politicians in this—should have any truck with terrorists. The conversation ended without any great conclusion.

However, there was a dramatic twist to Wilson's Dublin visit. I learnt from the Gardaí that Wilson later that afternoon had met Dr John O'Connell, then a Labour Party TD, in his home, and they were joined by three other individuals: Ruairí Ó Brádaigh, Dáithí Ó Conaill and Seán Mac Stiofáin—all senior IRA leaders and members of the Army Council. I immediately informed Lynch, who was shocked at Wilson's action. When I met the British Ambassador at a reception shortly afterwards I raised the matter. 'That man is a bloody fool,' the Ambassador replied. 'It is very embarrassing for me, but at least he is a member of the opposition.' He was very concerned that news of the secret meeting would not leak to the media.

As Minister for Justice I received daily confidential security reports. Although it was an illegal and secret organisation, we knew a great deal about the internal personnel within the Provos. By mid-1972 it was clear that a strongly militant leadership had emerged in the North and that they were in the ascendancy, although there was little general difference with the Southern leadership and such people as Ó Brádaigh and Mac Stiofáin over their support for violence.

In May 1972 a report came to my desk marked 'Report of IRA Activities'. Among the details in this briefing was a paragraph with obviously political interest:

Mr Charles Haughey T.D. is still in touch with the Provisional IRA through John Kelly and Joe Cahill. He told them he was not in a position to do anything for them at present but that he hoped to be back in the Government in a few months time and would press for a stronger line on the North. He told them that Special Branch, Dublin Castle were still receiving information from inside the republican movement but not as much as heretofore. He promised to pass on anything he hears on that aspect but to keep his name out of it.

This information was brought to Lynch's attention. In many respects it was not surprising. We had come to accept that Haughey was untrustworthy and was devious in his ability to play a variety of roles and push different agendas in his quest for personal political advancement.

———

Since the verdict in the Arms Trial I began to have concerns about the possible intimidation of jurors and witnesses. There was continuing internal debate about the number of cases involving republican suspects that delivered a verdict of 'not guilty'. In the summer of 1970 a member of Saor Éire, Patrick Keane, was arrested in England for Garda Fallon's murder. An extradition order was made, and it was appealed all the way to the House of Lords. Keane lost his appeals and was extradited. I did not get any request from the British for an undertaking that Keane would not be executed if convicted. He was subsequently tried before a jury in the Central Criminal Court. The jury decided to let him walk free.

As more and more of these types of cases came up, I decided that enough was enough. We were faced with unpalatable decisions. The move to establish the non-jury Special Criminal Court in 1972 had been under active consideration for some time, but the decision was not easily taken and followed lengthy Government deliberations.

The legislation allowing for a non-jury court was not new: it dated from 1939 and had been used during the 1940s and most recently during the IRA's border campaign in the early 1960s. It was a source of private amusement to me that in the case of the wartime legislation the Minister for Justice had been Gerry Boland and that later, after 1957, his son, Kevin Boland, had been Minister for Defence and in charge of internment!

The legislation was such that non-jury trials could only consider cases dealing with subversive activity against the state and organised crime. The main target was subversives; the use of the court against organised criminals became a feature in later years, especially when subversion and organised crime began to overlap. Those who were tried by the court after its reintroduction in 1972 were convicted of such offences as possession of firearms and explosives and membership of an illegal organisation.

I was unhappy with the previous structure whereby the court consisted of three military officers, and there was no objection to my proposal to get civilian judges to hear cases in the new three-member Special Criminal Court. There was great difficulty, however, in getting judges to serve on the new court. Several who declined told me the position was 'too dangerous', fear of the Provisional IRA and other republican terrorist groups had reached such a level. Threats against judges, and the possibility that thugs would picket their homes, were taken very seriously. Frank Griffin of the High Court and Charlie Conroy of the Circuit Court agreed to sit after many of their colleagues refused. I could not get a district justice, so the president of the District Court eventually said that he would take the position himself. We provided special protection for the three judges involved.

There was plenty of opposition; but I told the Dáil that the move was essential, given the serious security situation, and that I thought the need for the court would be temporary, probably for twelve months. The situation in Northern Ireland was so bad that there was a sense that it could not continue without some intervention to restore order. In such circumstances the need for the Special Criminal Court would be removed.

That was my genuine belief at the time. None of us envisaged that the conflict in Northern Ireland would last as long as it did, nor did we ever think that drugs-related criminals would become as dominant as they have been in more recent times. For these reasons the Special Criminal Court still exists today, more than forty years later, hearing cases involving serious organised criminal activity.

Not enough could be done to deal with people who were members of unlawful organisations. There were very real difficulties under the existing law. The Offences Against the State (Amendment) Act (1972) was intended to deal with the difficulty in gathering evidence against those who were openly appearing on public platforms and on radio and television as members of illegal subversive organisations. The legislation provided that the testimony of a chief superintendent would be admissible in evidence, but, as with any evidence tendered to the court, it would be for the court to determine what weight was to be attached to it in the light of all the circumstances of the case. It did not mean that just because a senior Garda officer testified to his belief that a person was a member of an illegal organisation the court had to convict unless the defendant proved him wrong: the court need not convict even if the defendant adduced no evidence at all, let alone convincing evidence to counter the Garda officer's testimony.

The citizens of Dublin had experienced in no uncertain way what was meant by these twisted brands of 'patriotism'. They found expression in the killing and maiming of the innocent and the wreaking of indiscriminate destruction of property. Two loyalist car bombs in the capital killed two people and left 127 others injured. It was the first of two loyalist attacks on Dublin during my time as Minister for Justice. The worst attack—the later Dublin and Monaghan bombings of May 1974—killed thirty-three people and an unborn child. The violence of loyalist and republican terrorists was the context for the measures that were necessary to protect the state and its citizens in that period. I argued strongly that the 1972 act was not a threat to individual rights and freedoms.

Paddy Cooney, who was Fine Gael's spokesman on justice, strongly opposed my actions. He told the Dáil that the legislation was unnecessary, excessive, and repugnant to the basic principles of justice and liberty and the long-established fundamental rights of citizens. I listened to his contribution—and those of other liberal champions— who defended civil rights while the Provos sought to undermine the very building in which we worked as democrats. Despite all the fuss there was no possible danger that an innocent person would suffer injustice as a result of these new measures. My opponents said it was a bad law and an excessive response; I fundamentally disagreed and believe that the passage of time has proved me to be correct. No one has repealed it.

The Government had serious concerns about how RTE was reporting the IRA. Terrorists were able to broadcast their activities and propagate their beliefs and objectives in a way that caused us grave concern. People known to be engaged in subversive and criminal activities were being glamourised, being allowed to use radio and television interviews as recruitment instruments. We saw this in the North—and that was why they were so keen on being on television and radio—and that was my argument in favour of limiting their access. I raised my concerns within the Government. It had appointed the RTE Authority, and I was frustrated that it was simply being allowed to sit back and allow television and radio programmes to be used by this small minority who wanted to brainwash the Irish public.

In June 1971 I was invited to take part in an RTE radio programme to discuss the situation in Northern Ireland. The programme-makers had decided to also ask two IRA members to be part of the programme. I found this situation outrageous. We were democrats who had been elected by the public; these other people used violence to achieve their objectives and had no public mandate. I made my views known to RTE and suggested that the programme be cancelled. There was obviously less concern at the state broadcaster about giving known members of an illegal organisation air time. The programme proceeded without a Government representative. But the law had to be enforced, and RTE had to be reminded of the law.

In September 1971 Lynch was returning from talks in Britain with his counterpart, Ted Heath, when RTE chose to broadcast an interview with two leading IRA figures, Cathal Goulding and Seán Mac Stiofáin. This time the Government was left with no choice but to act. I was very supportive of the decision to issue a directive under section 31 of the Broadcasting Authority Act (1960). The directive was clear: it was an offence to broadcast material that engaged in, promoted, encouraged or advocated certain objectives by violent means.

There was some opposition in RTE on the grounds that the directive was vague, but those running the station could not have failed to understand where the Government stood on giving air time to terrorists. Unfortunately, RTE continued to give the IRA and its views prominence. In November 1972, after the station again granted air time to the IRA's views, the Government was left with no choice but to replace the RTE Authority.

It is too easy to forget those difficult days. The duty of the Government was clear and beyond question. The men of violence were the enemies of society. They were not heroes or martyrs acting out of patriotic duty: their gospel was one of hatred and malice, and their only language was the language of violence. Lynch's Government acted to try to ensure that the community was protected against those who were dedicated to the overthrow of the democratic institutions of the state. By the time we left office in 1973 I think we had done enough to ensure that the state and its citizens had a reasonable degree of protection.

'
'WE HEARD THE
MINISTER PLAYS GOLF'

Affter sixteen uninterrupted years in government Fianna Fáil lost office at the 1973 general election, even though its vote increased. It was less of an adjustment for me, as I had only been elected to the Dáil in 1968, and in many ways I was happy to have a less demanding period. After the problems of the job of Minister for Justice I was glad to take a less onerous role as the party adjusted to life in opposition.

I wasn't totally free of my previous position. I remained under threat and continued to have Garda protection and to carry a personal firearm. Jack Lynch asked me to become frontbench spokesman on health, and I had time to return part-time to the legal practice in Limerick. But this quieter life was not entirely to my liking: the legal work had to consist of mainly dull probate cases, because there were no specific deadlines, and in health policy nothing of interest was doing.

The new Taoiseach, Liam Cosgrave, always gave me the impression that he was modelling himself on his father, W. T. Cosgrave, who headed the Free State government from 1922 to 1932. He was very interested in security matters and had less interest in economic or social affairs. In a sense it was no harm to have a man with this outlook as Taoiseach at that time. He had a dourness about him, a man of few words. I never considered him a man of great ideas either.

There were many members of that coalition Government who were men of ideas. On the Fine Gael side Garret FitzGerald was the big beast. If Cosgrave had few words, Garret was a man of many. The Taoiseach and his Minister for Foreign Affairs were on different wavelengths, and it was clear for all to see that there was an uncomfortable co-existence between them.

The Labour Party ministers included Conor Cruise O'Brien and Justin Keating, with whom I would spar over mineral exploration policy. The Labour Party was divided. You had intellectuals of the left and a country-and-western wing who wanted nothing to do with socialism. Deputies like Michael Pat Murphy from West Cork and Stevie Coughlan from Limerick were not interested in seeing posters with the Plough and the Stars on lamp-posts in their constituencies. It was said that in the 1969 general election campaign, when the Labour Party promised that 'the seventies will be socialist,' Michael Pat Murphy told his supporters to tear down their own party posters. Stevie Coughlan, whom I knew well from Limerick, proclaimed that the only version of socialism he recognised was that of the St Vincent de Paul Society.

The leader of the Labour Party, Brendan Corish, was Tánaiste and Minister for Health in the new Government. The health brief was nothing like it has become in more recent times; back in the mid-1970s it was a very dull department. To be honest, there was very little happening, and I found being opposition health spokesman very frustrating—although one way of measuring how the world has changed is to recall that both the Minister for Health and his opposition spokesman were enthusiastic smokers!

My style was to get stuck in to a brief; but it was difficult to work up any enthusiasm in shadowing Corish. He was not a man to cause great offence. When Lynch reshuffled two years into the Dáil term I was very happy to move to Industry and Commerce. I was again shadowing a Labour Party minister. Unlike Brendan Corish, Justin Keating was a formidable opponent. He had been a lecturer in UCD Veterinary College before carving out a career in the new television service during the 1960s as an expert on agricultural matters.

A great deal of time was spent on energy policy. Peter Barry intro-duced legislation to govern the development of gas and oil exploration. The commercial viability of natural gas, discovered off the coast of Co. Cork at the Old Head of Kinsale, was confirmed in

1973. Commercial finds of oil or gas obviously had—and still have—
the potential to benefit the economy hugely and in a profound way.

There was obsessive interest by those on the left in the profits that
transnational companies might generate from oil and gas finds off the
Irish coast. But they neglected to consider the huge investments needed
to find and bring ashore these hydrocarbons, and in most instances the
exploration work delivered either nothing or finds that were simply
not commercially viable. There was constant carping about the terms
offered to oil companies, claiming they were too generous; but we were
not overrun with companies seeking to drill off the Irish coast.

Policy in Ireland has not done enough to ensure that finds actually
get into production at the earliest possible date. After Kinsale in the
1970s we've had to wait until the Corrib find off Co. Mayo thirty years
later for another commercially viable gas find. We continue to import
a significant volume of gas from insecure Russian sources by way of
Britain. We have had no commercially viable oil find at all. We have
allowed professional agitators, many of whom have no local connections, to stir up trouble and delay production in Co. Mayo, at great
cost to the country.

In 1975 Keating decided to make the state a shareholder in Bula, the
company that had been formed to work the small part of the Navan
zinc ore body that was in private ownership. A mistake had been made
by the state in the acquisition of ownership. The ore body had been
discovered by Tara Mines, which had a lease entitling it to work the
remainder.

I opposed Keating's plan as a waste of money. He wanted the state
to share in the company's profits; I wanted the state to receive a gross
royalty for every ton mined. That way I felt the state had a guaranteed
income.

In the event, Bula never got into production, and the state lost all
its investment. Litigation dragged on for years and achieved nothing
but cost a lot. Tara's section went into production, and happily is still
in production many years later. Unfortunately, the state as such got
very little out of the mine, but at least the economy benefited, and the
exchequer got tax from the large Tara payroll.

The mine was never as profitable as forecast, because its costs of getting into production were very high. Ownership changed hands several times. Royalties would have given the state a nice steady income.

———

On 1 January 1973 Ireland's membership of the European Economic Community began. We had secured derogations in several products to give local industries time to adjust to open competition in the common market. There were immediate gains for the agriculture industry, with guaranteed market access and price increases. It was a shame that over the following decade the industry didn't take more advantage of its opportunities, such as the absence of milk quotas and the existence of beef subsidies and other aids.

Agriculture was conservative and insufficiently dynamic. For instance, when the milk quota system was finally introduced, about ten years after we had joined, the amounts allotted to each country were based on the average output for the previous few years. It wasn't based on, say, the previous six months, when you could have jacked up your output. I thought it was hugely disappointing that the increase in milk output had been so slight over a ten-year period, given the huge market now available to Irish farmers, and that we missed a splendid opportunity. It was not the only example of agricultural conservatism.

Membership of the EU has been exceptionally good for Ireland. It opened up minds and markets for us and helped in attracting external investment that has been hugely beneficial for the Irish economy. In the area of competition law—and to mention just one example, airline fares—the role of European law has been immense. The opening up of flight routes to other carriers and the arrival of cheap fares was against the wishes of Aer Lingus and the Department of Transport. I got heavy criticism from the likes of Charlie Haughey and Ray Burke—both of whom sat for constituencies in north Co. Dublin, where Aer Lingus was a premium employer: it employed five or six thousand people at the time. I was told by politicians and civil servants alike that nothing could or should be done to disadvantage Aer Lingus.

But while I got a lot of support from Seán Barrett, the TCD economist, and others, it was only when we invoked articles 84 and 85 of the Treaty of Rome to inject competition into the Irish air sector that opposition began to weaken. There are times when you just have to wave the big stick, but the point was that Europe had furnished the stick. The country has benefited enormously.

A great deal of social development has also arisen from EU membership. The attitude towards women is summed up in the Constitution of Ireland, which states that 'by her life within the home, woman gives to the State a support without which the common good cannot be achieved.' And while it is still unreformed in the text, I have no doubt this would be a more prevalent attitude if it hadn't been for the EU. The advances in equal pay and anti-discrimination laws arose from what is now the European Union. This is important: the transformation in our attitudes to women, issues of equality and simple fairness, might have happened by now under the social pressure of feminist advance, but it would have been a much slower and, I suspect, a more painful process politically had we not had enlightenment thrust upon us.

There is a lot of talk now from certain quarters—the usual people who are good at shouting and useless at doing—about bullying and dictation from Europe. They are not wrong about everything, although they are wrong about most things, but they fail utterly to remember that Europe has saved us from the worst of ourselves. It is depressing in particular to hear some women, who, more than any other identifiable group in Irish society, have benefited from our membership of the community, making Eurosceptic noises.

People now take Europe for granted. A lot of those under forty-five years of age can have no recollection of life before 1973. But accepting limited law-making from Brussels as part of how this state operates has been a great benefit. We have had to give up some sovereignty, but the leverage we have gained has been, in my opinion, of much greater importance. I always considered myself a supporter of the European ideal. Some, like the Labour Party, which opposed the 1972 referendum on membership, have come to change their tune. Paddy Hillery did a good job leading the Irish negotiating team. And in the following years the benefits of being part of the club have far outweighed the fears of critics.

There was no Council of Ministers in the justice area in the 1970s, so it was only when I returned to Government in 1977 as Minister for Industry, Commerce and Energy that I began attending regular European Council meetings. One of the features of these gatherings was the differing attitudes and abilities of British ministers. At that time, with the international oil crisis, energy policy was high on the political and public agenda. Tony Benn, the left-wing Labour MP, had ministerial responsibility for energy in the Callaghan government. His main objective at meetings was to obstruct business, sometimes simply for the sake of it. The British Labour Party was very much anti-Europe at that time, and Benn had led the referendum campaign against British membership. What was more, Benn also had a problem with the Germans: he wrote as much in his diaries when he said he 'loathed' Germany.

Remarkably, given how politics in Britain later changed, the Tories were at that time quite pro-European. Benn was followed by David Howell, a quiet and able Conservative Party politician who had been a junior minister in the Northern Ireland Office in the early 1970s. He eventually fell foul of Margaret Thatcher in a reshuffle in 1983—one of her so-called 'wets'—but, remarkably, I noticed how he was given a ministerial appointment as a lord when David Cameron brought the Tories back into government in 2010.

———

I worked closely with Jack Lynch in the period 1973–7 as Fianna Fáil provided effective opposition to Cosgrave's coalition while also preparing for the subsequent general election. We differed on one important decision in this period: the return of Charles Haughey to the party's front bench. Lynch thought he could control Haughey better from the inside. Perhaps he could.

Since the disgrace of the Arms Crisis, Haughey had been attempting to win favour with the Fianna Fáil grass roots. He was on what was called the 'rubber chicken circuit', attending every dinner dance and party function where there was an invitation open to him. While Haughey was loyal, in the sense that he wasn't breaking ranks with party positions, we were under no illusion that he was intent on building a support base for what seemed, at that stage, an unlikely bid for the leadership. Lynch felt he could keep a closer watch on him on the front bench, and also that Haughey would have less free time than in his present position on the back benches. It was a gamble, but by this time Lynch was in a much stronger position than at any point in his leadership. He had widespread support, and there was no threat to him in the party.

Bringing Haughey back was obviously questionable. But hindsight is wonderful; in all likelihood, given Haughey's ambition, and financial needs, he would have challenged for the leadership either way. We made the mistake with Haughey of assuming he was a normal individual. He had already acquired a taste for high living. His need for political office had little to do with serving the public interest but was more than just the drive of overweening personal ambition that was ascribed to him at that time: put simply, he needed political office as a way of ensuring a substantial income—at a level far beyond a ministerial salary—from his associates in the world of business. The revelations at the tribunals of inquiry after his retirement more fully explained his drive than anything previously.

Pressure came on me in Limerick to contest the 1974 local elections. I wasn't very keen but eventually agreed to be a candidate. From shortly after I was elected to Limerick Corporation, however, I was disappointed. I spent three years as a member, and I found it by and large a futile and rather pointless experience. I was wasting my time. It was difficult to make any kind of useful contribution.

The meetings were really of little value. They were poorly conducted and frequently descended into personal slagging matches between particular councillors. I found this very frustrating. The constant infighting left the City Manager free to do more or less what he liked. So much of the invective was of a personal nature that a fair share of the proceedings never appeared in newspapers. I had no intention of remaining on the council any longer than I had to, and once the general election was over, in 1977, I knew I could end my membership. Ministers couldn't be councillors; but even if Lynch hadn't appointed me to the Government I was still getting off the Corporation. I don't think anybody noticed, but I had resigned as a councillor before Lynch had formally asked me to become a minister.

Some of what went on was crazy stuff. It was suggested to the City Manager at the time that we should extend the city boundary. He agreed, and he got the support of the Corporation. He then drafted an application to go to the Department of Local Government for its approval. The application and the supporting map showed a proposed extension several miles beyond the existing boundary—away out in the country. I said I thought it was mad, but the City Manager reckoned that the department would cut whatever he sent up, so he hoped that what would be left was more or less what we really wanted. I thought the proposal was so outlandish that they would throw the whole thing out.

That was in 1974. The first extension of the city boundary did not happen until 2011 and then was only a tiny fraction of the original plan. That's how the system works, or doesn't work.

Another example was the disastrous planning of the city. For example, Southill was a greenfield development built—thrown up— by an outfit called the National Building Agency. There were about 1,600 or 1,700 houses, built with no facilities—no schools, no shops, no pubs, just the houses, into which were shovelled all sorts of people who had nothing in common. Within five or six years it was clear that it was a social disaster, and was acknowledged as such. But did that stop the disaster being repeated? It did not. Moyross was developed on the other side of the city. I tried to argue with the City Manager that the better course of action was to redevelop the various derelict sites in what was, after all, a very old city. But no, the manager had costed that option and it was more expensive to build in separate small lots than to plonk a whole lot of houses down on the one site.

Of course it was, because the manager was only looking at building costs and was ignoring the infrastructural costs, which would still have to be met, yet which were already present in the city: water, sewerage and suchlike. It would have been a chance to revitalise a city centre that badly needed it. But administrators can be very short-sighted in their thinking, taking a narrow, accountant's view of things like that. I said so at the time, but I was wasting my breath. And, of course, we all know what happened: it was decidedly not a success. They are now knocking down parts of both Southill and Moyross.

What was the point of being on a political body like Limerick Corporation when the city was in effect being governed by an administrator? We had a mandate to be impotent. The Corporation was mute on policy, but some members compensated for that silence by roaring and shouting personal insults at each other. I heard accusations of sexual indiscretions and of insurance scams. On one occasion I heard an exchange so outrageous that the reporters present just dropped their pens on the spot, because there was no way they could report stuff that was flagrantly defamatory. The mayor would let this go; because he only had a one-year term and would be back as a councillor the next year, he did not want to fall out with the lads. The Corporation's obvious dysfunction aside, it remains a source of some guilt that I failed to achieve anything worthwhile as a councillor.

There is too much local government in Ireland, and much of it is a waste of time. Even the reforms in process as I write—consolidating some bodies and closing others—are compromised, because the original intention was that the new bodies would be able to raise revenue locally—a bit like the old rates system, but fairer.

In reality, what has happened? All the revenue raised is now to go to the exchequer. All these talking-shops do hardly anything that is worth doing; all the executive powers are vested in the managers. For the councillors it is an apprenticeship that might lead to the Dáil or the Seanad, and the €30,000 they get on average must come in handy. (We got £2 a meeting.) Moreover, they have little incentive to cross the managers, who can outmanoeuvre them easily. You won't want to rock boats or spike guns if the manager says to you that there's a conference in Australia or America next year and it would make a nice trip for you and the missus!

There is a clear need to restore some appropriate democratic powers to local government; but the fear in central government is that devolved powers would be abused. While there is some historical evidence for that view, it is wrong to deny any effective power at all to local government. Either abolish it altogether or give it something useful to do.

———

Fianna Fáil as an organisation professionalised during its period in opposition from 1973 to 1977. A number of new staff members were recruited, including Séamus Brennan, who was young, energetic and keen to import ideas that he'd seen on visits to the political parties in the United States. As he had been with my own ministerial appointment and with Mary Harney's appointment to the Seanad, Lynch was willing to give younger people the opportunity to prove themselves. As the new general secretary, Brennan set about reorganising the party with gusto.

It has become fashionable to criticise Fianna Fáil's 1977 general election manifesto. At the time, however, the initiatives were not considered reckless. Most of what was proposed was necessary at the time. The country needed relief from a prolonged economic downturn, and the public needed some hope that the situation would get better under a new Government. The previous few years had been depressing and were best represented by Richie Ryan, the Minister for Finance, who was known on a satirical television programme as Richie Ruin, Minister for Hardship. Fianna Fáil's manifesto was designed to give the country a lift.

The two policy proposals that later caused most difficulty were the abolition of domestic rates and the scrapping of motor tax. Yet in 1977 these proposals were not considered outlandish, although the cut in car tax was added only at the last minute. If there was a 'stroke' in the manifesto, that was the sweetener for the voters. It is noteworthy that the abolition of rates was never changed.

The mistake was not the manifesto itself but rather that two years later, in 1979, we didn't reverse engines when the oil crisis hit. We didn't recognise early enough the problems that the oil crisis would cause. If we had acted earlier, people wouldn't be as critical of the manifesto commitments. It was hard to get people to pull back on spending in 1979. The economy was recovering and there was stronger investment. I suggested certain changes, as did some ministerial colleagues, but probably not strongly enough, although we had a difficult time making our arguments when there was a sense that the country was on the move. The economy would have continued to grow if it hadn't been for the shattering impact of the oil crisis.

Martin O'Donoghue had become a very influential member of Lynch's team. A professor of economics in Trinity College, he strengthened the policy team in Fianna Fáil. Individuals like him are taken for granted today, when all parties and governments employ specialist advisers, but in 1972 O'Donoghue was a rarity. He moved from the back room to front-line politics at the 1977 general election, when he contested, and won, a seat in Dún Laoghaire. But he wasn't really cut out for the rough and tumble of Irish politics. He found the post-1979 situation, when Haughey replaced Lynch, very hard. He was a true gentleman. We were united in our opposition to the politics represented by Haughey, and we both resigned from the short-lived 1982 minority Government when faced with a party motion of confidence in Haughey that neither of us could support. Several years later, when the Progressive Democrats were formed, O'Donoghue proved a very important adviser and counsel for me and other senior figures in the party.

The scale of the Fianna Fáil victory in 1977 was impressive. It won an additional 16 seats, to have 84 of the 148 seats on offer. Fine Gael were the big losers: they lost 11 seats; the Labour Party lost 2. The response on the ground in Limerick East had been very strong throughout the campaign, but I never thought we would win so easily.

Lynch, while very pleased with the outcome, was somewhat sombre about the consequences. He was worried about the size of the majority from the very first day of returning to power. The first time I met him after the election he expressed strong reservations. 'It will be hard to keep some of these fellows in tow,' he observed. I thought he was mad. 'The bigger the majority, the stronger you are,' I replied. But Jack was right, I was wrong. The results had brought a sizeable collection of Haughey supporters into the parliamentary party, and some went on to show a total lack of respect for the man who had secured the historic victory and won them their seats.

It wasn't an easy time to be in government. The economy was relatively weak. The manifesto promises were intended to stimulate activity, but there was no accounting for further external shocks. The second international oil crisis, predicated by developments in the Middle East and the overthrow of the Shah of Iran, caused huge global uncertainty. Yet compared with what I had experienced as Minister for Justice this period in office was still relatively straightforward. I was happy to be appointed Minister for Industry, Commerce and Energy. I knew what I wanted to achieve in the position. I was impatient to get things done, as befits the young and innocent.

I spent a lot of time in the period 1977–9 abroad, first with the IDA and Córas Tráchtála, the export agency, but also on European business. With Irish membership of the European Economic Community there were increased requirements to attend meetings with counterparts from other member-states. On top of this normal business Ireland held the EEC presidency in the second half of 1979. As Minister for Industry, Commerce and Energy I was chairperson of five different sets of Ministerial Councils, in such areas as energy, industry, research, the internal market and consumer affairs. It was incredibly time-consuming. Throughout that calendar year I made about forty visits to either Brussels or Luxembourg. The disadvantage of all this travel was that I was not in Leinster House enough to gauge the mood in the party and the emerging threat to Lynch's leadership from the constituency of deputies around Haughey.

Alongside the IDA and European work I was required to put in more and more time on energy policy as the international oil crisis took over the political agenda. On behalf of the EEC I had several meetings with Sheikh Yamani, the Saudi Arabian Minister of Petroleum and Chairman of OPEC, then regarded as one of the most powerful men in the world.

We had had early warning of trouble in Iran. When oil workers in the country went on strike in July 1978, production fell from 6 million to 1½ million barrels a day. The Iranian revolution, which led to the overthrow of the Shah in January 1979 and the assumption of power by the Ayatollah Khomeini, resulted in greater disruption of oil production. Even when supplies resumed they were at a lower level than previously. With shortages on the international market, the price of oil increased dramatically.

We were desperately looking for alternative sources of supply as queues formed at petrol stations around the country and the ESB ran short of heavy fuel oil. I went to a number of countries, including Norway and Iraq, to buy oil. I travelled to Baghdad in August 1979, only weeks after Saddam Hussein had come to power. We had no idea then what he would become. At that time the Iraqi capital was a fairly wealthy and cosmopolitan city, having benefited from the oil boom.

When I arrived in Baghdad the news was not good. Ireland was number 44 in the queue of countries seeking to do deals with the Iraqi Ministry of Oil. It was important to meet the right figures in the ministry, so patience was required. We were told that a meeting might be possible in three or four days. As we had time to waste, the Iraqis asked if I would like to see some of their country. The choice was a visit to the southern city of Basrah to view some oil installations or going to Kirkuk in the north, a big oilfield where a new tourism initiative was under way. It was insufferably hot in August in Baghdad. Logic told me that heading north would provide some relief from the heat, so we opted for Kirkuk, about 150 miles north of Baghdad. How wrong I was, as the hot semi-arid climate in Kirkuk brought temperatures over 40 degrees Celsius.

We set off on a magnificent motorway stretching northwards that had obviously been built for military purposes. A long line of tanks—

more than fifty in total—passed us heading south. There was a huge square embankment not far outside Baghdad, but it wasn't possible to see what lay behind it. We found out later that this was where the Iraqi regime was rumoured to have built a nuclear reactor and were keen to protect it from possible attack by Israel.

Kirkuk was the site of one of Iraq's main oilfields. An oil strike at Baba Gurgur, discovered in the 1920s by Gulbenkian, was known locally as the Eternal Flame. Flame coming up from the ground led Gulbenkian to conclude, correctly, that this was gas associated with oil which had been ignited by lightning millennia before. Baba Gurgur had been described by Herodotus and Plutarch.

Our Iraqi guide informed us about his government's plan to develop the local tourism industry. 'We heard the minister plays golf,' the guide said. My positive confirmation was followed by a request that I play a couple of holes. 'We're making a tourism film and we'd like to be able to show that golf can be played here in the summer,' he explained. I was incredulous. 'But it's 110 degrees Fahrenheit. I'd drop dead if I play a game of golf out there,' I replied. 'Just one hole,' the official pleaded as the camera crew waited in the wings.

They were excited about the tourism potential for this area and saw the video as a crucial part of selling the region to the outside world. I agreed to play a single hole. They had one poor fellow holding four clubs (there were no golf bags); another walked beside me carrying a bucket of water and three white handkerchiefs. As we walked outside, he would dip a handkerchief in the bucket and pass the soaked cloth to me to place on my head to stay cool. The sun was so intense that in less than two or three minutes the handkerchief would be bone-dry, and then he'd replace it. I played one hole. There was no real grass on the fairways: all that lay before me as I teed off were tufts of wiry grass. A player picked up the ball wherever it landed on the fairway and placed it on the nearest tuft of grass.

After three shots I was on what seemed a beautifully grassed green; but I quickly discovered that the grass was covered in a quarter of an inch of water to keep it alive. 'Take a practice putt,' my guide suggested. I took two putts to get near the hole. The heat was becoming overpowering. 'I can't go on,' I pleaded. My hosts were not too put out. 'We have all we need,' the cameraman said.

We were invited into the clubhouse for badly needed refreshments as the bizarre nature of the visit continued. The clubhouse was very elaborate for a building in the middle of a desert. Still recovering from the heat, I was baffled to find that there was a fireplace in every room. It turned out that the clubhouse had been built in the 1920s by the British, directly from the plans of a clubhouse in Kent, replicating the building brick for brick, including the fireplaces.

I doubt that the Iraqi tourism film with the Irish Government minister ever got made. Despite the enthusiasm of those involved, there was little chance of developing a tourist industry in Kirkuk, and after Saddam tightened his repressive grip on the country—and the war with Iran began in September 1980—the prospects for the region vanished. The day after my hole of golf we were back in Baghdad and meeting the Iraqi Oil Minister. After a round of negotiations we were offered 700,000 barrels of oil, which I gratefully accepted, and I undertook to form a state oil company and to ensure that none of this oil would ever reach any of the Seven Sisters.

———

Despite the economic challenges, I found this to be a very satisfying time as a minister. I worked hard in assisting the IDA in encouraging inward investment. There were some good successes. Securing foreign investment has never been easy, which makes even greater the IDA's continuing achievements. When I arrived in Industry and Commerce the agency was headed by Michael Killeen, an outstanding public servant who I got on very well with over the following few years. The target countries for investment were the United States, Japan and, to a lesser extent, Germany. Membership of the EEC made us a more attractive site for international companies seeking a base in Europe. In securing foreign investment, the early work is done on the ground by the IDA staff, but investors like to see ministerial involvement. As a result, I was travelling a lot in this period.

Japan was a harder market than the United States to break into, given the cultural and language differences. I made a couple of trips a year to Japan. Many company chairmen were in their seventies and eighties. They were revered for their age, but it was not always clear who was in control. Protocol required that the company chairman receive visiting government ministers. There was a similar protocol at official dinners; the further you were seated from the chairman, the less important you were in the internal power structure. At one meeting I was seated opposite the chairman, and our conversation was being interpreted. Fortunately, but unknown to our hosts, the local IDA man, Jim Cashman, a former Columban priest, could speak Japanese. He was able to eavesdrop on the conversation of the other company executives down the table, who were advising the chairman, and tell me what he would say to me a minute later.

There was increased competition for foreign investment. The global economy was in recession. Unemployment rates were high everywhere. All governments wanted investment that delivered jobs. The challenge was to know when not to proceed with a project, with local pressures to back any industrialist promising any worthwhile investment.

A case in point was the car manufacturing project promoted by an American businessman, John DeLorean. Not only would the DeLorean project be a glamorous acquisition but we had a ready-made site for a car assembly plant. The space had until recently been home to Ferenka, a Dutch manufacturer of components for radial tyres. Ferenka had employed 1,400 workers at Annacotty, outside Limerick. The IDA had invested more than £8 million in the operation, and it was the largest employer in the mid-west region.

But the Ferenka plant was loss-making throughout the 1970s, and it was besieged by industrial action. There was rivalry between two unions, which were engaged in a competitive tussle to recruit members. The unions were outbidding each other to prove their ability to defend the interests of the Ferenka workers. The outcome was increased militancy. There were repeated stoppages and regular strikes, official and unofficial. In November 1977 the Dutch owners pulled the plug. Despite the shock at the scale of job losses, there was a sense of inevitability about the closure. The impact was devastating on the Limerick area. I wasn't just a local TD but the newly appointed Minister for Industry and Commerce. I immediately asked the IDA to identify suitable alternative businesses that might take over the plant and replace the jobs lost.

The staff of the IDA's Chicago office made contact with John DeLorean in January 1978, and within weeks one of the senior executives of DeLorean Motor Company arrived in Ireland. DeLorean visited for three days in early April. An engineer by profession, he had made his name as an automotive executive, primarily with General Motors, which he left in 1973 to set up his own motor business and to seek investment for building his dream car.

By late 1977 a prototype of a two-door sports car was ready, at a cost of $7 million. The unique design featured 'gull-wing' doors as well as a stainless-steel and aluminium body and lightweight fibreglass under-body, with a 2.7-litre Renault engine. It was futuristic, and it was no surprise that some years later a DeLorean would turn up in the film *Back to the Future*.

Bringing the car to the market required significant investment, and DeLorean had been in discussions, without success, with the government of Puerto Rico as well as several American states.

The Ferenka plant and a site at Blanchardstown, Co. Dublin, were considered as possible locations. The Ferenka site had the added advantage that production could begin within twelve months. DeLorean was still in active discussions about setting up in Puerto Rico and so was very keen to get the deal concluded if his assembly operation was to come to Ireland.

The project required an investment of approximately £50 million. The Government approved the project in principle at a meeting in April 1978, subject to the submission of a substantial proposal by DeLorean. He was promising that, at full production within three years, the plant would build 30,000 cars a year. Questions were asked about how achievable this plan was. Crucially for us, however, DeLorean was also promising two thousand jobs.

Looking quite glum as I pedal around the family garden in 1941. This is the earliest photo of me in existence.

My career as an actor was short-lived. Here I am in costume (*right*), alongside my friend Bill McDonogh. We were playing twins in a production of *The Belle of New York*, 1956.

Donogh O'Malley, my uncle, on receiving his degree in engineering from University College, Galway, in 1943.

On the afternoon of my graduation from University College, Dublin, in 1962. A career in law beckoned.

My mother, Una, and I pose for a portrait in our smartest clothes. This could not have been taken much later than 1946.

On the campaign trail with my mother, probably in 1987.

Pat and I were married in February 1965. This photograph, taken before our reception at the Glencormac House Hotel, Kilmacanogue, Co. Wicklow, gathered two generations of the O'Malley clan. *Left to right*: my brother Joe; my father, Desmond; the newlyweds; my mother, Una; my brother Peter.

The wedding reception was disrupted by the unlikely arrival of Richard Burton, who was filming *The Spy Who Came In from the Cold* at nearby Ardmore Studios in Bray. He insisted on kissing the bride!

Deputy Paddy Clohessy welcomes Pat and me to Leinster House on my first day as a
Dáil deputy, 28 May 1968. (© *Irish Photo Archive*)

Pat and I in
technicolour
later that same
afternoon. The
steps of the
National Library
can be seen in the
background.

Alongside the President, Éamon de Valera, and Taoiseach, Jack Lynch, on the morning of my appointment as Minister for Justice, 7 May 1970. If we look a little tired, it's with good cause: the Dáil debate on the issue had concluded at nearly 3 a.m.

Meeting Richard J. Daley, long-serving mayor of Chicago and one of the most influential American politicians of his time, 1975.

On official business in Iraq, August 1979. A portrait of Saddam, then only weeks in power, hangs conspicuously in the background.

The most taxing photo opportunity of my career, August 1979: attempting to 'prove' that golf can be played in northern Iraq in August, when daytime temperatures soar above 40 degrees Celsius. I lasted one hole.

Celebrating re-election
in June 1977. Fianna Fáil
was swept back into
power with a twenty-
seat majority.

Lost in thought at a
press conference during
Fianna Fáil's 1982 election
campaign. (© *Photocall*)

Charlie Bird pursues me for a comment following my 'Stand By the Republic' address. Six days later I was expelled from the Fianna Fáil organisation for 'conduct unbecoming a party member'. (© *Photocall*)

Pat and I enjoy a stroll on the morning of 21 February 1985. My Dáil speech of the previous day effectively ended my parliamentary association with Fianna Fáil.

Charles Haughey and I during our period in coalition together in 1991. He would resign the following year. (© *Photocall*)

Martyn Turner's take on the political manoeuvring within the coalition during the 26th Dáil. I was always depicted with a cigarette smouldering at the corner of my mouth. (© *Martyn Turner*)

Turner once more. His subject here is the Progressive Democrats' fragile accommodation with Fianna Fáil, 1989. (© *Martyn Turner*)

And finally, a fairly downbeat assessment of my efforts throughout the 1980s. (© *Martyn Turner*)

1986: Eight years after our discussions with John DeLorean broke down—and five after the DeLorean Motor Company went into liquidation—I finally got behind the wheel of his infamous sports car. (*Left to right*) Hugh Coyle, manager of Renvyle House Hotel in Connemara; yours truly; the stylish owner of the DeLorean in question.

An unusual gathering: myself, Patrick Hillery, Jack Lynch and Bertie Ahern on the occasion of Lynch's conferral as an honorary doctor of law at the University of Limerick, 1995. (Courtesy *Irish Examiner*)

Pat and I with Máirín and Jack Lynch at a Limerick Chamber of Commerce dinner in 1993.

The guest of honour that evening was Ted Heath (*centre*), former Prime Minister of the United Kingdom and leader of the Conservative Party.

The 22nd Government of Ireland, formed in February 1992 following the resignation of Charles Haughey. Bobby Molloy and I, the only Progressive Democrats represented, are seated on the right end of the front row.

The Dáil horse, Arctic Copper, with its owners, trainer, jockey and lad, after winning at Navan on 11 December 1999. (© *Healy Racing*)

Pat and I on
our twenty-
fifth wedding
anniversary, 1990.

In 2003 the University
of Limerick chose to
award me an honorary
doctorate in law. Here
Pat and I share a joke
after the conferral
ceremony.
(© *Press 22*)

In 2002 my daughter, Fiona, was elected to the Dáil as a Progressive Democrat. It was a proud moment.

Two members of my family have served in Government, but the most famous member of the O'Malley clan is probably my cousin Dido Florian de Bounevialle O'Malley Armstrong, better known as Dido. This photo was taken after her concert at Marlay Park, Dublin, in August 2004.

Despite the IDA having first proposed contact with DeLorean, its senior executives were divided on the project. The Managing Director, Michael Killeen, was one of those with strong reservations, and he made his concerns known to me. The proposed deal was being put together in a very short space of time, and Killeen was not convinced about financial aspects of the business plan. I had great faith in his judgement, so, before progressing any further, I wanted to explore the project in greater detail.

The IDA organised a working lunch for me with DeLorean and his senior colleagues at the end of May 1978. Michael Killeen declined to attend; he had made up his mind, on the basis of the figures. I wanted to make a judgement on the promoter. We met in the Shelbourne Hotel in Dublin. DeLorean, as I quickly discovered, was a flamboyant character. Various aspects of the project were discussed, including employment numbers and production forecasts. A department memo of the meeting observed that 'on all these matters, Mr DeLorean appeared to be flexible in regards to his plans and confident of his ability to handle the situation.'

DeLorean was certainly a smooth character. He had an answer for every question I asked; nothing was a problem. 'If it's all this easy, then why are we here?' I asked myself. He was also very keen on having cash at the outset from the Government. When I expressed some reservations he immediately began talking about the possibility of establishing the assembly plant in Puerto Rico. He set 31 May as a deadline. It was a clear threat. If we didn't sign up he would go elsewhere, although he wasn't at all clear how solid were his alternative options.

The working lunch began at midday, and just before three o'clock DeLorean announced that he had to leave. 'I've a meeting at 4 p.m. in New York,' he said. He had a private plane waiting at Dublin Airport, and with the five-hour time difference he claimed he was on time for his appointment.

I walked back to my office now not convinced that DeLorean was someone we should do business with. I rang Michael Killeen and said I shared his reservations, and I cancelled a trip to Brussels so as to attend a Government meeting to brief my ministerial colleagues on the situation. There was an urgent need to replace the jobs at Ferenka;

but the DeLorean deal was very risky. The costs involved, in grants and equity, were considerable, and these had in fact increased since the Government first backed the project in principle the previous April. They were prepared to back the IDA in concluding a deal with DeLorean but without taking unnecessary or abnormal risks. We wanted the investment but also were conscious of protecting the taxpayer.

A letter setting out our terms was sent to DeLorean on 2 June. We were committing ourselves to $22 million in grants, with another $13 million in equity investment and $9¼ million in bank guarantees. During negotiations on these terms DeLorean sought to significantly change the package. There was also some confusion about what he was now proposing about the status of IDA shares. A line had been reached for the IDA, and I was very much in agreement with the decision taken at a special meeting of the Authority on 14 June. The terms approved by the Government were the final offer. In the light of DeLorean seeking to rewrite those terms, the IDA proposed terminating discussions.

Michael Killeen came to see me after the Authority meeting. I was happy to back the IDA decision. Investing was a huge risk. More than £50 million in public money was required in total.

DeLorean responded immediately by saying he was now willing to accept the original terms and wanted to meet me again to pursue the project; but there was no interest in reopening discussions. In politics, you never get thanked when you say 'no', but it is just as important to say 'no' as it is to say 'yes'. With DeLorean, 'no' was the correct decision; and it didn't take too long for that decision to be shown to be correct.

Within days of the ending of our discussions with DeLorean, newspaper speculation began to appear that a new car assembly plant could be established in Northern Ireland. Within weeks the Northern Ireland Development Agency, which was backed by the British government, completed a deal with DeLorean. The British side heralded the deal as a triumph for British diplomacy. The media reported that the IDA had lost out to its Northern counterpart in the 'race' to secure foreign investment.

Production began in early 1981, and about nine thousand of the DeLorean DMC-12 cars eventually came off the production line in Dunmurry, outside Belfast. But our initial suspicions about DeLorean's ability to deliver on his ambitious projections were correct. Breakdowns were frequent and difficult to repair; sales failed to reach the level needed to cover costs. Production ceased within a year, and by the end of 1982 the operation was bankrupt. The British government had invested nearly £100 million in the project.

Bizarrely, only a few hours after Margaret Thatcher called a halt, DeLorean was arrested in Los Angeles on charges of drug-trafficking, and in 1982 the company went into liquidation. DeLorean claimed the drug deal was only to generate capital for his ailing car operation. He was eventually found not guilty because of entrapment by the police.

Several years later, when on holidays in Renvyle, Co. Galway, I met a man who had bought a DMC-12 at the liquidation sale in Belfast. The cars by now were collectors' items, and this car was the man's pride and joy. He was very careful with it and hardly ever took it out on the roads of Connemara. 'I'd love to drive that car,' I said, explaining my history with DeLorean. It took a bit of convincing and a promise that I would not drive above 30 miles per hour. So, hardly going out of second gear, I finally had my spin in the car that, thankfully, hadn't cost the Irish state tens of millions.

————

In 1979 I led the first Irish trade mission to communist China. I was accompanied by officials from Córas Tráchtála and about half a dozen journalists. China was just opening up to the West; Mao was only three years dead; his widow, Jiang Qing, and the 'Gang of Four' had been arrested and disgraced; and Deng Xiaoping had just established himself as the new strongman.

We flew via Tehran just after the overthrow of the Shah and the return of Ayatollah Khomeini. We had a long stopover in Tehran airport, which in the Shah's day had boasted the longest bar in the world—about 150 feet—but of course it was very, very dry under the new regime, offering nothing more than sickly-sweet orange juice with no ice. This is what we used for slaking our thirst in the torrid heat.

Anyway, we got to Peking eventually. The first thing that struck me was the absolute uniformity of dress—blue or grey Mao jackets on men and women alike. As we drove in from the airport I noticed a group of maybe fifty people looking up in astonishment at men erecting one of the very first commercial advertisements seen in China. It was for Coca-Cola, as you might have guessed.

There were no hotels, so we stayed in a government guest-house that had previously been the Burmese embassy, an impressive and well-designed building. We visited the Great Wall and the Forbidden City, where we were objects of interest ourselves, because most Chinese had never up to then laid eyes on a Westerner.

The high point of the tour was a gala banquet thrown in my honour in the Great Hall of the People—not in the main hall itself, which is vast (it can hold five thousand people or more), but in one of the smaller rooms adjacent. Everything was done in nines—a lucky number: there were nine tables, with nine people at each. It was a meal of nine courses, of which the fourth or fifth was the *pièce de resistance*: a bear's paw. They had treated these by removing the claws and the fur but not the pads. We were eating with chopsticks, with which we were inept, so there was no question of cutting up the bear's paw. It was to be eaten whole; to leave it or to refuse it would have been considered bad manners.

It was awful. It was all fat and sinew, and we Irish must have been furiously chewing and chomping for about fifteen minutes before we eventually got it down. I was thinking, 'This is all for Kathleen Ní Houlihan.' However, to our horror, the Chinese had forgotten about their 'nine' rule, because there were still three bears' paws sitting in the middle of the table. We were, of course, offered first dibs on seconds, but we all politely refused, whereupon the Chinese fairly dived towards the middle to claim their prizes.

The Chinese Minister for Trade, our host, was about eighty-six and a veteran of the Long March, so he was made for life. It was a bit like being in the GPO in 1916.

We did get some positive results for Irish business from the trip. However, one potentially very big deal fell through. A company in Co. Clare that had a joint venture with an American company to manufacture a thing called a radome—a cover for radar equipment— sold six to China as a result of the trip, with a promise of more to follow. At about £300,000 each, that was good business. The Chinese wanted more for the protection of their long border with the Soviet Union; but they supplied their needs by stripping down the radomes, seeing how they were put together, and making their own. So the repeat orders for Co. Clare never materialised.

After the banquet we stood in Tiananmen Square, watching the vast empty space. There were no cars, but suddenly a set of traffic lights at one of the corners went green, and there issued from the side street what we reckoned was between five thousand and eight thousand bicycles. Eventually a car was spotted: the transport of a senior Politburo member. Chinese Mercs and perks.

The Chinese had a soft spot for Ireland, because Frank Aiken, when he had been Minister for External Affairs (as it was called then), had recognised communist China and urged its acceptance into the United Nations. It was hard to know who he displeased more, the Catholic Church or the American government, so it took some guts on Aiken's part. It wasn't forgotten in China.

We went on to Shanghai and later to Guangzhou (formerly Canton). In Shanghai I was struck by how alike its famous commercial street, the Bund, was to Dame Street in Dublin. The reason was that the buildings had been put up by the same sort of British financial institutions that dominated Dame Street, and possibly were built from similar plans. Outside our guest-house was a huge lawn, and I looked out on the first morning to see four men with little baskets down on their knees doing something. When we reached them what we saw was scarcely credible. They each had a pair of nail scissors, and each was cutting the grass, one blade at a time, which was then put in the basket! It took the four of them a week to cut the lawn—at which point they had to begin again. Full employment.

Not to be outdone, women's work was arranged with equal ingenuity.

Each woman had a section of street, about fifty yards long, which she was required to sweep about once an hour. They were fully employed as well.

The funniest moment on the trip concerned the journalists. One of their number was the legendary Raymond 'Congo' Smith. The journalists were sending copy by telex back to Ireland. Those who worked for other papers were being asked by their editors why they were not sending the same stories as Smith. They asked him to show them what he was sending. They protested that a lot of this never happened. Congo explained, 'The *Independent* likes a story they can put a bit of a headline on.'

We finally left China, travelling from Guangzhou to Hong Kong, after seven stimulating and valuable days. It was early in the morning when we got to our Hong Kong hotel. Of course Hong Kong was still a British colony in those days, and the British influence was pervasive. The hotel offered a slap-up English breakfast: bacon, sausage, eggs, beans, fried bread, puddings and God knows what else, with lashings of toast and coffee. It helped to erase the memory of the bear's paw.

Chapter 7 ~

'I'M NOT VOTING FOR YOU'

1979 proved to be Jack Lynch's *annus horribilis*. The local and European elections in June allowed the electorate to give vent to their frustration with the economic situation. There was industrial unrest and protests by taxpayers.

When the postal workers went on strike Charles Haughey, who was Minister for Health and Social Welfare, ensured that they were paid social welfare at once. It was a move intended not just to ease the burden on the strikers. The Taoiseach's critics in the parliamentary party—or, to put it more accurately, Haughey's supporters— were continually causing problems. A small group was carping about Lynch not being hard-line enough with the British government in relation to Northern Ireland. A relatively poor showing in the European Parliament and local elections and then two by-election losses in Lynch's home city of Cork only compounded a difficult political situation.

Lynch had intended to resign as leader early in 1980. He wanted to ensure that Haughey was not his successor, and he was persuaded by George Colley's belief that he had the numbers to win a leadership contest. For that reason Lynch brought forward his own retirement to December 1979. He and Colley believed they would catch Haughey unprepared; but those of us in the Colley camp had under-estimated the support for Haughey. We allowed ourselves to be lulled into a sense of complacency, mainly because we knew we had near full Government support.

George Colley had been an important member of the Government when I joined it after the 1969 general election. He was a man of great principle, and although Lynch had beaten him for the Fianna Fáil leadership in 1966 he had been a very important ally of Lynch's during the dark and dangerous period of the Arms Crisis.

Colley didn't seek to win friends, and I suppose he was set in his ways and somewhat inflexible on some issues. But if Fianna Fáil had had more individuals with his decency and honour it would not have ended up as the party of low standards. Colley had made an accurate assessment of Haughey long before others questioned his integrity. He knew him from boyhood, and they had shared for a time a constituency in Dublin. He used the phrase 'low standards in high places' even before the Arms Crisis.

When Lynch stood down I was asked by about ten Fianna Fáil deputies to stand for the leadership, and they pressed me strongly to consider. However, I had already pledged my support to Colley, and I actively campaigned for him. A few of those who directly approached me told me later that they had voted for Haughey. I felt a sense of commitment to George; I considered it would be unfair to him and rather dishonourable if I were to oppose him.

Colley was much more senior than me, and had more ministerial experience. I also thought he would win—an assumption made by others in the Government too. It was a big mistake. We thought that, as he had Government backing, the parliamentary party would follow with its support. Michael O'Kennedy was the only minister to back Haughey; but there was a sizeable constituency among the intake of new TDs from the 1977 general election who, for one reason or another, were prepared to back him.

The vote took place on 7 December 1979. I was confident that Colley would win and was shocked, therefore, when the result was announced. Haughey won by 44 votes to 38. I was worried for the future of the party, and also for the future of the country.

Enormous pressure had been put on people. Haughey used every tactic to secure support. It was only later that some of his more underhand methods became known. I didn't know it in 1979 but I heard later of cases where financial inducement was involved—not the direct payment of money but promises to pay off bank or other debts. We know now from tribunal inquiries that while Haughey was up to his eyes in debt at that time he also had an ability to get business people to give him considerable amounts of money. He used these funds well in his own interest.

There is much talk about TDs' financial assets but less talk about their debts. But whereas a few thousand shares in a public company gives the shareholder no influence in that company, a deputy's debts make him vulnerable to unscrupulous people, such as Haughey. He got at a number of people through this route. The essential reason why he insisted on an open roll-call vote in leadership elections was that he wanted to know exactly who was voting which way. I know of a couple of instances where TDs who voted the 'right' way had outstanding debts paid off, which was not just a reward for present conduct but placed those deputies under a very strict obligation for the future. I am sure that these were not isolated cases.

As the Haughey camp savoured their victory, a number of us, including Martin O'Donoghue, Pádraig Faulkner and Bobby Molloy, met in Colley's house. The mood was grim. The shock of defeat was only hitting us, but we were all too aware of the implications, not just for Fianna Fáil but more importantly for the country. We had every reason to suspect the sources of his wealth, although when the truth eventually emerged years later it was beyond anything we imagined in 1979. We guessed that he had benefactors whose welfare was bound up with his own. For example, how had he made his money in the first place? After all, he did not come from a moneyed background. In the 1950s he was a partner in a small accountancy practice in Amiens Street, Dublin, at a time when no-one had a bob and Amiens Street was no better an address than it is now. Yet out of this he was able to buy Grangemore, a country house in its own grounds beyond Raheny. When he sold that for development he was able to trade up to Kinsealy.

The suspicion was that he was very close to some people in the Gallagher construction empire, and it is possible that the initial funds came from that source. Certainly when the Grangemore lands were sold for development and were turned into what is now Donaghmede and environs the principal developers were the Gallagher Group.

He had begun as he meant to go on; the pattern was repeated both in government and opposition, when he showed extraordinary indulgence to certain agricultural interests. How else to explain his extraordinary trip to Libya, when leader of the opposition in the mid-80s, to lobby on behalf of those interests?

As to the Gallaghers, I was invited to dinner about 1980 by Patrick Gallagher (subsequently imprisoned in Northern Ireland for fraud but never even prosecuted in the Republic, even though the registered and head office of his bust bank was here). The whole point of the evening was to ask me to lay off Charlie. I replied that I wished Charlie would lay off some of his activities, so nothing came of the evening except a pleasant dinner.

On the days following Haughey's victory we began to work out who had supported the two candidates. I was flabbergasted at some of the people who had backed Haughey. Over the following weeks I made it my business to talk to some of these TDs. 'Can you please explain to me why you voted as you did?' I asked. Some of them decided that it was better that Haughey won because if Colley had beaten him Haughey would not have walked away but would have done everything to smash up the party, whereas Colley would accept defeat without causing terminal damage. It was a real perversion of democracy: voting for the candidate you don't at all want merely to keep the peace and avoid a violent reaction. This situation, where many votes were not genuine, freely given votes, would be repeated at two subsequent ballots on Haughey's leadership.

After the December 1979 leadership result I thought about not taking a Government position if I was offered one. But, having talked about this option with others in the Colley group, I decided it was better to be inside keeping an eye on Haughey than outside totally in the dark about what was going on. At that stage I wasn't even sure if Haughey would keep me in the Government. He dropped Jim Gibbons and Martin O'Donoghue.

I got the call to see him. He was proposing a new department by combining trade, commerce and tourism. Work on energy policy had been taking about half my time as a minister since 1977. The international oil situation was challenging, and shortages were a continuing problem. Power cuts and queues at petrol stations were politically difficult. Energy policy demanded full-time attention. I had previously told Lynch that energy needed to be split from Industry and Commerce, and I now explained the case to Haughey. Industry and Commerce were being neglected. In fairness to him I have to say that, despite our differences, he accepted my argument. He eventually assigned the energy brief to George Colley.

I was unhappy at his proposal to detach the industry brief from commerce. During the conversation it emerged that there was no policy logic involved: Haughey had simply promised the industry brief to Albert Reynolds during the leadership election. Already the debts were being paid off.

I said I was not interested in the proposed trade and tourism ministry; I would rather be on the back benches. I left him to consider my response, and really without hope of being a minister any more. But twenty-four hours later Haughey changed his mind, and I was reappointed Minister for Industry and Commerce.

Having lost the leadership contest, Colley felt that the rules of engagement had changed. This was particularly so given the lack of support Haughey and his backers in the parliamentary party had shown to Lynch over the two previous years. Loyalty was no longer provided automatically, and it could be divided: loyalty to the Taoiseach did not equate with loyalty to the party leader. I shared this view. Indeed being a member of a Government did not mean that you had to agree with the Taoiseach on each point. In a democracy it should be possible to hold different opinions from those of the leader. Unfortunately, under Haughey disagreement on any issue was regarded as synonymous with personal disloyalty. We had very different understandings of the Taoiseach's role.

Our knowledge of Haughey's involvement in the Arms Crisis coloured our attitude to him. We had good reason to be concerned. Colley secured a veto on ministerial appointments to the Departments of Defence and Justice. Michael O'Kennedy replaced Colley as Minister for Finance; but it was very clear that Haughey was intent on running the show.

The national economic situation was worsening as the international economy continued to slow. When Haughey addressed the
nation in early 1980 I was amazed at what he had to say. His message
about reining in public spending made complete sense. 'Maybe he's
going to act,' I said to Colley the next day. 'That would be all right if he
meant what he said,' Colley observed. 'But I don't think he meant it.
Just wait and see.' He was right to be sceptical. Within a few weeks it
was clear that Haughey had no intention of delivering the required
fiscal measures, and his talk was not followed through with the necessary action to lessen public expenditure. Like himself, the country
was living beyond its means.

There was now a different atmosphere from that in the Lynch
Government. There were different personalities at the Government
table. Haughey brought in quite a number of his own people. In another
sign of debts being repaid he increased the number of ministers of state
from ten to fifteen. If it hadn't been for the constitutional limitation on
Government members to fifteen I suspect Haughey would have headed
the largest government in any European country.

Lynch was treated shoddily after his resignation. Haughey did
everything possible to erase him from the party's history. It was petty
behaviour that even went as far as ensuring that Lynch's portrait did
not hang alongside that of other Fianna Fáil leaders in the party's
head office in Upper Mount Street. Lynch had led Fianna Fáil for
thirteen-and-a-half years; he had won two general elections, including
the historic absolute majority in 1977. As far as Haughey was
concerned, none of this had ever happened. His insecurity was as big
as his ego. There was no retirement lunch or farewell presentation for
Lynch. When I offered to organise a dinner in Limerick, Lynch
declined. He opted instead to fade into the background quietly.

——

It was hard to enjoy being a minister under Haughey. Everything, and
everybody, appeared to be on edge. There was considerable tension

within the party and within the Government. The leadership election, and the manner of Lynch's departure, had left a bad taste. Haughey knew that several ministers, including myself, were deeply suspicious of his intentions. A lot of documents were never brought before the Government, though it was clear that Haughey was involved in every financial or finance-related decision. In some ways it was nearly better not knowing what was going on.

Haughey had appointed Michael O'Kennedy as Minister for Finance, but within a year O'Kennedy was off to become an EU commissioner. The choice of his replacement was a huge shock. Gene Fitzgerald was in Government as Minister for Labour. It was just about his level. His promotion to be Minister for Finance was justified only by Haughey's desire to maintain a watchful and activist role in the Department of Finance.

Questions about the source of his wealth were asked in private among several colleagues. We had our deep suspicions, but without specific facts it was impossible for people, myself included, to prove anything.

In fairness to Haughey I have to say there was little enough interference in how I did my job. He was open to arguments on policy matters, provided they didn't interfere with his own plans. We tended to meet directly only when there was a fairly serious problem.

In the period before the 1981 estimates we had a serious run-in. He asked me to take £20 million out of my department's vote for industrial development, with a promise that the money would be returned after the general election. Having failed to deliver on his public pledge to sort out the national finances, Haughey was now intent on making the books look better with actions that avoided extra tax or cuts in expenditure. What he was proposing for my department's budget obviously had serious implications for how agencies such as the IDA operated, as they would have seen a large cut in their budget even if, as Haughey promised, the funds would eventually be restored. He said it would be an understanding between the two of us.

Such a move was not just wrong in itself: there were two other issues about what he was proposing. For one, he couldn't be relied upon to restore the £20 million; and secondly, everything was based on his being returned to office after the election. 'I won't do it,' I said. He was not pleased, but I think he managed to set up that type of arrangement with some other ministers. It was essentially an exercise in cooking the books, which was exposed by John Kelly after the election in June 1981.

The republican hunger-strike candidates facilitated to some extent Garret FitzGerald's election as Taoiseach in 1981 when Fianna Fáil lost seats in constituencies where there was strong support for what was happening in the Maze Prison in the North. But Haughey's pledge when defeating Colley that he was the man to deliver electoral success proved unfounded. The total number of TDs had been increased from 148 to 166, but Fianna Fáil still managed to lose seven. By comparison, there were twenty-two new Fine Gael TDs, although, with the Labour Party losing two seats, FitzGerald was only able to put together a minority Government that was three seats short of a Dáil majority.

The Government formed by FitzGerald in June 1981 was reliant on independents for its survival. Its collapse on a budget vote in January 1982 was not a great surprise. Haughey called a meeting of the Fianna Fáil front bench. The idea of a change of Government without an election—permissible under the Constitution—was discussed. The power to refuse an election rested with President Hillery. The idea of an opposition communicating its availability to form an alternative Government is perfectly legitimate; but what happened later that evening, when Haughey threatened staff members in Áras an Uachtaráin when he was refused access to the President, was an absolute scandal; and years later it hastened the end of his political career.

Haughey was the prime mover behind the phone calls. Poor Brian Lenihan, whose sheer good nature was taken advantage of—his biggest problem in life was that he couldn't say No to anyone—made the actual calls. Sylvie Barrett, a Clare TD, was reluctantly pressed into service as well, on the grounds that he had shared a constituency with Paddy Hillery.

This was not the only time that Haughey traded on Brian Lenihan's good nature. In 1985, when Garret FitzGerald concluded the Anglo-

Irish Agreement, one of the finest achievements of any Dublin government, Lenihan was despatched to America to drum up opposition to it. He failed; the leading Irish-Americans, such as Ted Kennedy and Tip O'Neill, were much better informed about Irish realities than some of their over-excitable constituents.

So the phone calls proved to be a fiasco. The subsequent general election led only to minor changes in party strengths in Dáil Éireann. The Labour Party had the same number of seats, at 15, Fine Gael came back with two fewer, at 63, while Fianna Fáil increased by four, to 81. In this era, when Fianna Fáil would not consider a coalition arrangement, another minority Government was the only outcome. In the messy circumstances in which FitzGerald's Government had collapsed, Fianna Fáil's failure to secure an absolute majority was disappointing. For a second election Haughey had proved not to be the vote-winner that was one of the trump cards of his supporters in the leadership contest with George Colley in December 1979.

Haughey was scrambling around to put together support for a minority Fianna Fáil Government with backing from independents such as Tony Gregory and Neil Blaney as well as Sinn Féin the Workers' Party (previously Official Sinn Féin). Two years previously I had backed George Colley for the leadership. In early 1982 I would have happily stepped aside if another candidate had emerged. Colley was not interested in contesting again, so pressure came on me to challenge. Many of what I would call the 'middle-ground' TDs wanted Haughey out, but they were fearful of the consequences for the party of a leadership challenge. These deputies would say things to me like 'The timing is wrong,' 'Be patient,' 'Keep your head down, it will come your way.'

But my motivation in trying to remove Haughey was not a desire to take his job. I was not personally driven to become party leader or Taoiseach; I would be quite happy to have someone reasonable there. I wanted him out because of what he represented and the malignant force that he was. As was revealed many years later by the tribunals of inquiry, what Haughey was involved in was far worse than what we thought at the time.

I agreed to challenge for the party leadership; but, in truth, we were not fully prepared for a contest. The issue was never put to a vote at a meeting of the parliamentary party. That morning two of my strongest supporters sat down beside me in the members' dining-room in Leinster House. They now favoured calling off a challenge. I knew immediately that there was no chance of defeating Haughey at that time.

The formation of the second Haughey Government brought more of his supporters to ministerial office. A number of these were insufficiently qualified to be in government. He had so many debts to repay that ability was not high among the criteria for ministerial promotion. He attracted blind loyalty from these people.

Haughey wasn't interested in narrowing divisions. He proposed dropping Colley as Tánaiste. With this decision, and without consultation on the appointments to Justice and Defence, Colley opted not to take a Government position. I considered following him onto the back benches, but to have done so would have given Haughey a totally free hand. He attempted to achieve a show of balance by giving Martin O'Donoghue, who he had dropped from the previous Government, a ministerial role. But it was a short-lived appointment, as the minority Fianna Fáil Government formed in March 1982 didn't see out the year. O'Donoghue and I had resigned even before it collapsed.

It was a desperately unhappy period in government. It was clear that little was going to be achieved, given the conditions we were working under. Haughey was prepared to spend a limitless amount of money—most of it borrowed—to stay in power. The deal with Tony Gregory in exchange for his support on the formation of the Government was only the start. There was no attempt to rein in public spending. The country was running up an ever-increasing deficit.

Haughey's reaction to Argentina's invasion of the Falkland Islands showed how much of an opportunist he was. For short-term gain with diehard republicans he was prepared to criticise the British government for driving out the intruders and to stand alone within the European Community. His action totally and unnecessarily set back Anglo-Irish relations seriously. He had made a mess of the situation.

He generally stayed clear of my departmental agenda, although he was always in the background. The PMPA, a cut-price motor insurance company, collapsed just after I resigned from the Government in October 1982. That was no surprise. I had had several difficult meetings with Joe Moore of the PMPA. I had got as far as threatening to withdraw the company's licence. Moore was an aggressive character. He warned me that he controlled 44 per cent of the private car insurance market, so I couldn't take away the licence. He was less vocal when I suggested that the department could stop him writing new business. As he was paying claims from new-business premiums, that would have been a problem for the PMPA. 'How you are behaving is wrong, and you know it's wrong,' I said to him. His trump card was always that there was a higher authority than me. Even when he didn't have a leg to stand on, Moore would aggressively argue his case. After one of these bruising encounters I turned to my department official and said, 'I hope I'm not here when this thing finally blows up.'

Just how close Moore was to Haughey is illustrated by one of the more notorious forms of pressure that Haughey was able to employ to secure support in the heaves against him. David Andrews TD was a barrister who received a lot of work from the PMPA, to the degree that he was unwise enough to become over-dependent on this single client. But Andrews was also firmly in the anti-Haughey camp. Haughey asked Moore to withdraw the work from Andrews; Moore passed the word along, and it was made clear to Andrews that he would lose the PMPA account if he didn't vote for Haughey. He didn't: he voted for me instead and duly lost all the PMPA work.

The strength of Haughey's desire to remain in power is better understood by the information that emerged from the various investigations that reported long after he left political life. Protecting his own financial position was his primary motivation. We would speculate, but we had no idea of the scale of the corruption; all we knew was that it was impossible to square his life-style with his official salary. On one occasion I was approached late one evening in the Dáil bar by an ardent Haughey supporter. 'Why can't you leave Charles J. Haughey alone?' he asked. 'What did he ever do to you?' The man in question was Tom McEllistrim from Kerry North. He was one of the backbenchers who had agitated against Lynch and was rewarded for his efforts by elevation to the ranks of junior ministers in 1979 and again in 1981. I had heard him drone on enough. 'Tom,' I said, 'could you tell me how he can live as he does on his public salary?' McEllistrim had no answer to my question. 'That's treason,' he replied. 'That's treason, to talk like that about the great leader of our country.' And with that observation he walked away.

Many TDs who backed Haughey in the leadership election in December 1979 and in the confidence votes in late 1982 and early 1983 did so out of fear. Many were threatened. Sometimes the intimidation related to their constituency and the prospect of being replaced as a party candidate; in other cases the threat was of a direct economic or financial nature.

For others the threat involved family members. One of the cases I know about involved the brother of a Fianna Fáil TD whose business was dependent on three main customers, about 60 per cent of his business being with them. He was told that if his brother did not vote for Haughey these contracts would not be renewed. I was told that this man rang his brother late the night before a confidence vote, begging and pleading with him to vote for Haughey, regardless of what he thought of him. The poor man voted the 'right' way, hating everything about it, rather than see his brother ruined. No-one was in any doubt that Haughey's goons would have carried through their threats.

In October 1982 I was on ministerial business with Bord Fáilte in Spain when I heard that Charlie McCreevy had tabled a motion of no confidence in Haughey. The news reached me in the middle of the night. McCreevy was one of the new TDs elected in 1977 who had backed Haughey, but his enthusiasm waned after witnessing Haughey's performance as party leader and Taoiseach. The timing of the motion was terrible, and I was furious with McCreevy for acting as he did. He was on a solo run and had not consulted anybody. What was most galling was that he knew that planning for a leadership challenge was under way. We had agreed what needed to be done.

Unlike the previous February, we were going to move in a planned and co-ordinated way. McCreevy breached that agreement. It was a self-indulgent act that I have never understood. Haughey was increasingly vulnerable but we needed another fortnight to be sure of a majority in the parliamentary party. As news of McCreevy's action was relayed to me by phone, I felt physically sick. 'That's it,' I said to myself, 'that's the end of it.' McCreevy's solo run ruined the challenge, and ultimately kept Haughey in place as leader.

I arrived back from Spain to find Haughey seeking public declarations of support from his Government colleagues. The no-confidence motion had put Martin O'Donoghue and myself in a difficult position. I told Haughey bluntly that I had no obligation to support him in a vote on the leadership of Fianna Fáil. That had nothing to do with my membership of the Government, as every deputy had an equal vote. He was equally blunt: if I wanted to remain as a minister I had no choice but to vote for him openly on the confidence motion. 'I'm not voting for you,' I said. 'Well, then you'll have to resign as a minister,' he replied.

I left his office and had consultations with colleagues, including Martin O'Donoghue, who was facing the same choice. O'Donoghue and I returned to meet Haughey together. We handed him our resignations. 'Well, fuck you anyway,' he responded. 'I didn't think you'd have the guts to do it.' We resigned as ministers on 6 October 1982.

There was a sinister undertone to dealing with Haughey. Some days later his driver turned up at O'Donoghue's house. A gift-wrapped box was presented. 'A delivery from the Taoiseach,' the driver announced. Inside the box were two dead ducks and a card that read, *Shot over Kinsealy.*

———

Haughey announced that the leadership vote would take place by means of an open roll-call. I spoke against this idea, as did five or six other members of the parliamentary party; but we were already openly in the opposition camp. Others were now being forced to show their preference in public.

Haughey had his argument worked out. In summary, he declared that there was terrible disloyalty to the party leader, people were working against him, and the grass roots were furious with those involved. He claimed that the party membership was entitled to know who was voting against him as leader. As a compromise, he proposed holding an open vote to decide whether the confidence motion would be determined by a secret ballot or not—even though the party rules prescribed a secret ballot. There were howls of protest in the room, as this suggestion amounted to the same thing as the original proposal.

The vote took place on 6 October 1982. There was an unpleasant and uncomfortable mood in the room. The meeting went on for almost fifteen hours. Haughey got his open roll-call and duly won the motion of confidence, by 58 votes to 22. Before McCreevy's premature move I had been hopeful of victory, but, given the way the voting system was manipulated and the tremendous pressure people were put under, the outcome was not a great surprise. Haughey had won, but not in accordance with the rules.

As for the pressure used by his supporters, it was beyond anything previously known in Irish politics: sinister late-night phone calls; financial manipulation, threatening livelihoods on the one hand and discharging debts on the other. It would have been neither contemplated nor tolerated in earlier days, even among battle-hardened veterans in what was always a rough game. But that was a game played by the rules; Haughey threw the rule book away and stopped at nothing to get what he wanted.

Over the following days several TDs came to see me. Some had voted against their own preference because of the roll-call vote. Some were actually in tears. I came to the conclusion that democracy could exist in its purest form only when there was a large electorate. Where the electorate is relatively small, as it was in the Fianna Fáil leadership votes, those casting their votes were more vulnerable to manipulation by ruthless people like Charles Haughey and his cronies. In such circumstances voters are identifiable and open to being pressured and bullied.

There was a menacing mood after the result was confirmed. While the marathon meeting of the parliamentary party was under way, many Haughey supporters had spent the day drinking in the Dáil bar. Their intense hostility towards those of us who opposed Haughey was typified by the assault on Jim Gibbons. There was a strong dislike for Gibbons among the Haughey camp because of his giving evidence in the Arms Trial against Haughey; he was also a critic of Haughey's leadership. He was hit and knocked to the ground by a group who surrounded him inside Leinster House. The situation was nasty. Some of this mob followed Gibbons out of the building, and as he was getting into his car—still within the environs of Leinster House—they attacked him again. Having knocked him to the ground they proceeded to kick him in the chest and stomach. A friend of Gibbons eventually frightened them away. A few days later Gibbons suffered a heart attack. He was never in good health afterwards.

A sinister aspect of this affair was that the assaults on Gibbons took place in front of several members of staff and gardaí, who did nothing to intervene. No-one was arrested or ejected. About the same period an excessively pious but harmless woman was bundled out of the public gallery and barred for life because she asked the Ceann Comhairle to say the Angelus at 12 o'clock.

A terrible atmosphere existed within the party throughout this period. People would cut you in the corridor. Some TDs were fearful of even being seen talking to me or to others opposed to Haughey. One day I was walking down Dawson Street when I bumped into another Fianna Fáil TD. 'I'm sorry I can't be seen talking to you in Leinster House,' he said. 'It would be reported upstairs.'

Haughey's minority Government limped on for a few weeks after the meeting on the confidence motion. In the November general election Fianna Fáil lost six more seats. It was the third election in a row where the voters had failed to give Haughey an absolute majority. Unlike the 1981 election, however, Fine Gael and the Labour Party had sufficient seats this time to form a coalition Government with a comfortable majority.

Garret FitzGerald was back as Taoiseach. He was a hands-on type of person who got involved in all sorts of detail, much of which he should have stayed out of. He bogged himself down. That's why Government meetings when he was Taoiseach went on for so long. I marvelled at FitzGerald's extraordinary energy. His output was amazing. He had a political shrewdness but no personal guile or malice. Throughout the 1980s, in the sinister atmosphere that pervaded Leinster House, Garret was an antidote. He showed great tenacity in delivering the Anglo-Irish Agreement in 1985. Most of the progress made in later years in the North would not have been possible without it. Neither the British nor Haughey's Fianna Fáil wanted the agreement, but Garret believed in its potential, and he made it happen, against the odds.

He was also a very European politician. His enthusiasm for the EEC and European integration was motivated by a belief that it would make it easier to liberalise many of the social attitudes in Ireland. He saw Europe as much more than a source of cash. As Taoiseach, however, he had far less success with the Irish economy.

We were back in opposition, and I believed the party had had enough of the turmoil that existed since December 1979. There was no justifiable reason for continuing with Haughey as Fianna Fáil leader: he was not just an electoral liability but his behaviour in government showed him to be unfit to hold the office of Taoiseach. I had had concerns about economic management and saw the damage his actions did to Anglo-Irish relations. The entire period was typified by the farcical 'GUBU' affair, when a double murderer was found in the flat of the Attorney-General. Those of us who had opposed Haughey during the 1979 succession and in later leadership votes had great reservations about his suitability for office. In early 1983 we were presented with even more evidence of the accuracy of this view.

————

Revelations about phone-tapping were made public in late January 1983. As Minister for Justice, Seán Doherty had requested taps on the phones of two journalists, Geraldine Kennedy and Bruce Arnold. The action was totally illegal. Haughey denied any knowledge of what Doherty was up to, and it would be another ten years before Doherty finally admitted what we all believed to be the case, that Haughey was not just aware of the illegal taps but that he had directed that they be put on, and had also read the transcripts.

Several of my colleagues had been suspicious for some time that our own phones were being tapped. For that reason I was already careful about what I said on the phone. The night before the abortive heave in February 1982 my home phone went dead. There was a large group of supporters in the house. We were ringing members of the parliamentary party. In a world without mobile phones and the internet, making immediate contact with people was not always easy. This final 'ring around' was important in consolidating support and convincing waverers that the best interests of the party and of the country were served by removing Haughey from office. There was huge frustration when the phone line went dead.

The next day a friend of mine got a colleague who worked with Posts and Telegraphs to visit the exchange in Rathmines, which covered the area where I lived. What this man discovered was extraordinary. A matchstick, bent in two, was jamming the entry point to my phone number. As soon as the match was removed the phone line began to work again. Given the events taking place in Fianna Fáil, this was clearly a deliberate act of sabotage of my home phone.

In the same period there was also a series of burglaries at my house. Strangely, in two of these burglaries nothing was taken. The investigating gardaí agreed that the events were highly suspicious. They feared that listening devices had been planted. The house was swept twice, but no bugs were discovered. I've often wondered if it was simply that the equipment used by the Gardaí was not sophisticated enough to find the device.

About the time of my resignation from the Government in October 1982, but just before Haughey's beleaguered minority Government finally collapsed, I received a warning about the type of activity sponsored by the Taoiseach and his cronies. Early one morning

Michael Killeen, recently retired as managing director of the IDA, called to my house. I had worked closely with Michael in my first period as Minister for Industry and Commerce. He was now chairman of Irish Distillers. He declined to come into the house. He said he had been asked to deliver a message to me, and handed over a sealed envelope. 'I don't know what's inside,' he said. 'Garret FitzGerald asked that I deliver it to you.'

This was very odd. Although I was not personally close to Garret, he was a neighbour—living about 150 yards away in Palmerston Road—and we also saw each other most days in Leinster House when the Dáil was sitting. He had obviously decided to use Michael as a courier, as he knew I got on well with him and trusted him. When Killeen departed I opened the envelope. Inside was a short note, written in pencil and in capital letters. The import of the message was very sinister. My phone was being tapped; I was being warned to be careful about talking on the phone, and especially careful in talking to journalists. The author of the note also suggested that I deliver a similar warning to George Colley and Séamus Brennan.

In sorting through my papers at a thirty-year remove for the purposes of writing this book I was not able to find the piece of paper, but from what I can remember Martin O'Donoghue's name was also mentioned as someone who needed to be careful in what he said in telephone conversations. The note was unsigned but had clearly come from within the Gardaí. The envelope was addressed to me in the same writing. It had apparently not been opened by Garret, who may or may not have known its contents. I imagine he did.

Within months of this anonymous note it was publicly revealed that the phones of two political journalists, Geraldine Kennedy and Bruce Arnold, had in fact been tapped by the Gardaí at the request of Seán Doherty. The newly appointed Fine Gael Minister for Justice, Michael Noonan—also a TD from Limerick East—confirmed the phone-tapping scandal in January 1983. The revelation also confirmed the authenticity and accuracy of the anonymous note I had received through Garret FitzGerald and Michael Killeen.

It was some consolation to know that there were people in the

Gardaí who fundamentally disagreed with the illegal actions of unscrupulous politicians, aided and abetted by senior members of the force. I wrote to FitzGerald about the revelations, stating that

> the reports of the 'unofficial' tapping of deputies are consistent with information I received privately from an anonymous source, through reliable intermediaries, at the beginning of October 1982. I was unable at that time to verify the truth or otherwise of the information. When I received this information, I was a member of the Government. It was and is therefore a cause of great concern to me. That concern has been heightened by the press reports and is compounded by the apparent accuracy of other related matters in the same reports.

The Haughey-Doherty explanation for phone-tapping was a lie. They thought it would sound credible to explain the tapping as a means of tracing Government leaks; they were in fact breaking the law and only wanted to find out who was opposed to Haughey, and what his opponents were going to do and when. Their actions had nothing to do with the security of the state or monitoring organised crime, which were the only legitimate, and legal, reasons for telephone-tapping. This was all about internal Fianna Fáil disputes, and it was a serious abuse of power.

What we knew in early 1983 was that an ambitious deputy commissioner, Joe Ainsworth, allowed himself to be used in an illegal spying activity by a ruthless Taoiseach and an unscrupulous Minister for Justice. One wondered where the Commissioner, Patrick McLaughlin, was in all this activity. He had to sign the application for the warrant.

Over the following weeks one consequence of the revelations was that both the Commissioner and his deputy left the force.

In a normal government there was no way that an individual like Seán Doherty would have been appointed Minister for Justice in the first place. He was only a minister because Haughey wanted someone in the position whom he could control and who would do his bidding. With the phone-tapping revelations there was now enough evidence to prove the case that Haughey was unfit for office, even with those who feared a party split. Four months after the unsuccessful attempt to remove him—prematurely prompted by McCreevy's foolish action—the leadership issue was once more open for discussion.

The parliamentary party met on Sunday 23 January 1983 to discuss the phone-tapping revelations and a disclosure that Ray MacSharry had secretly recorded a conversation with Martin O'Donoghue, using equipment supplied to him by Deputy Commissioner Joe Ainsworth. The perception was generated that O'Donoghue was the wrongdoer, whereas in fact he was the injured party. I had an opportunity to read the transcript, and it speaks for itself. Martin did nothing wrong. He came under attack, and he had to defend himself, which he did.

The meeting adjourned at 9 p.m., after six-and-a-half hours of speeches. In his contribution Haughey denied any knowledge of phone-tapping but also bemoaned leaks from Government meetings during 1982 and listed off stories in various newspapers that were an obvious source of irritation to him.

In a bizarre twist I ended up sitting next to Doherty. I was keeping notes, but with Doherty sitting beside me I had to be careful about what I wrote down. After a host of members had had their say, an internal party committee was set up to investigate further.

We met again four days later, when the leadership issue was discussed. Haughey knew he was in real trouble this time. He was clinging to his job. While he declared that he would not be run out of office, he promised to consult the party before making a decision about his future.

We were to meet again on 2 February, but the day before, news came through that Deputy Clem Coughlan from Donegal had been killed in a road accident. Clem was supporting my bid for the leadership. Haughey took advantage of the situation. Amid uproar, the parliamentary party meeting was abruptly adjourned after a minute's silence for Clem Coughlan. I retain a vision of Jim Tunney, the chairman, scurrying out the door, followed by Haughey, and shouting back over his shoulder in Irish that the meeting was adjourned for a week.

Haughey and his supporters were buying time. Requests for another meeting were ignored, so Ben Briscoe tabled a motion of no confidence. Haughey had mishandled the economy, he had failed at the polls and, most importantly, his behaviour and misuse of power made him unfit to hold office. I believed we would win.

At the party meeting on 7 February 1983 the vote was by secret ballot. Haughey won by 40 votes to 33. A swing of four votes would have removed him, and saved the country a lot of trouble in later years. In the days before the vote Haughey's troops had used every possible means to secure victory. As in previous challenges, political and financial threats and inducements were part of their approach. 'Dirty tricks' were central to Haughey's strategy and his motivation to win at whatever cost.

Three days after that party meeting I received a phone call from John Devine, a journalist with the *Sunday Independent,* who was investigating a story that had been given to his editor, Michael Hand, the previous weekend. This was to the effect that before the 1977 general election I had employed a civil servant to steal a document from the desk of the then Minister for Industry and Commerce, Justin Keating. The source had obviously been hoping that the story would be published in the *Sunday Independent* on the eve of the Fianna Fáil meeting on the no-confidence motion. There wasn't an ounce of truth in it. The source was a member of Haughey's staff, who passed on the story when drinking with Michael Hand in the Oval Bar in Middle Abbey Street, near the paper's offices, the previous Saturday. Ringing his newsroom from the pub, Hand had instructed one of his journalists to write the story; but as Keating could not be contacted the story never made the paper. Devine picked up the story later that week, but with no success. Keating dismissed the story and told him that it looked like the 'use of the dirty tricks department against O'Malley.' And so it was, with a direct connection back to Haughey.

After the 1983 heave Haughey offered me a frontbench role as spokesman on energy. Again I was minded not to accept; but, upon reflection, I decided that by declining the position I would be cutting myself off totally from front-line politics. Keeping myself in the public eye was helpful later when the decision to form the PDS was taken. I decided to accept the role also because I was genuinely interested in the energy policy area.

Haughey and FitzGerald had been outbidding each other in this period. The 1983 abortion referendum was the result of this competition, each party leader trying to outdo the other's perceived piety. But Haughey was also highly opportunist, and from 1983 onwards he was in hyper-opposition mode. He would oppose even the smallest proposal from the FitzGerald Government, irrespective of its merits. It didn't cost him a thought to oppose measures that were obviously in the public interest, as was the case with the Anglo-Irish Agreement in 1985. There was one decision, however, that he took in this period that mystified me but that, with the benefit of hindsight and the later financial revelations, made complete sense—at least for him, that is.

In March 1984 Allied Irish Banks announced that losses at its wholly owned subsidiary Insurance Corporation of Ireland were in the region of £86 million, and that it intended to place ICI in liquidation. The amount was a huge sum at the time, and was in fact a gross underestimation of the final losses. The acquisition of ICI in the early 1980s left AIB on the verge of collapse. There were fears of a 'run' on AIB and, as a result, concerns for the stability of the whole banking system. The Fine Gael-Labour coalition decided to rescue ICI by purchasing the company from AIB. In effect, the state took over the ICI's sizeable losses and so allowed AIB to continue to pay dividends to its shareholders.

Haughey arrived at a Fianna Fáil frontbench meeting following a briefing from FitzGerald. He had not only agreed to back the Government's decision on ICI but was very positive about the proposal. I was baffled by this stance. 'Why is he agreeing to this?' I asked myself. It was a significant departure from his 'oppose everything' policy. He said that backing the Government's decision was in the public interest; but this was not a concept that troubled Haughey too often. A few questions were asked at the meeting but, to be honest, I never for one moment thought he had a personal interest in the decision.

In the late 1990s it emerged that shortly before Haughey was elected leader of Fianna Fáil in December 1979, and when he was first elected as Taoiseach, he owed Allied Irish Banks some £1.14 million in the form of an overdraft. His mansion at Kinsealy, Co. Dublin, and the adjoining lands were held by AIB as security. But shortly after he defeated George Colley, AIB settled the overdraft debt by writing off almost £400,000 of the £1.14 million. When the report of the Moriarty Tribunal was published in 2006 Mr Justice Moriarty concluded that AIB had shown an extraordinary degree of deference to Haughey, despite his financial excesses. Moriarty also concluded that AIB's leniency amounted to a benefit to Haughey from the bank.

Obviously, Haughey's decision on the ICI bail-out must now be seen in a very different light when set against our knowledge of his relationship with AIB, as revealed by the tribunal of inquiry.

The tribunal figures may possibly be understated. I base this belief on what I was told by the late Niall Crowley years after he had retired as chairman of AIB. I got the impression that the deal with Haughey was done by the bank's management without his knowledge and that he found out later. He thought the overdraft was well over £1 million, and that £1 million of it was transferred to Guinness Mahon Bank, where Des Traynor was managing director. AIB wrote off the balance, which he thought was well over half a million.

———

My breaking point with Haughey arrived over his attitude to the report of the New Ireland Forum when it was published in May 1984. The forum was established to find an agreed nationalist viewpoint on the North. All the main parties had been involved, although the unionist parties declined the invitation to participate. The Forum's final report presented three options that might provide a peaceful settlement in Northern Ireland: a unitary state, joint authority between Britain and the Republic, and a federal arrangement.

Haughey signed the report on behalf of Fianna Fáil, but half an hour later he called a press conference and rejected the report. He saw Irish unity as the only solution to the conflict; the other options in the report were not for discussion, he decreed. In my opinion, a federal solution was very worthy of consideration. Senator Eoin Ryan backed my view; but Haughey insisted that he was the only person in the party who would comment on the report.

I found this preposterous and said I wanted to comment publicly. I also criticised the lack of debate in the party. Ray MacSharry's name appeared on an article in a Sunday newspaper criticising the report. I saw no reason to remain silent. I didn't think it was right that one person should lay down all the rules for everyone on such a funda-mental policy area. I wanted to debate the really important issues in the report. But my contribution to public debate and my support for the Forum report were not welcomed.

Haughey moved immediately to have the party whip withdrawn from me. The vote was by open roll-call (contrary to the rules). By 56 votes to 16, I was thrown out of the Fianna Fáil parliamentary party and told I was now an independent deputy, free to act as I liked.

In the circumstances, I was surprised at the level of support I received. A number of this group—which included Mary Harney—were prepared to resign the whip, but I advised against this action.

———

A number of years later I had my own confrontation with AIB. When I was Minister for Industry and Commerce again in 1989, AIB applied for a licence to set up a life assurance company. Bank of Ireland was already in this profitable market. I didn't see why, in my capacity as a Government minister, I should grant a licence to AIB to help it to make more money when it had cost the state a fortune over the bail-out of Insurance Corporation of Ireland. The ICI deficit was by that time estimated to have reached £240 million. I was of the view that AIB's application for a licence to conduct a life assurance business should be used as a lever for extracting a higher contribution to fund the continuing ICI deficit. I argued for a higher financial contribution from AIB; but this proposal met with opposition from the Department of Finance, which repeatedly raised legal advice that questioned my proposal to link the ICI affair to the life assurance licence.

My position didn't go down very well with AIB either. Its then chairman, Peter Sutherland, made the bank's position very clear to me: it threatened to sue me. No support was forthcoming from Albert Reynolds, who was now Minister for Finance. He wrote to me in February 1990 saying Haughey was also of the view that it was impossible to recoup a further financial contribution from AIB. I continued to press the issue in government, but there was no Fianna Fáil support.

During 1991 the state had to borrow £75 million from the banks, at normal lending rates, to fund the continuing costs of the ICI administration. I still favoured getting AIB to pay more by means of a bank levy that could be included in the Finance Act in 1992. The Attorney-General, however, did not favour my approach and said that AIB could sue.

Together with Haughey and Reynolds I met senior AIB figures in January 1992. There was little progress. Sutherland said AIB had no legal or moral responsibility for ICI, and this position was reiterated in subsequent correspondence. I wasn't their favourite minister. In a letter to Haughey in February 1992 Sutherland said that AIB took grave exception to my suggestion that legislation could be introduced to force the bank to pay a levy to cover the ICI costs. He warned that even knowledge of the threat could gravely damage the bank. The threat of a legal challenge to my proposal was confirmed.

I wasn't impressed and wanted a hard-line Government response. I wrote to Reynolds, who had just replaced Haughey as Taoiseach, and to the new Minister for Finance, Bertie Ahern, pressing for the AIB levy to be included in the Finance Bill. I continued to press the Fianna Fáil side of the Government to remain tough in discussions with AIB. My presence at the Government table—and the involvement of the PDS in government—ensured that Government policy did not roll over in the face of AIB's resistance to paying more for the ICI losses that were their responsibility.

By this time the Department of Finance estimated that the total cost of the ICI administration was more than £250 million. My proposal would have required AIB to pay £20 million per annum; but even that amount was resisted by AIB, which initially proposed paying £4.2 million per annum over twenty years, a figure it later increased to £8.8 million per annum.

———

The Fianna Fáil-PD coalition collapsed on 4 November 1992 when Bobby Molloy and I resigned after Albert Reynolds accused me of perjury at the Beef Tribunal. He had achieved his aim of ending what he called 'a temporary little arrangement.' The country went to the polls on 25 November 1992.

The minority Fianna Fáil caretaker Government signed a deal with AIB on 28 November 1992 that saw the Department of Finance settling for £8.8 million annually for twenty years, with the Central Bank providing an interest-free loan of £32 million to ICI. It wasn't the last loan advanced to ICI. I argued strongly that what was being asked of AIB was an inadequate and inappropriate deal for the state. Throughout this period, in which the taxpayer and the insuring public were picking up the bill for AIB's ill-fated acquisition, the bank racked up growing profits, and dividends for shareholders increased. And so the cowboy culture of Allied Irish Banks continued without restraint until it carried the bank and the country to disaster in 2008.

Chapter 8 ~

| 'BREAKING THE MOULD'

With the withdrawal of the whip in May 1984, for the first time in my political career I was outside the Fianna Fáil parliamentary party. I became an independent TD in the Dáil although I was still a member of Fianna Fáil. John Kelly of Fine Gael declared that I was 'sleeping under political bridges,' but my intention was still to contest the Fianna Fáil convention in Limerick East for the following general election. I was extremely fortunate in having strong support from the local party organisation and was confident of being selected by the majority of my constituency colleagues. And if elected to the next Dáil I would automatically have become a member of the parliamentary party again, without having to make any application for readmission.

Remaining silent in the face of Haughey's continued opportunism on important policy issues—many of great national importance—was, however, hugely problematic. When he set Fianna Fáil against Barry Desmond's contraception legislation in early 1985 I was faced with the choice of backing another cynical action or taking a stand. The legislation was an attempt to sort out the ambiguity arising out of the law conceived by Haughey himself as Minister for Health in 1979. Legally, condoms were available for sale only with a doctor's prescription, but the law was not being enforced: not alone were condoms being distributed from family planning clinics but they were available in student unions in most colleges. About nine million were being imported into the country every year.

There was a significant lobby to have the bill defeated. The strength of the Catholic Church could still be felt in Ireland at that time, and deputies were put under huge emotional and, at times, moral pressure.

I experienced this when lobbied in my Limerick East constituency. The Bishop of Limerick, Jeremiah Newman, was one of the last of the autocratic bishops. He was outspoken and not shy about courting controversy. As I was outside the Fianna Fáil parliamentary party, and therefore not subject to the party whip, the issue of how I would vote on the contraception legislation was raised. I indicated that as the bill made sense I saw no reason to oppose it.

Shortly afterwards I had two separate visitors to my home in Limerick. Both visitors were people I was friendly with, and both had been sent by Newman. First, a priest whom I knew arrived at the house but declined to come in. He said he had been asked to deliver a message from his lordship the bishop. 'I know what you're going to say, but I have to be able to say I delivered the message,' he said. I replied: 'I have a fair idea what that message is, and the answer is No.' The priest was clearly uncomfortable with the task he had been given. 'His lordship feels you should vote against this legislation. He feels that as a Catholic you should abide by his guidance.' The conversation on the doorstep was short and friendly. 'Go back and tell him that I will use my own judgement,' I said.

The following day I had another visitor, this time a cousin of mine, who called to the house on Newman's behalf. He told me he was embarrassed but had been asked to talk to me. The conversation was similar to that of the previous day.

Pressures forced me to agonise over the political and personal implications arising from how I would vote. I spoke on the second stage of the legislation on 20 February 1985. It was my twentieth wedding anniversary. There was a touch of irony in this, in that two decades earlier I had married a woman from Northern Ireland, and now here I was about to address the wild claims that the free availability of contraceptives resulted in people becoming degenerate. Contraception laws had been liberalised in other places, including Northern Ireland, without the collapse of society. But a vocal and influential conservative lobby refused to accept this reality.

As I waited my turn to speak, Alice Glenn of Fine Gael was on her feet. Glenn was on the extreme conservative wing of Fine Gael and was a vocal critic of FitzGerald's liberal agenda. She warned that contraceptive 'devices' would be very damaging to the health of young people. Next to speak was Noel Tracey, a loyal Haughey supporter, who staunchly followed the Fianna Fáil party line. He predicted that the legislation would increase the rate of marital breakdown and the incidence of sexually transmitted disease and 'illegitimacy'. If you were to accept the warnings of people like Glenn and Tracey the world was about to end.

Pádraig Flynn took offence when I was called to speak before him. He rose to his feet to ask the Ceann Comhairle if Deputy O'Malley was a Fianna Fáil speaker. He didn't receive an answer.

I had decided to approach the debate from two viewpoints: firstly, the issue of the legislation itself, and secondly, the wider context in which the availability of condoms to eighteen-year-olds and over had to be considered. The wider context, and the relationship between church and state, was for me much more important. I predicted that if the bill was defeated there would be two elements on the island that would rejoice to high heaven: they were the Unionists in Northern Ireland and the more fanatical Roman Catholics in the Republic. I viewed this curious alliance in the context of partition, the possibility of Irish unity and an understanding of 'republicanism'. In my opinion, without a broader outlook we could forget the possibility of ever succeeding in persuading our fellow-Irishmen and women in the North to join in a 32-county republic.

The most extraordinary and unprecedented extraparliamentary pressure has been brought to bear on many members of the house. This is not merely lobbying. It is far more significant. I regret to have to say it borders on the sinister. We have witnessed the public and private agonies of so many members of the house who are being asked not to make decisions on this bill in their own calm and collected judgement but to make them as a result of emotional and at times overwhelming moral pressure. This must constrain their freedom in certain respects.

I spoke for about twenty-five minutes and concluded my contribution with the following words:

> The politics of this would be very easy. The politics would be, to be one of the lads, the safest way in Ireland. But I do not believe that the interests of this state, or our Constitution and of this Republic would be served by putting politics before conscience in regard to this. There is a choice of a kind that can only be answered by saying that I stand by the Republic, and accordingly I will not oppose this bill.

In respect of the 1985 legislation—and later when we founded the Progressive Democrats—I tried to adopt a common-sense point of view towards social and economic policies without an ideological hang-up that you have to start from one particular point or that you always move towards one particular point.

I did not vote on the legislation in the hope that my speech would prevent a parting of the ways with Fianna Fáil or out of deference to some of my colleagues: I made my decision after numerous conversations with party colleagues. Pádraig Faulkner pleaded with me not to vote against Fianna Fáil. He was also opposed to Haughey, but he argued that I would damage the party and my own future. I explained that my decision was motivated by a sense of having been trapped in Haughey's Fianna Fáil. As I was not a member of the parliamentary party I was not covered by the party whip, so I could vote as I liked.

But Haughey was not interested in technicalities, and the speech was used as an excuse to get me out of the party. In truth, I had come to accept that there was no future for me in Fianna Fáil while Haughey remained as leader. I certainly didn't want a future on his terms. Some supporters were urging patience, but there was too high a price involved in waiting for him to be gone—five, maybe ten years of endurance. I had nothing to lose. And, to be honest, I was glad when the break eventually came.

The bill was narrowly passed. Fianna Fáil claimed it would have been defeated if I had voted with them.

Haughey moved quickly. A motion was submitted to the National Executive seeking my expulsion from the party. The grounds were described as 'conduct unbecoming' a member of the party. The motion was dealt with at a meeting in Fianna Fáil head office on 26 February 1985. Haughey had set himself up as presiding judge and chief prosecutor. I was not permitted to attend the meeting; after Haughey had stated the case against me I was then invited to come in.

I recognised many faces. A young Mícheál Martin, who was the Ógra Fianna Fáil representative, was among the ninety National Executive members entitled to vote on the motion. I was given ten minutes to defend myself. At the outset I remarked that it was impossible to deal with the allegations against me, given that I had no idea what exactly had been said. In fact if I had been Robert Emmet I doubt if it would have made any difference. I asked for a secret ballot, but I knew that ran contrary to Haughey's strategy.

After I left the meeting Haughey moved to expel me without any dissent. He wanted a unanimous decision, arguing that it was for the good of Fianna Fáil. When it was clear that this was not going to be forthcoming, he called a vote by open roll-call. To their credit, nine members of the National Executive broke ranks, including Mary Hanafin, a future minister.

Supporters from Limerick and other parts of the country had travelled to Dublin and were waiting outside the Fianna Fáil head office, as was Pat. I had joined them after I finished speaking and had been asked to leave the meeting. This bizarre situation was typical of the Haughey era. We waited, knowing that voters were highly unlikely to go against the leader.

Pádraig Flynn eventually arrived out on the front doorstep to tell the world the good news. Before he spoke, word reached me. 'You're out,' I was told. Afterwards there were kisses for the cameras, and I joked that kissing Pat might be described as 'conduct unbecoming.'

I could have stayed in Fianna Fáil. I could have remained quiet. I would certainly never have approved of Haughey as leader, but I would have been a reminder internally that there was another route open for the party. In time the leadership might or might not have come my way. Former colleagues who remained in Fianna Fáil, such as the late Séamus Brennan, often said I would have become Taoiseach if I had stayed. But I didn't have the naked hunger to be Taoiseach, or to lead Fianna Fáil at any cost. In many respects I failed because I didn't have the overwhelming desire for personal power. In the end I didn't need, or want, the leadership so badly that I was prepared to sacrifice looking myself in the mirror. As Colley had said, the rules had changed. You now needed to subordinate literally everything to achieving your objective.

———

My political status now was that of an independent. The idea of joining Fine Gael was mooted; I had at least one formal approach. A senior Fine Gael figure acting on behalf of Garret FitzGerald came to see me. The invitation to join Fine Gael came with the prospect of ministerial appointment. I turned it down, and I repeated my decision a few days later when I spoke to Garret in Leinster House. Moving from Fianna Fáil to Fine Gael would have meant substituting one large populist party for another large populist party. Both were also slightly vague conservative organisations. I wanted to make a clean break with politics shaped and dominated by the civil war era. Fianna Fáil and Fine Gael were still fighting those battles, and they were also outdoing each other in an attempt to curry favour with the electorate. FitzGerald led a coalition that could not control public spending, and every day it was met by criticism from Haughey's Fianna Fáil that spending was not high enough. The public were in despair.

The option of setting up a new party began to become a possibility from the moment I was expelled from Fianna Fáil in February 1985. I had not considered this option during the various battles since Lynch had stood down as leader of Fianna Fáil in December 1979, but from March 1985 onwards the idea was discussed with several of those in the anti-Haughey group. Conversations involved Mary Harney, Séamus Brennan and David Andrews, among others.

Barra Ó Tuama, a Cork businessman who had been a supporter of Jack Lynch, commissioned an opinion poll in April 1985 to gauge public opinion about a new party led by me. I wasn't aware of it until after it was completed. The results were personally gratifying and reassuring to me. Some 39 per cent of voters would support a new party being established with me as leader. The breakdown of the results was very positive: 22 per cent were strongly in favour of a new national party, 17 per cent were slightly in favour, 13 per cent were slightly against, and 22 per cent were strongly against, while 26 per cent were neither in favour nor against or didn't have an opinion. Support was evenly spread around the country, with slightly stronger backing in Munster, which was not surprising, given my Limerick base. From the data it was clear that younger people backed the idea: 47 per cent of those under 25 favoured a new party, as did 42 per cent of those in the 25–34 age group.

The findings were given to the national newspapers. Taken in conjunction with the hundreds of messages and letters I had received over the previous two months, I was convinced that they reflected a growing and heartfelt dissatisfaction with established politics. When I was asked to comment on the opinion poll I remarked that consideration had to be given to how the aspirations of so many people for a fresh approach could find expression in political structures.

Harney was the strongest and most consistent promoter of the idea of a new party. Others among my former colleagues in Fianna Fáil wavered in their enthusiasm every time the idea was discussed. Among my supporters in Limerick East there was divided opinion. Despite what had just happened at Haughey's behest, many still hoped to see me back in Fianna Fáil at some point. While Harney persisted with the idea, my own thoughts on a new party were not fixed. There were all sorts of considerations, involving not only finance and organisation but also who would actually join, and whether the public would back it at the ballot box. I wanted to ensure that if a new party was set up it was going to be a success. There were too many examples in party-political history of well-intentioned ventures that never went anywhere, not to mind ever achieving anything.

It seemed that our discussions went on for a long time. But making a decision to set up a new party is not one to be taken lightly. It was a gradual build-up.

In the aftermath of my expulsion from Fianna Fáil my office received more than two thousand letters of support. One anonymous writer even wrote a poem for me. Titled 'Unbecoming conduct', the two-verse lyric was ironically handwritten on the torn-out cover of a chequebook. There were few moments of levity in the early months of 1986, which may explain why I kept the 'poem' from all the items of correspondence I received: 'You may cook the books and be on the fiddle | And on every principle piddle | But as the stormy seas we cross | You must be loyal to the Boss.'

Michael McDowell, who I had never met, was one of those who contacted me, as did Paul Mackay, a businessman who was involved with Fianna Fáil in Haughey's constituency. He had been a supporter of George Colley but had parted ways with Fianna Fáil in 1983. Like Harney, both McDowell and Mackay were keenly interested in establishing a new party.

I first met McDowell at his home in early May 1985. He later wrote a long memo to me about how a new party might be structured and what it should stand for. The ethos was consistent with the thrust of later PD values, including an emphasis on business and enterprise. While not a national figure, McDowell was a very strong figure within Fine Gael in Garret FitzGerald's constituency of Dublin South-East. He had enormous energy and a great intellect.

During the summer months Mackay drew up a financial plan for a new party. I took soundings from a variety of people around the country. Meetings with important colleagues took place in September and October. There were a few heated moments, and it was by no means certain that a new party would be established. Pat wasn't too keen on the idea; she had come through some terribly tough times because of my political career. There was great pressure when I was Minister for Justice, and later I had been travelling a lot as Minister for Industry and Commerce. The constant battles with Haughey had taken their toll on all of us. But despite her reservations, when the decision was made to establish a new party she was a huge support.

Charlie McCreevy was also involved in discussions by this stage. He was very friendly with Harney, who had invited him to various meetings that were taking place. I wasn't hugely happy with his involvement. Since his solo run on the no-confidence motion against Haughey in October 1982 I believed McCreevy wasn't totally reliable. I felt that his actions had helped keep Haughey as leader, and he had never once expressed any regret for the mistake he had made. McCreevy was involved in discussions until the end of November; he even wrote a document setting out some principles for a new party. But he never formally applied to join the PDs, and he certainly never indicated to me that he wanted to join the party.

Harney was keen to have McCreevy as a member. She was also pushing the case for involving Michael O'Leary, the former Labour Party leader who had joined Fine Gael. I disagreed with her, and I know she was not pleased with me. But I felt that opportunists had to be kept away, irrespective of their name recognition. Unfortunately, we still picked up our share of them.

A private opinion poll of Fianna Fáil supporters was commissioned in October 1985. Half the participants expressed opposition to a new party, while 28 per cent said they were in favour. Of that 28 per cent some 15 per cent favoured it strongly and 13 per cent favoured it slightly. Surveys published in the newspapers showed that about a quarter of the electorate were undecided about how they would vote in the next election. I took comfort from these responses.

In early November 1985 I was involved in a car accident while driving from Limerick to Dublin and was laid up for several weeks. While I was recovering, Garret FitzGerald and Margaret Thatcher signed the Anglo-Irish Agreement. Haughey opposed the development. It was a continuation of his opposition strategy. He even sent Brian Lenihan to the United States to campaign against the agreement. I thought Haughey's response was an act of treachery. Fianna Fáil's willingness to exploit a hugely positive policy development on the North prompted Mary Harney to finally leave the party. She voted for the Anglo-Irish Agreement in November 1985; for her action she was duly expelled from Fianna Fáil.

In many respects the discussion about forming a new party had reached a crucial point. Paul Mackay had found premises suitable for a head office at 25 South Frederick Street and some funding to pay the rent and other bills. We researched the names of political parties in other countries before finally settling on Progressive Democrats.

We announced the new party to the wider world just before Christmas 1985. The press conference took place in the party's head office on 21 December. Seated at the top table were Mary Harney, Michael McDowell and myself. I had a short speech prepared in which I spoke of 'breaking the mould of Irish politics.' We had talked for almost a year about this day; now it had finally arrived. All of us were conscious of the widespread feeling of disillusionment and power-lessness to deal with the economic and social problems engulfing the country; the Progressive Democrats were presented as an alternative. As I outlined it:

> Irish politics, which sought to be about choice, is more and more a competition between power blocs whose principal or even sole aim is office. Of course there are many honourable men and women in politics today; but it is labouring the obvious to point out that their political allegiances have more to do with history and birth than with ideals or beliefs. This generation of Irish men and women will no longer accept the legacy of division that history has given us. For the past year I have been struck by the strength of feeling throughout the country in favour of breaking the mould of Irish politics and giving the Irish voters a new and real alternative. I believe that the old loyalties on which the present parties feed are no longer enough to sustain them.

As I sat at the top table alongside Mary Harney and Michael McDowell I was fully aware that our decision to establish the Progressive Democrats was very much a leap in the dark. We had taken a high-risk decision. The record of parties that challenged the dominance of

Fianna Fáil, Fine Gael and the Labour Party was not good; but I was confident that support would be available for a party that sought to replace cynicism and despair with hope and optimism. Despite past experience with new parties and also the enormous task involved, I was keen to stress my confidence in the PDS.

> Thousands of ordinary men and women have come to me offering support for such a change. They want to replace cynicism and despair by trust and hope. I believe that they are right. I believe their courage can be rewarded by change. I believe as a politician that they cannot be denied such change. If I can in some way be a vehicle for facilitating that kind of change, I do not feel that I have the right to deny my services, limited as they are, to that growing segment of the public requiring such change.

In December 1985 we didn't have a range of detailed policy documents to put before the people; nevertheless there was a clear sense of what the PDS would represent.

> I believe there is a great consensus in Ireland which favours a peaceful approach to the problem in Northern Ireland; which favours fundamental tax reform; which favours enterprise; which favours a clear distinction between Church and state. I believe that many of the problems we face today result from an unwillingness on the part of the politicians to make any hard decisions or to risk losing any electoral support. For these reasons, I believe that Irish politics must be transformed. Experience tells me that no such transformation will come from within the existing parties. It must come from outside. There must be a new beginning.

The party needed members, and donations, and there was no guarantee that the response would be positive. We took out advertisements in the national newspapers in early January 1986. In the first few days of the PDS' existence there were almost 5,000 requests for membership applications, and we had 13,000 signed-up members by the end of January; that number would eventually hit 20,000.

The reaction at public meetings was equally gratifying. I was amazed at the thousands of people who came to those first meetings throughout the country. One journalist called it 'PD fever'. Almost three thousand people came to a meeting in Cork in early February, and a fortnight later an even larger crowd gathered in Galway. In my opening words I quipped: 'I thought Cork was great, but Galway wins the All-Ireland.' These people all wanted to volunteer to make the party a success. They were enthusiastic and committed. And they came from all age groups, and all walks of life.

Early opinion polls showed there was a considerable appetite for the PDS. We captured the public mood. FitzGerald's Fine Gael-Labour coalition was unpopular, but large sections of the electorate simply did not trust Fianna Fáil under Haughey. People wanted hope. The economic situation was a disaster.

There was a real possibility of the International Monetary Fund arriving. The implications of what that eventuality would have meant were probably not fully realised at the time but would be clearly seen later. The post-2008 troika bail-out has shown what life under an IMF programme is like, with a so-called sovereign government being told what it can and cannot do. The country was close to having the IMF arrive in 1985 and in 1986.

We tried to be honest with people. We would be neither left nor right: rather we would be a party that was socially liberal and economically responsible. As the months went on we published several radical reform policy documents. Our message was consistent: we had to sort out the economy by cutting government spending and reducing income taxes. We wanted to fundamentally reform the taxation system. Personal tax rates were at punitive levels, many people on moderate incomes paying over 60 per cent. The rates were an absolute killer of employment and enterprise. Rates of capital tax were equally high and had a stifling effect on reinvestment in the economy.

Alongside tax reform it was necessary to reduce the government deficit. We were proved correct in the argument that by bringing public spending under control the ensuing confidence would create sufficient economic growth to pay for cuts in income tax. We also wanted a new type of politics, beyond the politics of the Civil War parties. On Northern Ireland we accepted the recommendations of the New Ireland Forum and the ethos of the Anglo-Irish Agreement. We accepted the principle of consent.

A variety of names were linked with the party. These included people in Fianna Fáil who were fed up with how the party was being run under Haughey and everything he represented. Pearse Wyse, a TD for Cork South-Central, resigned from Fianna Fáil to join us in late January. He had first been elected as a Fianna Fáil councillor in 1960 and had held a Dáil seat at each general election since 1965. He was close to Jack Lynch.

There was even greater shock in Fianna Fáil when Bobby Molloy left to join us. The party would never have done as well as it ultimately did in Galway had Molloy not joined. He had been a TD since 1965, and Jack Lynch had promoted both of us to ministerial positions. Molloy had opposed Haughey, although his decision surprised many in the party. There was a huge reaction when he turned up at the inaugural PD rally in Galway.

Having existing TDs as members was very important. It meant that in several constituencies we now had a PD organisation, as each TD brought supporters with them. It also meant that we had a presence in the Dáil. With TDs in Leinster House it was difficult for the media to ignore us. I think it would be much more challenging to establish a new party without any sort of national parliamentary representation.

Several other Fianna Fáil TDs thought about joining, and I was disappointed that they were unwilling to take the risk. I really thought David Andrews was going to join, but then he went to a rugby international in France and changed his mind after spending the weekend wandering around Paris. For him, family ties to Fianna Fáil were stronger than leaving Haughey behind. Séamus Brennan faced a similar dilemma. The political choices made at that time unfortunately affected personal relationships, and I regret that our families were never as personally close again.

There were two or three other Fianna Fáil figures who were deeply unhappy in the party under Haughey, but for some the pressures of the previous few years meant they decided to opt out of political life altogether, and rather than join the PDS they did not seek election again. That was one of the overlooked consequences of Haughey's tenure: many good people simply walked away from political life. We were keen that the PDS would not be labelled as a rump of Haughey opponents. Some in Fianna Fáil were keen to have us seen in that light, and others in the media were quick to describe us as the 'anti-Haughey party'.

Michael McDowell was one of the driving forces in the PDS from the outset; but he was not an elected representative, and we were conscious of being a group of former Fianna Fáil TDS in the Dáil. That said, there were some people who I didn't want to have join. I was adamant that the PDS would not be a home for the disillusioned and disaffected from other parties. A new party full of those who had fallen out with other parties was not something I was keen on. I was certain that I didn't want the party to be a refuge for all sorts of oddballs from other parties and organisations.

I had conversations with people who might be sympathetic to joining the PDS, although I didn't spend too much time pursuing recruits. Harney did most of those meetings. She was more suited to that role. She was in many respects the driving force in the new party; I was almost the nominal head. We were also joined by two Labour Party senators, Timmy Conway from Kildare and Helena McAuliffe-Ennis from Longford-Westmeath.

The recruitment of Michael Keating was a bit of a surprise in April 1986, although it has to be said he didn't last long with the PDS. He had been a junior minister in Garret FitzGerald's 1981–2 coalition Government, and he had been Lord Mayor of Dublin in 1985. He had been overlooked by FitzGerald and joined the PDS more out of a need to shore up his own political career. To lessen the perception that the PDS were a Fianna Fáil rump, Keating was appointed deputy leader. Mary Harney had earned the role but she did not object to Keating, as he reduced our anti-Haughey image. With hindsight I know I should have gone with my instinct in making Harney deputy leader. Not only had she earned the position, given the tremendous work she put in to getting the party established, but she also had the ability for the job.

A few days after Keating joined the PDS—and it was a fairly big story that we had recruited a sitting Fine Gael TD—I received a phone call from Joan FitzGerald, Garret's wife. I didn't know her very well, and I don't think she had ever phoned me before. She wanted to warn me about Keating. 'Be careful for your own sake and for the sake of your party,' she said. At the time I thought it an odd phone call, and put it down to sour grapes in Fine Gael. But she proved to be right. Keating held his seat at the 1987 general election but two years later opted out of national politics, without giving any notice. He wasn't the most reliable of individuals, and he ultimately added little to the PDS. He was later caught up in all sorts of business trouble.

We had great support in the background. Adrian Hardiman, an emerging barrister who would later be appointed to the Supreme Court, produced a volume of policy papers. In the pre-launch phase I had asked Pat Cox to join the discussions. I knew him from Limerick, where he had contested the 1979 local elections and was working with RTE. He became the PDS' first general secretary. He worked closely with the *Irish Independent* journalist Stephen O'Byrnes, who became the party's director of policy and publicity.

Over the following years this small team would give great cohesion to the party organisation. They were also invaluable in preparing all the elements necessary to allow a modern party not just to function on a day-to-day basis but also to plan strategically, in particular for elections.

This party infrastructure did not come cheap. Paul Mackay had organised a £5,000 overdraft, but to be a serious political party we needed access to continuing financial support. State funding was at that time limited, and as a new party we were not entitled to any public money. Personal and corporate donations were necessary to support the PD organisation. We had to pay for a head office and staff; we also had to prepare for contesting a general election. Without these donations the PDS could not have competed with the main parties, including the Labour Party, which received generous financial support from the trade unions.

In the first few months, donations arrived before we even asked for them; but that comfortable position didn't continue, and after the first year or so it was necessary to actively seek donations. I never found it easy to ask for money. It was a distasteful aspect of running a party; but there was no choice. We were reasonably well resourced, but most of our activities were operated on a shoestring.

———

I doubt if what we achieved in 1986 could be done today. As a result of the bribery and corruption scandals that emerged in the 1990s, political parties and their political activity are now predominantly financed from the public purse. These funds have largely replaced private donations as a source of political funding. It might seem a sensible solution, but the consequences are serious. Most of this money is distributed to political parties in accordance with performance at the previous general election. One of the effects of this in practice is to inhibit the formation of new parties and to strengthen the pre-dominant position of the existing ones. It has had, and will continue to have, the effect of propping up and prolonging the status quo. It is hard to see how a new party could succeed when it can obtain access to none of this public funding and is also virtually banned from receiving any significant private donations, even if they were available. Permitted private funding of political parties is very low, although some special cases seem to exist—I refer of course to Sinn Féin—with money coming from criminal activities and from abroad.

In my view, the present rules are essentially anti-democratic. They act as a barrier to newcomers in the world of electoral politics. The difficulty in setting up a new political party or political movement was seen before the 2011 general election when several groups of people toyed with the idea of launching a new party; but well-known figures like Fintan O'Toole and David McWilliams quickly hit a brick wall. New parties are more than intellectual exercises: they need money to sustain an organisation on the ground. I believe the protection of the party-political status quo is sinister and harmful to democracy.

The established parties always seek to protect the status quo. We experienced this reality immediately after establishing the PDS. By April 1986 we had five Dáil deputies and two senators. There was a reluctance to provide the party with adequate working facilities in Leinster House. We were allocated office space in 16 Molesworth Street, about a hundred yards from the main gate of Leinster House. There was just about enough space, but after the 1987 election there were serious problems when we were told that our new total of fourteen TDS would have to occupy the space that previously housed five. With secretaries and other support staff, thirty-one people were expected to work from the allocated space in this building.

The cramped working space for politicians and staff was not the only issue. There was no security on the premises, and we had concerns for personal safety coming and going several times each day to and from Leinster House. Towards the end of 1987 there were continuous protests in Kildare Street over the extradition of republican suspects to stand trial in Britain. I have no doubt that people listed by the Gardaí as members of the Provisional IRA were among the protesters outside the gates of Leinster House. When there were large protests of this kind we were prevented from exercising our right as deputies to vote in divisions. The Molesworth Street building was also at risk of occupation by protesters.

The matter was raised at the Committee of Procedure and Privileges, but at meetings when our concerns were to be discussed the Fianna Fáil representatives on the committee failed to turn up. I wrote to Haughey seeking appropriate and adequate accommodation within the Leinster House complex but I never received a reply, or even the courtesy of an acknowledgement.

Twelve months later, with no progress and after the Gardaí had made me aware of their concerns for the safety of the fourteen PD deputies, I wrote to Gerard Collins, the Minister for Justice in Haughey's minority Government. I reminded him of the constitutional and legal issues involved.

Under Article 15 Section 10 of the Constitution, members of Dáil Éireann have an absolute right to travel to and from the House and be protected against any person or persons interfering with or molesting them in the exercise of their duties. A section in the Offences Against the State Act 1939 prohibits the holding of any meeting, parade or protest within half a mile of Leinster House and makes it a criminal offence to hold such a meeting, parade or protest.

Unlike Haughey, Collins replied. In a bizarre solution, he pledged Garda support for cordoning off footpath space to ensure our 'unhindered passage to and from the Dáil.' This unsatisfactory issue was resolved only when we entered government in 1989.

The fact that I was advised to write to the Taoiseach about a parliamentary matter—the allocating of accommodation to members— is indicative of the way the Dáil had become totally subservient to the executive. It failed to assert itself or its independence from the Government. Its employees were not prepared to protect a member from a criminal assault because to do so would have annoyed Mr Haughey, whom they regarded as their boss.

Even today, more than twenty years after the end of the Haughey era, the Government continues to have contempt for the Dáil. Important announcements are made by way of press conferences in Government Buildings, even when the Dáil is sitting a hundred yards away. Imagine the uproar if that was attempted in London!

———

The success of the Progressive Democrats rattled both Fianna Fáil and Fine Gael. We attracted members from both parties, although the opinion polls showed that from the outset we hurt Fine Gael more in public support. As in the accommodation dispute, Haughey's attitude was to try to ignore us. All he would say was that we were not in the national interest. His Fianna Fáil cronies, such as Pádraig Flynn, Ray

Burke and Tom McEllistrim, attacked us for being 'right-wing'; they even called us 'Thatcherite'. These were lazy descriptions. The PDS were in the classic European liberal tradition. When we joined the European liberal group in the European Parliament we were very much at home with their values.

One of the early milestones in the party's development was our first national conference, held in May 1986. It was a historic occasion. The National Stadium was full to its capacity of two thousand, and because of its main use as a boxing arena the stage was in the centre of the audience. This 'theatre in the round' effect added to the atmosphere. I paid tribute to my new colleagues, including Bobby Molloy and Pearse Wyse, noting that they

> had risked much and have forsaken much cosier political homes because they too accepted that the time for blandishments and catch-all politics had to end.

There was loud applause when I acknowledged the role of Mary Harney in the party's foundation.

> From the outset, the principal inspiration and driving force behind this party was Mary Harney. She needs no introduction. Her eloquence and political courage are unparalleled. Others sought to silence that voice of concern and determination, but they failed.

In my leader's address I placed tax reform as the cornerstone of PD policy.

> The taxation problem is the key to tackling all the other major problems. An equitable tax system will generate economic development and enterprise. That is the key to resolving the unemployment crisis. That problem, in turn, feeds the drugs and violence epidemic. And the present tax regime is also a major ingredient in the general disrespect for law. It has fuelled a massive black economy, and made tax dodging respectable and acceptable.

We were clear that the income tax system had failed. Some 40 per cent of workers were paying tax above the standard rate; for every pound of taxable income above £7,500 a single person had to pay 65 per cent in PAYE and PRSI. This system was crushing and debilitating; it destroyed the incentive to work an hour's overtime, to accept promotion, to take a business risk or to invest in industry. We proposed a five-year reform period during which the standard rate would be cut from 35 to 25 per cent, with a surcharge for high-income earners.

I had long championed the idea of removing the state from various areas of economic activity. 'Rolling back the state' became a catch-phrase. I expressed the view that in such policy areas as posts and telegraphs the best thing the state could do was stand back to allow private enterprise to provide services. The state's role had to be concentrated on maintaining control over monopolies, to promote competition, to root out cartels and price-fixings, but it did not need to provide services that the private sector was well capable of providing and in many cases doing so better than the public sector. The sale of commercial state-sponsored bodies was proposed. Workers in those companies would be given shares.

There was no ideological zeal underpinning these proposals. Most people did not feel any practical or philosophical involvement with the state-sponsored companies. Our proposals were practical and sensible, and though we were accused of being dogmatically right-wing, few on the left would have wanted to return to a time when it took several months to get a telephone connection. There was the constant accusation that we were driven by ideology. It is instructive that in Ireland this would be regarded as a criticism. Why else would somebody stand for election except to promote a certain ideology?

I was very clear that we would be pragmatic in considering what was best for the country. The most important factor for the Irish economy is the climate in which it operates, rather than whether it is geared towards the state or towards the private sector. The killing thing in the 1980s was that the environment was absolutely wrong both for the state sector and for the private sector. Neither was encouraged to expand and generate the wealth and jobs so badly needed. The Government's approach was hostile to every form of enterprise. In changing the official mind-set it was also necessary to get people to accept that the state didn't have to dominate the economy in order to raise the revenue to provide necessary social services. Ireland was in the eastern European league in the matter of state involvement in the economy. This situation had developed gradually over the previous ten to fifteen years. My view was that we needed to get to a position where the state had to let the private sector get on with its main task of creating wealth in a pro-enterprise environment.

———

The PDs were about much more than the economy. We also had a distinctive social and political reform agenda and made many interesting proposals for refreshing and renewing Irish life. Politicians would lead by example: the number of ministers of state would fall from fifteen or twenty to seven, the number of TDs from 166 to 130; serving Oireachtas members would no longer receive a ministerial pension. We also proposed the abolition of the Seanad; three decades later others would eventually see the merit in our case.

In the liberal and moral debates in the 1980s we offered a progressive voice. I am a Catholic, but I believed that Pope John Paul II was far too conservative. He had appointed several conservative bishops in Ireland, and their presence was an obstacle to the modernisation of the Catholic Church's attitude to social and moral issues. We saw this reality in the debate on contraceptive legislation and also in the defeat of the divorce referendum in June 1986.

The PDs wanted a pluralist, inclusive society. In that regard we focused on the need for a new constitution. I remain of the belief—as I argued as PD leader from 1986 onwards—that the 1937 Constitution has certain serious defects that must be addressed and remedied. It was an unpopular argument with some people in the 1980s, who still clung to more of the traditional values in the 1937 text. I believe that the Constitution has to be judged not only as the basic framework of citizens' rights but also as a plan by which our affairs are governed and as a framework within which change and growth can occur. For a start, the Constitution as enacted was a document of an explicitly Catholic ethos. It was not intended by the drafters as a minimalist document, which set out in bare republican form the framework of rights and institutions, which any republic should have: on the contrary, it embodied as the basic law of Ireland parts of contemporary Catholic social thinking.

We had already deleted article 44, which contained the 'special position' of the Catholic Church, but throughout the text there is still implicit acknowledgement of its primacy. The articles on the family and education as well as the 'directive principles of social policy' all resemble a fading snapshot of Catholic social theory from the 1930s. On one occasion in the mid-1980s I described this situation as the 'left luggage' of a generation past. Remarkably, despite the removal of the constitutional ban on divorce in 1996, my assessment still holds in the second decade of a new century.

The ethos of the Constitution has a view of Irish nationhood that is very predominantly Catholic and Gaelic. As opposed to a basic minimum law on which people of different creeds and none could agree to establish and regulate their civil liberties, its thrust is not pluralist. Many people do not feel that the Constitution is a genuinely republican constitution; indeed we would do well to remember that it was adopted by a plebiscite in which only 76 per cent of the electorate of the Free State participated. Of the 1.2 million votes cast, 685,000 were in favour and 525,000 were against. Of the 1.6 million electors only 42 per cent asserted the 'right' of their new parliament and constitution to hold sway in Northern Ireland. If all the people on the island had been consulted in 1937 the Constitution would not have been carried. The PDs wanted to rewrite articles 2 and 3 to express an aspiration 'for unity to be achieved by peaceful and democratic means.'

There are many other areas in the Constitution that require change. It is not desirable that bills referred to the Supreme Court under article 26 should for ever be free from constitutional challenge. I believe the role of the President is too weak in the event of a hung Dáil. The 1967 Constitution Committee and other reviews examined this issue, but nothing has ever been done about it. The private property rights in the Constitution seem to me, rightly or wrongly, to have given rise to indefensible abuses of the environment and our heritage. They could do with restating. In 1987 I posed the question, 'Should we not give reasonable priority to children's rights?' It was a long time coming, but finally in 2011 we amended the Constitution to reflect the rights of children. There are other articles in the Constitution that need change. Is it true that 'by her life within the home, woman gives to the State a support without which the common good cannot be achieved'?

Having considered the scale of revision necessary to the 1937 text, the PDS arrived at the view that a programme of gradual reform was not the best approach. For example, our proposal to abolish the Seanad would have entailed amending scores of articles; so we argued for a new document that would embrace the best of the 1937 text, remove the social theory ethos of the 1930s and reflect an Ireland that was pluralist and tolerant. With our proposal we wanted a new text that would not have discarded the great bulk of our constitutional case law and traditions but would have been a major recasting of our constitutional law. All these years later I still believe the PD approach to be correct.

Of the various faults and shortcomings of the Government elected in 2011, one of the most culpable in my view must be its failure to make any real effort to promote its own proposal to abolish the Seanad. One minister made a few half-hearted speeches; that was more or less it. Yet the proposal was lost in the referendum by just over 1 per cent. If they had made any kind of effort it would have been carried comfortably. Now we are stuck with an institution that is not democratic and serves no worthwhile purpose.

The Constitution has serious defects. To provide contemporary Ireland with a basic legal framework that assists and encourages desirable change rather than inhibiting the growth of our nationhood, we need a new constitution. We first made this argument in 1986.

There was a lot of media fuss about revising the text so that it was pluralist and inclusive. Our critics latched on to the idea that we wanted to 'take God out of the Constitution' without considering the wider context of our proposals, or even reading our draft.

————

On several occasions at private functions the Bishop of Limerick, Jeremiah Newman, made his views about the party's policies known to me. Unfortunately, he was a man who was fond of alcohol, and sometimes he was under the influence when he approached me. I especially recall a scene he caused at the opening of a new bridge in Limerick in May 1988. The PDS were well established, and we were promoting the idea of a new Constitution without the Catholic ethos that is in the existing text. Charles Haughey had been invited to open the bridge, and his handlers let it be known to the local authority that my presence on the platform would not be welcome, so despite being the senior TD in the constituency I was standing among the crowd during the proceedings. There was a large crowd, swollen by noisy protesters who were objecting to the decision of the Government to impose a rod licence.

Despite being snubbed at the official opening, I had been invited to a lunch afterwards. When the ribbon was cut, those present were invited to walk across the new bridge, which was on the way to the hotel where the lunch was taking place. As I was walking across the bridge I heard a roar behind me. 'If you think you're going to separate church and state you're very wrong. You'll only be able to do that over my dead body.' The voice was that of Bishop Newman. He came up beside me and continued a torrent of criticism. I quickly realised that he was 'tired and emotional' and eased away from him into the crowd.

At the lunch Newman was asked to make a speech. It was bizarre, consisting of a talk on why the new bridge might not have been such a good idea, as it displaced some ducks from local swampland to the pond in front of the Bishop's House. As I recall, one local newspaper did not report Newman's speech, or his general disposition. Another reported some of the speech, and it was possible to read between the lines to discern that the bishop was probably the worse for wear.

———

I found running a party much more difficult than being responsible for a Government department. Being party leader was far more unpredictable, especially with the range of issues than could arise. I was probably not the best choice as party leader. I didn't really have the personality for the role, and I didn't enjoy the limelight. There was a lot of nonsense, especially the emphasis on personal matters. If things had worked out differently I would have been content to be the number 2—or even the number 3 or 4—to Jack Lynch or George Colley. I realised that if it was difficult to run the Progressive Democrats it would have been well-nigh impossible to run Fianna Fáil, with so many people implacably opposed to me.

Unfortunately, politics had become more about the leader and his personality. The previous few elections had all been about 'Garrett versus Charlie'. The PDS could not ignore this reality. My colleagues had commissioned opinion polls that showed that I was seen as the PDS' prime asset, and the election strategy was to build the party's image around me. Stephen O'Byrnes had brought in an advertising agency, and between them they came up with the slogan 'Dessie can do it.' O'Byrnes thought it was marvellous. I didn't; I hated the concentration on personality. I said I didn't really agree with this approach; but Stephen went ahead and plastered posters with the slogan all over the country.

Midge Burridge, an Englishwoman who was part-owner of the legendary steeplechaser Desert Orchid, made the best use of the 'Dessie can do it' posters. Desert Orchid was universally known as 'Dessie'; so she acquired several PD posters and brought them to English meetings when Desert Orchid was racing. Whenever the television cameras came near her a 'Dessie can do it' poster was held high.

The opinion polls published in the first few months after the party was founded indicated that it could win about thirty seats. But elections are different situations from opinion polls. Many of our members were new to politics. There was a lot of inexperience in the party ranks. We were also seeking out candidates around the country, sometimes without having any real sense of how well a particular individual might do at the polls.

When the election came, in February 1987, we nominated 51 candidates in 33 of the 41 constituencies. Some were very late additions. To her credit, Mary Harney had continued to seek other new candidates. Before the 1987 election she recruited Geraldine Kennedy, a political correspondent with the *Sunday Press.* Several PD candidates had family roots in Fianna Fáil, including Anne Colley, Martin Gibbons and Frank Aiken. Máirín Quill had previously contested two elections for Fianna Fáil. Peadar Clohessy had been elected in 1981 for Fianna Fáil for nine months. But many of our candidates were new to politics and unknown to the electorate. The media concentrated on this perceived weakness of too many inexperienced candidates. One article in the *Sunday Tribune* was headed: 'Dessie can do it but can the PDS?'

I worked very hard to try to help all those candidates, and during the campaign I travelled to various constituencies to canvass with them. We even had a helicopter to save travelling time. For a new party we ran a highly professional campaign.

I thought we had a realistic chance of winning twenty seats. In the end, fourteen seats was a remarkable achievement for a party established only fourteen months previously. We probably should have won four or five more. We had obtained nineteen quotas. Greater strategic thinking would have delivered more seats, but we were under pressure to establish a national organisation in a short space of time, so we nominated some candidates without the benefit of proper research.

There was some satisfaction when we won seats in rural Ireland. I was delighted that John McCoy was elected in Limerick West and Peadar Clohessy in Limerick East, which disproved the lie that the PDS were an urban yuppie party. Support in opinion polls had fluctuated from an initial maximum of 19 per cent in one IMS survey to a minimum of 9 per cent in October 1986. Our support eventually settled in the low teens. At the February 1987 election we won 12 per cent of the first-preference vote. It was a level of support that the party would not attain again.

But there were successes throughout the entire history of the party. We contested five general elections and spent in total thirteen years in government. We existed for nearly twenty-five years; that was far longer than we ever envisaged when we were set up to deal with the problems of the mid-eighties. The PDS had an influence on public policy not achieved by any new party before or since.

One of the overlooked aspects of our success was the gender mix in the party. From the outset, half the PD membership were women. There was an equally strong mix in the parliamentary party elected in 1987. Energetic and principled people like Geraldine Kennedy, Anne Colley and Máirín Quill now joined Mary Harney in the Dáil. These women succeeded in their own right, without any artificial quota system. They were excellent, intelligent individuals who were well able to hold their own with anyone in the Oireachtas. In fact they were among the best parliamentary performers the Dáil has seen. In later years two talented women, Liz O'Donnell and Mary Harney, defined the PDS' ministerial presence. In my view Harney has to rank as one of the most successful women in the parliamentary arena since the foundation of the state. I was mistaken in not promoting her sooner.

Chapter 9

'I WOULDN'T UNDERESTIMATE YOUR SELLING ABILITY'

The PDS' result in the 1987 general election was one of the biggest frights Charles Haughey ever got in his political life. The Progressive Democrats were preaching a message directly opposite to what Fianna Fáil was telling the public. Reform of the income tax system and control of public expenditure was our mantra; Haughey's Fianna Fáil promised more spending and had nothing novel to say about taxation.

I have no doubt that the PDS' electoral achievement in winning fourteen seats (and nineteen quotas) caused Haughey to rethink his attitude to policy. From the outset, the new Government's economic policy was at variance with the Fianna Fáil election manifesto.

With eighty-one seats, Fianna Fáil formed a minority Government, but its parliamentary position was helped by support from Fine Gael. Its new leader, Alan Dukes, pledged not to oppose economic measures consistent with reducing the deficit. The so-called Tallaght strategy has been much praised, but what is frequently overlooked is that this support for Haughey was to a great extent a sign of Fine Gael's weakness. Many Fine Gael supporters, frustrated at the performance of the 1982–7 FitzGerald coalition, had switched allegiance to the PDS. Fine Gael had lost twenty seats in the election.

As a new leader, Dukes was keen to avoid an early election. Backing Haughey made short-term political sense for Dukes and for Fine Gael. I experienced this Fine Gael weakness to the cost of the PDS at the 1989 general election. I made a strategic mistake in agreeing a pre-election pact with Fine Gael, when the correct decision was to have maintained our full independence.

While Dukes clung to his Tallaght strategy, I was unwilling to give Haughey *carte blanche*. We dealt with issues as they arose and were happy to see in general that Fianna Fáil was following a PD-led agenda. I led an incredibly talented and hard-working front bench. We left Fine Gael in the traps, and as we had not signed up to support Haughey we were much more effective in critically examining Government policies. Although an opposition party, we were intent on following through on the policies included in the party's election manifesto. With that in mind we published a private member's bill to end the payment of ministerial pensions to former ministers who were serving TDs, members of the European Parliament or judges or who held the office of President.

In October 1987 Bobby Molloy and I surrendered our ministerial pensions, worth about £8,800 and £7,100, respectively. Fianna Fáil and Fine Gael, for all their talk about fiscal prudence, voted against our motion. The other parties adopted this policy twenty-one years later, in the aftermath of the 2008 economic crisis and in response to considerable public anger.

The local nature of Irish politics came to the fore in this period when the Government proposed closing Barrington's Hospital in Limerick. A well-organised campaign in opposition to the move quickly emerged. I had no difficulty with the need for cuts in expenditure, but I could see that the wrong hospital in the city had been singled out for closure. Unfortunately, it wasn't easy to get across the message that closing the more inefficient St John's Hospital would have made it possible to keep Barrington's open. The media and our political opponents jumped all over my position without properly considering what I was saying. The issue wasn't helped by the actions of the local bishop, Jeremiah Newman, who lobbied the Government to close what he called the 'Protestant Barrington's Hospital' so as to keep open St John's, which fell within his own jurisdiction, as it was owned by an order of nuns.

The Fianna Fáil Government that came to power in 1987 remained in office for only two years. It was the last single-party Government, as coalitions have become the norm since 1989. It was a curious Government. I would give Haughey—and MacSharry—credit for beginning to tackle the serious deficit problem. Haughey was highly opportunist in opposition up to 1987, opposing all cuts and promising to spend money everywhere; but he implemented the correct fiscal policies when in office, even if it was a U-turn of massive proportions.

But there was a deeply disturbing aspect to what was going on in private in the period 1987–9. As would be revealed in later years, there was a 'Golden Circle' at work, and its members ultimately did very well for themselves in what were difficult times. Decisions taken by that Government benefited an elite group of private citizens; and all the while Haughey—and several of his ministers—were on the take. The reputations of Charles Haughey, Pádraig Flynn, Ray Burke and Bertie Ahern were all tarred by subsequent scandalous revelations.

Despite the information that emerged from the various tribunals of inquiry, far less information has ever emerged on what was done for this Golden Circle in return for the money they handed over. There's no doubt that some people were given the inside track over their competitors. Significantly, the 1987–98 period was the only time when Haughey did not have people at the Government table willing to stand up to him. He had full rein, and the outcome was the most corrupt Government in the history of the state.

We had some sense at the time that all was not right. For example, disturbing information began to emerge about the Government's allocation of export credit insurance and that its policies in relation to the beef industry were questionable, at the very least. What emerged from probing by politicians, including some of my PD colleagues, was fraud and corruption of massive proportions. We also asked questions about a highly dubious 'passports for investment' scheme, as it was officially known when it was introduced in 1988. This scheme became better known as 'passports for sale', as many of those issued with passports gave money to Fianna Fáil or to some of its senior figures.

Haughey was not just in breach of established guidelines—which he simply didn't care about—but it was clear that he had a very confused sense of the difference between what is private and what is public. This was exemplified by a curious episode when very expensive gifts from a member of the Saudi royal family, a diamond dagger and a diamond necklace, ended up in Haughey's private possession. My PD colleague Geraldine Kennedy questioned Haughey in the Dáil about the appropriateness of the holder of a public office accepting such gifts. His reply only further confirmed what we knew about his attitude to such matters: he simply dismissed her queries, as if taking such expensive gifts was a normal activity. He stated that these were like other gifts he had received—a memento of his public life, from which he would never personally profit!

We had early signs of a cosy relationship between Haughey's Government and certain business people, including Larry Goodman. The detailed nature of the latter relationship would emerge later at the Beef Tribunal; but in early 1989 the PD deputy Pat O'Malley raised concerns that Liam Lawlor, who Haughey had appointed to chair the Oireachtas Joint Committee on Commercial State-Sponsored Bodies, was also on the board of Goodman's Food Industries. When Goodman's business expressed an interest in buying the state-owned Irish Sugar Company, Pat O'Malley drew attention to Lawlor's conflict of interest. In a response that said everything about standards in Fianna Fáil, neither Haughey nor Lawlor saw any problem. We persisted with the issue until Lawlor was eventually forced to resign as chairman of the committee.

One of the problems of coalition was that it ultimately depended on the 'nuclear option' of being able to withdraw from the Government. But many controversial issues—even important ones—were not always ones on which we realistically could fight an election. We were frequently accused, therefore, of appeasing Haughey, whereas in fact we fought harder against him and his Government than any other party.

In the course of the Lawlor controversy Haughey attacked us in Dáil exchanges. He accused us of resorting to a game of personalised politics and damaging the interests of Irish Sugar. What really worried him was that we were damaging the interests of his friend and benefactor Goodman. At the core of the debate were questions of appropriate standards in government and of the proper role of elected representatives who found themselves entrusted with positions of public care and responsibility. In defining where the public interest lies we needed to decide on the necessary and proper boundaries that must exist between big business and government in their complementary, and sometimes competitive, roles. My argument was that if we failed to retain truthful accountability to Dáil Éireann as an integral part of parliamentary democracy our whole system of government would be threatened. This was not mere constitutional theory: it was necessary in practice if we wanted to avoid an executive that could act arbitrarily, and secretly, in its own interest rather than in that of the public.

By this point, in the late 1980s, it was clear that there was a growing feeling that there was one law for the great bulk of citizens and a much more selective, à la carte legal code that a wealthy elite could avail of. There was understandable outrage and dismay as details emerged about these various scandals. Decent people were rightly outraged at the Golden Circle and the privileged elite unmasked by the scandal surrounding Telecom Éireann's Ballsbridge site and the insider dealings in the former Sugar Company.

When these scandals came to light the PDs sought to act decisively and effectively in investigating their causes. We insisted that the scandals be tackled and not swept under the carpet. A good deal of my time after the PDs entered government in 1989 was consumed in getting to the bottom of wrongdoing associated with the minority Fianna Fáil Government that was in power from 1987 to 1989. We had increasing evidence of abuse of power, but never did we comprehend the scale of the corruption sponsored by some senior Fianna Fáil figures.

Haughey's single-party Government lasted only two years. In going to the country in a fit of pique in 1989 he thought he would secure the additional numbers for governing with a secure Dáil majority. Thankfully for the country, that ambition was not realised.

Unfortunately, however, the wave of support that helped in the election of so many new PD deputies in 1987 was not repeated two years later. I had kept reminding my colleagues that large sections of the electorate rewarded constituency work more than parliamentary performance, and many voters put constituency effort above work on national policies. It was not as I would have wished Irish politics to be but was—and remains—the reality for those who want to have a sustained political career. My new PD colleagues were immensely talented in legislative matters but they got little reward for excelling in the mundane but important legislative aspect of a TD's work. This work was even more important when there was a minority Government, but the voters did not see this, in part because the media tended to concentrate their coverage on rows in the chamber rather than on meaningful contributions in shaping legislation and policy. I urged and warned them that they had to take care of the constituencies.

For the 1989 contest we agreed a pre-election pact with Fine Gael. The idea was to offer the electorate a clear alternative to a Haughey-led Government. But Fine Gael wasn't in a great position. Alan Dukes had failed to reinvigorate the party since 1987, and his near-uncritical support for the minority Fianna Fáil Government had failed to win public support. He had little love for the PDs; in fact his stated priority was to destroy us, as we had taken what he called Fine Gael votes and seats in 1987. But in politics, pragmatism is needed, and an alliance of Fine Gael and the PDs was considered the best available way of removing Haughey from office.

The deal backfired on us. Instead of standing on our own distinctive policies and our record of independence we blurred with Fine Gael. People who favoured this governmental option were presented with the option of backing the larger party. It was a bruising contest for many of my colleagues. We received 6 per cent of the vote and six seats—down from the fourteen won two years previously. We lost good people, such as Michael McDowell, Anne Colley, Geraldine Kennedy and Pat O'Malley. The Dáil was a poorer place for their absence. Michael came back, but the others took different career paths, away from electoral politics. There was a small consolation in the party's performance in the European Parliament election, taking almost 12 per cent of the vote. Pat Cox polled strongly in Munster, and won a seat.

Once more Haughey had failed to get the seats required to form a majority single-party Government; but with the six PD seats he could still be elected Taoiseach. Speculation began immediately. There was talk that we might offer support to a minority Fianna Fáil Government; there were also calls for a Fianna Fáil-PD coalition.

Harney was the first to reach the conclusion that an absolutist position was not tenable. There was considerable anger in the party when she suggested that the PDs might support a minority Fianna Fáil Government. McDowell, although having lost his Dáil seat, agreed with her argument but went further in suggesting that we should consider a coalition arrangement. It took three days of talks among the six PD deputies and other senior party figures to come around to that point of view. In truth, none of us wanted to go into Government with Fianna Fáil. We were all opposed to the idea of working with Haughey.

After the election I went on a short holiday to the south of England. I was still on this break when I received a message that Harney had spoken on radio about options for forming a Government, including the PDs agreeing to back Haughey as Taoiseach and the feasibility of a coalition arrangement. I was annoyed that she had gone public. I later discovered that she had apparently been urged to do so by McCreevy. There was still huge shock in the PDs at our losses. Harney saw reality earlier than most of us, and in fairness I must say she articulated the unthinkable before anybody else.

Many people were later critical of us for ending up in a Government with Fianna Fáil. But the numbers did not add up for a stable arrangement involving Fine Gael, the Labour Party and the PDs. We were faced with the reality of life. Politics is not an academic profession but rather one in which decisions have to be made that involve compromise and adaptation to changed and changing circumstances. We were faced with an impossible choice. I summed up the position for my colleagues: 'If we don't go into government there will be another election in four weeks' time. The people of Ireland won't thank us for that. Yes, we didn't create this situation, but it's the arithmetical result of the election. We either have to take it or leave it.

But if we leave it we'll cause an immediate election, and in all likelihood the Progressive Democrats will be wiped out.'

When the Dáil first met after the election none of the candidates nominated for Taoiseach secured a majority of votes. It was the first time such a situation had ever arisen. We voted for Dukes, in keeping with the pre-election pact; but with that vote concluded we were free to act in whatever way we thought best for the country. When the first discussions with Fianna Fáil began I deliberately chose not to get centrally involved. My contact with the Fianna Fáil side was kept to a minimum. Bobby Molloy and Pat Cox met their counterparts, Albert Reynolds and Bertie Ahern, then two stout allies of Haughey. The talks took a week to reach a conclusion. We deliberately refrained from saying too much in public. Haughey also remained silent, but several of his colleagues were openly talking about the party's core value of not participating in coalition Governments.

It took Fianna Fáil several days to accept the reality that we were not going to automatically put Haughey back into the Taoiseach's office. They baulked at first at even talking about coalition. We were not interested in propping up a minority Fianna Fáil Government. They were six seats short of a Dáil majority, and we had six seats. We made it clear that the alternative to agreeing a deal with us was another election.

The talks stopped and started for a few days before real negotiations got under way. I eventually met Haughey to discuss the options. He had never said anything to me about the PDs, but I knew he did plenty of 'effing and blinding' about us in private. At our first meeting the atmosphere was businesslike and cordial. I was accompanied by Molloy and Cox. As the discussion was coming to a close I raised the coalition issue. 'Des, even I couldn't deliver that inside Fianna Fáil,' Haughey replied. I remarked: 'Well, Charlie, from my knowledge of you inside Fianna Fáil I wouldn't underestimate your selling ability.'

Twenty-seven days after the election a Government was eventually formed. I still had serious reservations about being in government with Fianna Fáil but, like my PD colleagues, I recognised that the electorate had made its choice and the numbers pointed to a Fianna

Fáil-PD coalition. In the end we secured two Government positions and one junior minister post. I returned to the Department of Industry and Commerce, Bobby Molloy was appointed Minister for Energy, and Mary Harney became the country's first Minister of State with Responsibility for Environmental Protection.

The programme for government was an ambitious document. The objective was to pursue policies that were pro-jobs and promoted tax reform. PD policy was very strongly represented in the proposals, including an emphasis on greater enterprise and competition. Our policies on ending state monopolies and cartels were also accepted by Fianna Fáil. Getting so much PD policy into the programme for government lessened somewhat the internal party concerns about entering government with Fianna Fáil. We quickly came to realise that for Fianna Fáil, power took precedence over policy. Office mattered; ideology did not. Thus it was not so hard to get your way with them.

Over the life of the Fianna Fáil-PD coalition significant progress was made on income tax reform. In the coalition's first budget the standard rate of income tax was reduced from 32 per cent to 30 per cent, while the top rate was cut from 55 to 53 per cent. A year later those rates were reduced further to 29 per cent and 52 per cent, respectively. In a mid-term review of the government programme economic growth was sufficiently strong to allow us to set the target of a standard rate of 25 per cent and top rate of 44 per cent, to be implemented before the next election. We also pushed through reforms in environmental protection and competition law. And we helped to abolish the death penalty.

Job creation was my priority. Working with the IDA was once more very satisfying, and the agency continued to produce some world-class executives. I was fortunate in having worked with Michael Killeen in a previous term as minister; now I found another in Kieran McGowan. In very many respects, but specifically in influence and importance, Killeen and McGowan were to the state-sponsored world what T. K. Whitaker had been in the civil service.

In this period I also asked the businessman Jim Culliton to chair a review of industrial policy. A raft of radical measures to strengthen indigenous industry emerged from this review process. We also made progress on deregulation of the aviation industry. I was very taken by the economic proposals for liberalisation of aviation put forward by Seán Barrett, an economics lecturer at Trinity College, and the idea that high air fares could be cut to increase air travel. The resistance to the emergence of Ryanair was huge, and not just from Aer Lingus, but the merits of breaking the stranglehold of a single airline were proved very quickly as fares fell and passenger numbers increased greatly.

Ryanair's tremendous achievement in becoming Ireland's most successful business is now well known. Back in the 1980s it was all very different, when I was one of the few voices promoting the case for airline competition. Aer Lingus had a stranglehold on the market into and out of Ireland. It had remarkable arrangements with other airlines, including paying some of them not to fly into Dublin. The customer was the real loser. Fares were kept high and flight options restricted. This situation was ably facilitated by the Department of Transport. During one Dáil debate I coined the term 'downtown office of Aer Lingus' for the Department of Transport. I pointed out that the Minister for Transport was not just the sole shareholder in Aer Lingus but was also the market regulator. It took some time to secure widespread political acceptance that this was a serious conflict of interest. Seán Barrett produced figures to show how much preventing competition was costing not just the travelling public but also the economy. I was happy to use this information in encouraging support for competition that ultimately facilitated the growth of Ryanair and enabled other airlines to fly routes to and from Ireland.

It is hard to believe now, but back in 1984 legislation was published to make selling discounted air fares a criminal offence. Jim Mitchell of Fine Gael, who was Minister for Transport, admitted that one of the objectives of the legislation was 'to prevent the charging of fares that are too high or fares that are too low, where they would be disruptive.' I strongly argued for allowing the market to arrive at fare levels and for pro-competition measures to increase flight activity. Fianna Fáil fully supported Mitchell. Charlie Haughey and Ray Burke, as North Dublin TDs, took their lead from the trade unions at Dublin Airport.

I was outside the Fianna Fáil parliamentary party at that time, so I had no obligation to follow the party's anti-competition line. I contested every line of the legislation, which I argued was ridiculous, and was the only TD to express my opposition to the proposal in the Dáil. When the debate concluded, Mitchell took a swipe at my contribution. 'He is a lone ranger jumping fences that are figments of his imagination. The points he has raised have no validity.' Well, time is the judge of all things.

My status *vis-à-vis* Haughey had changed: I was now dealing with him as the leader of a party in government rather than just a member of his Government. In fairness, I must say he acknowledged this position, in that our dealings were always businesslike. But I never trusted him; in fact when I saw him taking an interest in a particular topic or policy area I tended to keep an even closer eye on proposals. Despite these reservations Haughey was well suited to running a coalition Government. He was businesslike and worked to ensure that the coalition functioned properly. The greater problems were often with some of his senior ministers, who resented the PD presence at the Government table. Pádraig Flynn was positively repulsive; Ray Burke was hardly pleasant; Albert Reynolds saw an opportunity to enhance his prospects of capturing the Fianna Fáil leadership by stressing his hostility to the PDS. Unfortunately, Reynolds continued with this hostility even after he succeeded Haughey as Taoiseach in early 1992.

Flynn gave Mary Harney a terrible time in the Department of the Environment, where he was the minister. He treated her like absolute dirt. She was left off the top table at functions, and was even advised not to use the main entrance at the Custom House. Her every attempt at progressing policy was thwarted. Despite Flynn's hostility, one of Harney's greatest achievements was in passing the smokeless-coal legislation. Smoke pollution was a serious problem in Dublin and other cities and towns; asthma and other lung diseases were the main consequences. Harney wanted to introduce a ban on the polluting coal. Flynn was opposed. He said it would never happen; he had some spurious argument about protecting the Irish coal industry. Despite Flynn's obstructions, Harney persisted and eventually got her policy implemented, which was a great achievement for a minister of state.

———

After we went into government I began to learn more about what had been going on in the 1987–9 period, especially in relation to the beef industry. I set up an internal departmental inquiry into the administration of the export credit insurance scheme. The scale of the wrongdoing when Fianna Fáil had government to themselves in those two years gradually emerged. I've no doubt that Haughey had to act differently after 1989 because of the coalition arrangement with the PDS. We challenged him when information emerged. For example, he had to concede on setting up the Beef Tribunal. There is no doubt in my mind that the Goodman situation was a landmine under the Government.

Matters came to a head in May 1991 when UTV broadcast its 'World in Action' investigation into the beef industry. There was not a huge deal that was new in Susan O'Keeffe's programme, but by making the story accessible to the public, and by making it visual, the programme-makers created a powerful piece of television.

There had been resistance to a full-blown inquiry up to that point, but now that the issues had been aired so dramatically I was able to insist on the establishment of an independent inquiry. I went to see Haughey. 'Look, there are highly unsatisfactory and improper things going on in the beef industry,' I told him. He told me to 'get stuffed.'

While this discussion was taking place in Government Buildings, Michael O'Kennedy, the Minister for Agriculture, was on his feet in the Dáil defending the beef processors. I informed Haughey that the PD ministers and deputies would not support the Government view in the Dáil. With this information he finally accepted that without a tribunal there would be a general election. He was obviously not prepared to collapse the coalition. A message was sent to O'Kennedy to reverse gear. From an initial position of opposing the motion on a tribunal, Fianna Fáil accepted that an inquiry was necessary. He made O'Kennedy look very foolish. It seemed as if Haughey would concede anything to avoid a general election.

——

As the Government entered its second year there was already a real sense of Haughey's waning powers. He had fallen out with many of his former diehard supporters. The drip-drip of scandal weakened him. His sacking of Brian Lenihan during the 1990 presidential election lost him considerable support within Fianna Fáil.

We had formally remained outside the election, although there was considerable support in the party for Mary Robinson's candidacy. Lenihan's contradictory statements on whether or not he had put pressure on President Hillery not to dissolve the Dáil in early 1982 placed us in a difficult situation. It was not a problem we made, but it was a very real problem. Letters of resignation were prepared; we put the party on an election footing. But Haughey was not keen to face the electorate, and when Lenihan refused to resign he was duly sacked.

It was hard not to feel sorry for Lenihan. If he had admitted the truth over the taped interview—that he wasn't well and had made a mistake—the matter would not have been so serious. But despite pleadings to do so he declined, and the matter was brought to an unfortunate end.

Throughout 1991 there were further business-related scandals that kept the focus on Fianna Fáil's association with certain business people, and the reality of a Golden Circle remained in public debate. As Minister for Industry and Commerce I was drawn into several of these controversies. I appointed an inspector, John Glackin, to investigate the purchase for £9.4 million of a site in Ballsbridge by Telecom Éireann. There was a whole series of unusual transactions involving several well-known business people. It seemed an inflated price was paid for the site by Telecom Éireann. Glackin finally concluded that the two principal hidden beneficiaries were Dermot Desmond and J. P. McManus.

There were other controversies involving Celtic Helicopters, which was owned by Haughey's son Ciarán, and also Greencore, the privatised sugar company. An official investigation into the latter affair established that certain directors and executives of the sugar company had made significant profits at the apparent expense of the taxpayer. For example, the Greencore chairman, Bernie Cahill, who was by no means the closest of the cronies, was also chairman of a mining company set up by another of Haughey's sons.

Haughey was clearly entering the final phase of his political career. But it had been close to being over on many occasions, from the Arms Crisis in 1970 to the phone-tapping revelations in 1983. I sometimes wondered if he would ever leave. There were ministerial resignations in late 1991, and as the leadership battle moved into what looked like its final phase Haughey proposed nominating Jim McDaid from Co. Donegal as Minister for Defence.

We had concerns about the nomination. McDaid had been photographed outside the Four Courts during a republican extradition case. He said he was only giving support to a constituent, but in the context of the times, when the IRA was terrorising people, he was the wrong choice for the still highly sensitive department. The crisis was eventually resolved when, honourably, McDaid declined the nomination.

The last straw came when Seán Doherty confirmed what we always suspected was the truth behind the telephone-tapping in 1982. The revelation during a television interview that Haughey was centrally involved brought the end within sight. I've no doubt the Doherty intervention was orchestrated. I went to see Haughey, and our conversation was brief and to the point. I said, 'This can't go on.' He told me he'd think about the situation; but he was realistic enough to recognise reality. There was no real fight from him this time. The threat of a general election wasn't available to him. He knew he couldn't carry a majority in the Fianna Fáil parliamentary party. If he somehow had attempted to carry on he would have been removed as leader by his own colleagues. It was our final meeting, and one of our final conversations.

Haughey was hugely able as an administrator and as a politician, but he compromised himself politically and personally. And, as the

tribunal revelations would later reveal, he disgraced political life in
Ireland. He didn't go to many public functions after his retirement,
and that was before the tribunal process began. We last met at Jack
Lynch's funeral in Cork in 1999. Lynch had in many ways been my
political mentor, and we had stayed in regular contact socially after he
resigned as Fianna Fáil leader in 1979. Our wives were very friendly.
He was interested in what was happening, although he never really
offered advice on political issues. I think he wanted to stay out of
politics. He had been there long enough.

I was honoured to deliver the graveside oration at Lynch's state
funeral in October 1999. It was an opportunity to remind the country
that Lynch's legacy was the existence of the democratic state in which
we lived. When confronted with some of the most difficult decisions
to face any Taoiseach of the modern era, Lynch took determined and
resolute action to defend democracy and uphold the rule of law. For
that alone he deserved his place in Irish history. In my speech I said
that I hoped 'the life and career of this wonderful man and dear friend
will inspire younger people to seek to follow his example and to be
publicly generous of themselves at a time when the commitment of
integrity is so badly needed.'

There was reserved seating in the North Cathedral in Cork. Because
of a diplomatic *faux pas,* when I arrived at the church I was put sitting
between Haughey and Reynolds. There wasn't much conversation
between us, although there was a fair amount of chatter in the seats
behind.

After the Mass, on the journey to St Finbarr's Cemetery I could
hear the crowds booing Haughey, whose car was near my own. As we
approached the roundabout at Wilton his car took the right turn out
of Cork. The people lining the streets that October day in Cork not
only honoured the legacy of Jack Lynch but in their reaction also
delivered their verdict on Charles Haughey.

———

The transition from Haughey to Reynolds was swift. From the outset there was a change in mood and tone in the working relationship in the Government. Reynolds had been openly hostile to the PDs in private and, on occasion, in public since the Fianna Fáil-PD coalition had been formed in 1989, describing the coalition as a 'temporary little arrangement.' It was good rabble-rousing talk for the Fianna Fáil grass roots in his campaign to succeed Haughey. As he saw it, Haughey had let the party down in ending its 'core value' of opposing coalition Governments.

Unfortunately, Reynolds brought this hostile attitude into the Government room. I know that several of his newly appointed Fianna Fáil ministers disagreed with his approach, but they kept their opinions to themselves. Reynolds simply wasn't interested in compromise or in achieving consensus between the coalition partners. He made it clear that the two PD ministers—Molloy and myself—were in a minority.

On one occasion I was registering my opposition to a proposal. I was speaking for about five minutes when Reynolds intervened. 'You can speak for as long as you like. I don't mind how long you take, because when you finish we'll take a vote, and the result will be thirteen to two.' He might as well have said, 'We're not listening to you, so you should stop now.'

There had been meetings from time to time with Haughey, and where necessary there were pre-Government discussions to resolve problem issues. That all stopped under Reynolds. Haughey was too clever to create avoidable division; Reynolds simply did not consider the effect of his divisive attitude. His hostility came through at every opportunity. When I nominated Mary Harney to be the PD representative on the Government team for talks with the Northern parties at Stormont, he raised an objection. The talks were sponsored by the British Secretary of State for Northern Ireland, Peter Brooke, and were a precursor to later progress. In the summer of 1992 Sinn Féin was still outside the process, given the continuation of IRA violence. Ian Paisley and Jim Molyneaux came and went. With Reynolds refusing to allow Harney to be a member of the Government's delegation, I ended up having to go to the talks myself. It wasn't as if I wasn't busy enough at that time.

The talks were going nowhere. I hadn't had direct involvement in policy on Northern Ireland previously but I was happy to be reacquainted with Ken Maginnis of the Ulster Unionist Party. We knew each other from attending rugby matches. At lunch one day at Stormont he invited me to sit at his table. The various parties to the talks had tended to sit in their own groups. Although our conversation was primarily about rugby, my presence at a 'unionist' table caused concern with one of my Fianna Fáil counterparts. In effect I was 'consorting with the enemy.' A report was telephoned to Reynolds immediately by Flynn. It was an extraordinary mentality.

It was a short-lived Government but one that involved a number of controversies, including the Supreme Court judgement in the X Case. The initial mood in government was to let the matter settle so as to give a more considered response. It was a classic example of the Supreme Court making a decision that caused more problems than it solved. It was a complicated situation, but I didn't think it would take until 2013 for the legislature to finally offer a response to the judgement.

I had served in government under two Taoisigh, Lynch and Haughey, and I had seen two Fine Gael leaders, Cosgrave and FitzGerald, hold the position in my time in the Dáil. These four individuals had different strengths and weaknesses; but they were all head and shoulders above Reynolds, politically and intellectually. Personally, I don't think he was up to being Taoiseach. His singular motivation seemed to be to end the Government's life as quickly as possible—which is exactly what he did. Seven months after he was elected Taoiseach the Government collapsed after he accused me of committing perjury at the Beef Tribunal.

———

One of my last trips abroad as a Government minister was to South Africa in 1991, on Ireland's first trade mission there. Those were the dying days of the apartheid regime, and the dawn of South African democracy was already visible. Nelson Mandela had just been released. I remember the trip for one thing in particular. When in Johannesburg I wanted to visit Soweto but permission was refused. It was dangerous, and the authorities did not want to take any risks with the personal safety of a visiting minister—or maybe they just didn't want me to see the reality of the place.

I could not persuade them, but the day was saved by Fergal Keane of the BBC, even then one of the most distinguished journalists in the world. I had known him of old, because he had begun his career on the *Limerick Leader* and we had had common resort to two places: Limerick District Court and Limerick Corporation. He was on assignment for the BBC in Johannesburg and he came over to see me. When I told him about Soweto he said not to worry, he would take me there in the morning. I said I'd have to tell the police; he was a bit displeased but said all right but tell them they are only to send in one unmarked car after you.

So I told them all that. The following morning we set off, with Fergal driving, and when he looked in the rear-view mirror he said, 'There are six police cars behind us.' We headed to a Convent of Mercy run by Irish nuns, who would give us the low-down on Soweto. We found it with some difficulty. Soweto is enormous, with a population of 5 or 6 million—nearly as much as all of Ireland. The buildings were shanties for the most part, the streets were confusing and unnamed and it was very easy to get lost. The convent was about two or three miles inside Soweto.

Finally, after some wrong turns and other difficulties, we found it. But the nuns there were mostly American, not Irish. They explained that the Irish nuns were up at the convent school, about a mile away. One of them came with us to show us the way. It was the end of the school year and the nuns were busy in the school, marking exam papers.

It was a big school. We met the head nun, whose name I can't remember but she was from Waterford. She apologised for them all being so busy but they had been going to start that morning at seven o'clock. She got there before seven to open up, but she couldn't open the gates and had to wait.

The reason was that there were about a dozen dogs beside the front gate, and when she saw them she realised what they were doing. They were eating a human body.

She knew because she had seen it before. People were always getting shot at night in Soweto and the bodies were dumped. The police and emergency services dared not enter the township in the hours of darkness, so that by dawn the body was eaten—or most of it. Only then could an ambulance get in to remove what was left.

I asked her how much support the school got from the state. The answer was that they received nothing at all: the apartheid state did not care about black people, whether they lived or died. There were hundreds of well-turned-out girls, wearing uniforms and all. The school was looking forward to the post-apartheid regime in the hope that the state would now support education for everyone in South Africa.

We visited Cape Town as well—a place less charged than Johannesburg—and the beautiful wine country nearby around Stellenbosch. I liked the Cape—most people do—but I have never been able to forget that awful image of the dogs in Soweto.

———

We entered into the 1992 general election as an independent party. We hoped to increase our number of seats, but it was hard to judge what the voters would think, given that we had pulled the plug on the Government. We had perfectly valid reasons for leaving office, but our challenge was to ensure that those reasons were clear to the public.

The results were gratifying. We won four extra seats, taking our total to ten deputies. There was no possibility of going back into a Government led by Reynolds. There was a slight possibility of an alternative Government without Fianna Fáil's involvement; but a government of Fine Gael, Labour Party, Democratic Left and PDS would not have been ideal. Dick Spring had this idea of being Taoiseach; the Labour Party was clinging to an idea of Spring rotating the role of Taoiseach with the leader of Fine Gael. Not surprisingly,

John Bruton wasn't too keen on that proposal, and to be honest I wasn't either.

That said, I still think the four-party coalition option would have been better than the arrangement that did emerge. Spring effectually threw Reynolds a lifeline by agreeing to lead his party into government with Fianna Fáil. It was a very odd combination. The parties had little in common, and right from the outset the Beef Tribunal was a shadow over the arrangement. A great deal of my time between 1989 and 1992 had been consumed with export credit insurance. The dodgy activity of the beef industry was responsible for the collapse of the Fianna Fáil-PD coalition, and ultimately it contributed to the collapse of the Fianna Fáil-Labour Government too.

One particular policy initiative was introduced by the new Government that confirmed my belief that the Labour Party and the country would have been better served keeping Fianna Fáil out of power. I was appalled when news emerged in May 1993 that Fianna Fáil and the Labour Party were proposing a second tax amnesty. I regarded the idea as immoral and one that went to the root of a lot more than the collection of taxes. It also gnawed away at the very fabric of a democratic society. The amnesty rewarded those who had deliberately broken the law, and penalised those who observed the law. The principle of equity between citizens and of compliance with one's duty as a member of society were simply not a consideration for those proposing the amnesty.

What was even more galling was that the previous amnesty in 1988 (also introduced by Fianna Fáil) was sold on the grounds that it was a one-off event. The idea of a second amnesty had never been raised in the 1989–92 period, when the PDS were in government. But obviously, with the Labour Party as their new coalition partners, Fianna Fáil found a more receptive audience.

Reynolds was the main author of the amnesty. The Labour Party were said to have reservations, and also Bertie Ahern, who was Minister for Finance, but ultimately they went along with it. It was argued that the exchequer would not lose out, and that as the money concerned was already out of the reach of the Revenue Commissioners it would remain so without a scheme like the one proposed. I found this a crazy way to run a country. I repeatedly reminded people of the consequences when Reynolds had last ignored the best professional advice available to him in 1987 and in 1988.

The first tax amnesty had been an example of an abuse of power. It emerged within a year of Fianna Fáil forming the 1987 Government; but the terms were not over-generous, although there was a waiver of all interest charges and penalties if all outstanding taxes were paid. The 1993 amnesty was altogether different: it was structured to allow people to pay 15 per cent of their outstanding tax liabilities; the other 85 per cent owed, together with all penalties and interest, was written off.

When I spoke against the amnesty in the Dáil in June 1993 I reminded the Government parties that many of the tax-evaders escaped liability of 60 per cent in the 1980s. Now in the case of an individual who had hidden £10 million, a liability of £6 million was legitimately owed to the Revenue Commissioners. With their amnesty proposal, Fianna Fáil and the Labour Party were saying to such people: With interest and penalties you owe a lot more than £6 million, but we'll settle for £1 million.

It was a crazy situation. Imagine a bank robber taking £6 million plus but then being told, It's all right, just give us back £1 million and you can go free. That was the message the amnesty was sending to wealthy tax-evaders. The amnesty was brought in for all the wrong reasons and for the wrong people. Even the Revenue Commissioners made known their concerns about the vast amounts of tax being written off. The taxation system was undermined. Michael McDowell did great work in drawing attention to the problems with the amnesty. It was yet another example of the type of policies favoured by that generation in Fianna Fáil; but what made the 1993 amnesty so appalling was that the Labour Party willingly facilitated its introduction and its passage into law. Never before or since were secret political donors so richly rewarded.

Chapter 10

' 'GROSSLY UNWISE, RECKLESS AND FOOLISH'

In one important respect we have got ahead of ourselves. We need to wind back about six years, to the formation of the last single-party minority Fianna Fáil Government under Haughey, in order to trace the story of Larry Goodman, the Fianna Fáil bigwigs, the export credit insurance scheme and the scandal that was the Irish beef industry.

Many people find agriculture, insurance, intervention and similar subjects a big turn-off. Put them all together and add Haughey, Reynolds, Burke and Lawlor and it's easy to lose concentration. But this was a major scandal, a product of the very worst type of crony capitalism and an early indicator of the culture that led Ireland to disaster in 2008.

In June 1987 the minority Fianna Fáil Government held a press conference to announce the central plank of its strategy for employment creation. More than a thousand jobs were promised, arising out of an investment of £260 million in the beef industry. This industry was important to the economy, claiming to contribute more than 5 per cent of GDP. It had progressed from producing cattle for export and subsequent slaughter in other countries to one that by the late 1980s exported three-quarters of cattle output as beef to intervention or to destinations around the world.

Unfortunately, membership of the EEC, and access to various support schemes, undoubtedly contributed more to the increased beef production than had access to the large European market. In my view Ireland had manifestly failed to penetrate the increasingly valuable Continental market to any significant degree. One of the consequences of this reality was a reliance on volatile Middle Eastern markets as outlets for much of our beef exports.

The investment programme announced in June 1987 was going to transform the industry. That was the promise. But it was a remarkable plan for other reasons. At the press conference Charles Haughey sat at the top table alongside the businessman Larry Goodman. Joe Walsh, Minister of State at the Department of Agriculture, was also present; but the minister was not. It was a very odd arrangement.

It made no sense that one company—Goodman's Anglo-Irish Beef Processors—was getting preferential treatment. As I saw it, the greater the dominance of the Goodman group, or indeed of any other single group, the more vulnerable and insecure was the position of the beef-producing farmer. The less effective competition there was in the beef-processing trade the less Irish farmers were assured of a fair price for their output. I was suspicious about what was going on between Goodman and the Government, and what exactly they were up to.

There were some remarkable features about the Goodman five-year development plan as approved by the Government, first in June 1987 and subsequently, as amended, in March 1988. Firstly, the cost per job to the state was £90,000, which was approximately five times the average cost per job at that time and about six or seven times the average in indigenous industry. Secondly, Haughey's Government and the IDA agreed, as part of a total package, that Goodman should be allowed to avail of £120 million in highly advantageous section 84 loans. Even though the Beef Development Plan, as the package was called, never went ahead, and even though the package was announced in June 1987 and the grant agreement not signed until March 1988, we later learnt that £106 million of this £120 million was actually drawn down on the date the grant agreement was signed.

Much of this information came to light during the subsequent Beef Tribunal; but my suspicions about the deal were raised from the outset when word reached us that the IDA was terribly unhappy with what the Government was proposing. The Government originally considered the five-year plan on 26 April 1987 but, remarkably, without the knowledge of the IDA. The Industrial Development Act (1986) makes it clear that the IDA dealt with all industrial development proposals. The Government only got involved with larger deals where its consent was required. The tribunal of inquiry would later conclude that the Government's action was 'wrongful and in excess of their powers.' This was a startling finding of direct illegality. The order to do so—the tribunal said—was made 'either at the instigation of the then Taoiseach or the Secretary to his Department.' It seemed most unlikely that a very senior civil servant, entirely on his own initiative, would give an illegal direction to the IDA. If he was not the instigator there was only one other person who could have instigated this illegal action, according to the report, and that was the Taoiseach, Charles Haughey.

With my knowledge of the serious misgivings about the plan within the IDA—and, from what I gathered, reluctance at being involved at all—I kept a watchful eye on what the Government was proposing. Little did I realise the scale of the wrongdoing. Knowledge of this wrongdoing emerged as we became more aware of the closeness of the relationship between senior Fianna Fáil figures and Larry Goodman. My PD colleague Pat O'Malley TD was instrumental in extracting crucial information. When the Government decided to sell the Irish Sugar Company, Pat took a keen interest in the people involved in the deal, including Goodman's Food Industries, which expressed an interest in acquiring the state asset.

After the 1987 general election Haughey had appointed Liam Lawlor chairman of the Oireachtas Joint Committee on Commercial State-Sponsored Bodies. Lawlor had numerous business interests, including operating as a non-executive director of Food Industries. So when Goodman's company sought to acquire Irish Sugar it was obvious that Lawlor—as chairperson of the committee with responsibility for the company—had a direct conflict of interest. Not that Lawlor, or Haughey, saw it that way.

Pat O'Malley, who shared a constituency with Lawlor in Dublin West, was well versed in Lawlor's questionable business activities. He pursued the conflict of interest, and tabled a number of Dáil questions. For his efforts he was the subject of bitter criticisms from Lawlor and

Haughey. Lawlor claimed that those who publicised issues about his 'dual role' were engaged in a 'witch-hunt' and that Pat O'Malley had pursued 'a personal vendetta and erroneous campaign' against him. This inability to even acknowledge a conflict of interest said much about the Fianna Fáil approach to ethics at that time. The PDs' attention ultimately forced Lawlor to stand down from his Goodman role.

But our suspicions had been further raised. We began to delve a little further into Goodman and his relationship with the Fianna Fáil Government. We were given some information about the handling of the export credit insurance scheme. Thanks to persistent questioning by Pat O'Malley and myself, some very disturbing facts emerged, particularly in relation to beef exports to Iraq. There were good grounds for believing that substantial abuse had occurred, leading to a potential liability of the state that was unprecedented.

———

Export credit insurance was a valuable scheme that enabled exporters not just to insure against the non-payment of export contracts but also to raise cheap finance in respect of sums due to them where the credit had been insured. It was in effect a state aid to exporters, as the risks associated with export contracts were underwritten by the taxpayer. Before 1987 the amount of insurance for beef exports to Iraq was small: in 1986, for example, cover was less than 30 per cent of total Irish beef exports to Iraq. In fact the Fine Gael-Labour Government decided in 1986 not to continue to underwrite any further beef export cover for Iraq, because of the high risks involved. Following the formation of the single-party Fianna Fáil Government in 1987 there was a dramatic change in policy. Cover was increased substantially to more than the amount of beef exported. This trend became even more pronounced in 1988, and huge potential liabilities were undertaken at the expense of the taxpayer.

The reversal of policy from 1987 was extraordinary. In my view there was an obligation on Haughey and his ministers to explain why the decision was taken to restore cover for Iraq, exposing Ireland to potential liabilities well in excess of £100 million. I wanted to know why they had encouraged an expansion of the insured beef trade to Iraq despite the huge risks involved. Albert Reynolds, as Minister for Industry and Commerce, championed the policy. He told the Dáil in 1988:

As a result of successful growth in business contacts in Iraq and in the context of the Irish-Iraqi Joint Commission, it was decided to provide export credit facilities to Iraq. This is a positive development in terms of sustaining growth in the long term.

I believed back in the late 1980s—as I still do today—that Reynolds was not simply doing Haughey's bidding. In questioning the operation of the export credit policy I was on a collision course not only with Haughey and his immediate successor as Taoiseach but also with the wealth and influence of a businessman, Larry Goodman, who boasted some year or two later that he constituted 5 per cent of Ireland's GDP.

It was exceptionally difficult to get information from the Government. Answers to parliamentary questions were frequently unsatisfactory, and it was obvious that a policy of non-cooperation was operating. It emerged later at the tribunal of inquiry that one of the officials responsible for drafting replies was actually complimented by a senior official for preparing an answer that 'succeeded in confusing the deputy [who asked the question].'

Other TDs at this point began to ask questions about various aspects of the Goodman enterprise and its political relationship with Fianna Fáil. Barry Desmond, Pat Rabbitte, Tomás Mac Giolla and Dick Spring were also receiving information and asked questions in the Dáil about what increasingly looked like a scandal or, more accurately, a series of scandals.

Further delving into the export credit policy revealed two incontrovertible facts. The first was that at different times during 1987 and 1988 most of the available insurance provided for all Irish exporters of all goods to all countries was made available to two companies and in respect of one product, beef, being exported to one country, Iraq. Well over 80 per cent of that cover was made available to a company that was part of the Goodman group. The policy was of considerable assistance to Goodman in increasing its dominance within the Irish market and with suppliers and putting other companies in the same industry at a considerable disadvantage. The policy also put a large number of exporters in all other industries producing all kinds of goods and services at a great disadvantage.

We wanted to know how the Government could justify giving such an enormous proportion of all our export credit insurance to two companies, one getting 80 per cent or more of the beef cover, when hundreds of exporters and would-be exporters were left without this facility and without the indemnity and cheap finance that it provided. We also wanted to know how it was that such a high proportion of export credit insurance was afforded for the high-risk Iraqi market, which was not covered at all by most western countries. The lengthy war between Iran and Iraq was the source of this risk. Many countries began to withdraw credit—and the Fine Gael-Labour coalition in 1986 had displayed caution—but incredibly, once Fianna Fáil came into government in 1987 Ireland went into expansion mode. For example, in November 1988 an Irish minister stated at the Baghdad Trade Fair that we would further increase our export credit insurance limits for exports to Iraq in 1989 (a decision that was later rescinded).

Haughey and Reynolds, as the main drivers of this policy, were ignoring internal official advice. In 1988 the Department of Finance reviewed the history of export credit insurance and noted: 'We oppose successive increases in the Iraq ceiling which, because of the extremely volatile Iraq situation, we regard as too much of a gamble with the Exchequer's resources.' The gamble taken by Haughey and Reynolds was taken with well over £100 million in public funds. Most of it was for the benefit of Larry Goodman, who was close to both politicians and who subsequently acquired the Reynolds family's pet-food factory, to which he had been a supplier.

The second issue that needed clarification from the Government was the fact that the amount of beef in respect of which the state provided insurance on its sale to Iraq in 1987 and 1988 actually exceeded the amount of beef exported from the Republic to Iraq. According to official cso figures, this excess was approximately £57 million. Despite all our questions, the discrepancy remained unexplained. The only credible explanation was that beef from sources other than Ireland was given cover under the Irish scheme. If this was so, then the cover was in breach of the terms of the scheme and was a flagrant abuse of the scheme. It was nothing short of a fraud on the Irish taxpayer.

The Government at first refused to deal with our queries. We were fobbed off with the line that the matter was being investigated within the Department of Industry and Commerce. But the point was that the Department of Agriculture and presumably the Department of Industry and Commerce had to have been aware of this discrepancy long before it was raised in public by the PDs.

Ray Burke succeeded Albert Reynolds as Minister for Industry and Commerce in November 1988. The change in minister made little difference in attitude. We continued to have to drag information from the Government. In early May 1989 Burke dismissively remarked that PD deputies, including myself, had put down twenty-four Dáil questions on the export credit scheme; but if proper information had been forthcoming we would not have had to push so hard.

In my view the public were entitled to be informed of the facts. They were entitled to a full and frank explanation. It was simply not sufficient to adopt a 'no comment' approach, or to threaten litigation against those who wished to throw the spotlight of public attention on an area of serious suspicion. Specifically, people were entitled to know whether beef from outside the country was used to fill insured contracts, and they were entitled to know the level of financial risk arising from the Government's preferential treatment of one private business.

In April 1989 Pat O'Malley put down a series of questions, asking the Minister for Industry and Commerce to explain the discrepancy that had emerged between the trade statistics for beef exports to Iraq and the amount of insurance cover for beef exported to that country. We now know from evidence given to the tribunal of inquiry that the explanations given by the minister were spurious, and were known to be spurious at the time. For example, on 20 April and 3 May 1989, in response to questions put by PD deputies, Ray Burke told the Dáil that in relation to export credit insurance decisions 'the first two companies to apply had at the time of their applications firm contracts for the supply of beef to Iraq.' We later found out that this answer was false. In September 1987 Reynolds allocated export credit insurance for beef to Iraq to two companies, neither of which had a contract at the time, and indeed one of them never did any business in Iraq.

I raised the operation of the scheme in relation to beef exports to Iraq on an adjournment debate in May 1989. I focused on the provision of this extraordinarily generous support to the almost entire exclusion of everybody else in that trade and to the considerable detriment of hundreds of other exporters in other sectors of business. In my speech I specifically said that the provision of export credit insurance on the sale of beef to Iraq in 1987 and 1988 of an amount greater than the amount actually exported was not only in breach of the terms of the export credit insurance scheme but constituted a substantial abuse amounting to a fraud on the taxpayer, the scale of the abuse and of the potential liability of the state being unprecedented.

The way an adjournment debate was structured at that time was to allow the opposition deputy twenty minutes, with the Government representative having ten minutes to reply. Ray Burke was then at the height of his Rambo phase. A few days previously he had described me as a 'dirt-thrower'; now he continued in a similar abusive vein. He accused me of making 'reckless charges' and of being 'out to get the Goodman Group.' But for all his roaring and shouting he failed to confront the issues I had raised. He was almost apoplectic in his effort to condemn me for making these points, even though he knew them to be true. His behaviour was a dramatic example of the unwillingness of ministers, and of some public servants, to be properly accountable to Dáil Éireann, a factor that ultimately contributed to the necessity for an expensive extra-parliamentary inquiry.

At the end of the adjournment debate I was more convinced than ever that there was a real public interest in pursuing this topic, and that an independent inquiry was necessary.

———

A few weeks after the adjournment debate the Dáil was dissolved. Haughey cut short the life of his minority Government in a dispute over health funding. In calling an early general election he was banking on securing an absolute majority, whereas the outcome actually led to the formation of a Fianna Fáil-PD coalition.

In the discussions on the allocation of ministers Haughey was insistent that the Department of Industry and Commerce would be broken up, with responsibility for industry going to a Fianna Fáil minister. I informed him that this was unacceptable, and after a 24-hour stalemate he backed down. But he was unwilling to agree to my request for an immediate public investigation into the beef industry. 'We'll have to have an inquiry into the beef industry,' I told him. His reply was dismissive. 'You'll find out all you want in the department,' he said. 'There will be no need for an inquiry.' 'We'll see,' I replied. With considerable misgivings, I deferred the issue of an inquiry, and Bobby Molloy and myself took our places at the Government table.

I arrived in the Department of Industry and Commerce to find that the officials had anticipated the appointment of a new minister, and the possibility that that individual would ask questions about the export credit scheme. A draft report was near completion. I got a sense that some officials were relieved that finally a huge problem was going to be addressed. I sought access to all the relevant files, and was given sight of the internal report. The contents confirmed all the claims we had been making from the opposition benches. If anything, as I read the documents it became clear that the situation was more serious than we had envisaged. Irish companies were owed about £60 million from Iraq, and some of these payments were more than twelve months overdue. A large number of claims against the exchequer were likely. The state was potentially facing huge losses, and there was evidence of fraud.

I knew then there had been a major scandal in the period 1987–9. I became increasingly convinced that the truth could be established and made public only through the medium of a sworn inquiry. In particular, it was clear to me that I faced a difficult choice: I could insist on some form of inquiry being established into the conduct of serving ministers, or I could expose the portion of the truth known to me and bring that Government to an end. The problem, as I saw it then and see it now, was that by my leaving the Government without establishing all the facts, those responsible for misconduct in public office would quite probably conceal their responsibility and comprehensively suppress the truth.

The files contained evidence that the previous Government was fully aware of fraudulent activities. A note dated 2 May 1989 between officials in the Department of Industry and Commerce and the Attorney-General's office confirmed that it was clear that shipments of beef to Iraq insured under the export credit scheme included beef processed in Northern Ireland. The discrepancies indicated that approximately 38 per cent of insured beef by volume in 1987 and 1988 had been processed either in Northern Ireland or in Britain. Goodman had been confronted with this evidence, and the response from his company was noted by officials in the files as 'extraordinary.'

The company accepted that over the two previous years it had exported insured beef to Iraq that had not originated in the Republic—some of it coming from Northern Ireland—but total exports by the group of beef processed in the Republic would match the value of those exports insured under the scheme. The department note of this meeting in May 1989 stated: 'The exporter had asked that the Department should, in considering their position on the policy of insurance, consider the overall position and reconcile the overall value of exports insured with the company's overall exports of beef sourced in the Republic.' It was an amazing request, especially as the situation was so clear-cut. From a legal point of view, the insurance policies covered specific shipments, and if the origin of the beef in those shipments did not comply with the terms of the policy, the Government was perfectly entitled, indeed duty-bound, to declare the policies void.

By the summer of 1989 Goodman was owed about £200 million for business in Iraq. It was unlikely that these debts would be paid. The taxpayer was badly exposed from export insurance that should never have been granted, given that beef from outside the country had been included. Having considered the matter thoroughly, I decided to void Goodman's policies in October 1989. The action was the taxpayers' only defence to a claim for a sum between £120 and £200 million.

Our legal advice was that action could not be taken without first hearing Goodman's explanation. He was informed that serious matters had emerged and that I, as minister, was minded to void the insurance policies. A series of meetings took place in August and September 1989. It became clear that Goodman and his representatives had become used to getting their way with the Government, and they did not like what I had to say.

I outlined the advice available to me, and I concluded that as there had been a serious breach of the cover I now considered the policies to be void. There was clearly a serious problem for myself as minister, for the taxpayer and for the company. I wanted Goodman to know the position at that stage before we began the technicalities of voidance. There was also the related matter of bank guarantees, which were unconditional and therefore unaffected by the voidance of the policies. I suggested to Goodman that he start making arrangements with the banks to clear all the guarantees. There was an understanding between the company and the department that Goodman would not make any claims in respect of Iraqi guarantee business, although his representatives had recently revealed potential problems with guarantees about to fall due.

Goodman was antagonistic and at times almost hysterical in his contributions. Most of what he had to say was irrelevant to the problems he faced, although he accepted that total exports from Ireland were less than the amounts insured. I reminded him several times that the gist of the matter was that the policies required that Irish beef be used, and that a declaration to that effect had been supplied by the company. This had obviously not been complied with. He thought my response was extreme, that the issue was a technicality, and asked that I reconsider my position. I found myself having to explain that it was not a matter of reconsidering my decision but dealing with the policy, the law, and the facts—all of which gave rise to this situation.

The meeting was exceptionally tense. I was impatient with the bluster and the refusal to concentrate on the core issue. Goodman explained that he had spent ten years building up business in Iraq, sometimes when it was dangerous to do so, and that it was vital for his company to hold on to the market there. My concern was to protect the Irish taxpayer. If the Iraqis weren't paying Goodman, then the insurance credit scheme left the Irish taxpayer exposed, and potentially paying for the sale of beef that did not originate in Ireland. I pointed out that Iraq was a very large risk when the huge increase in export credit insurance had been approved, and that it remained a risky place in which to do business. We needed to deal with the matter of the bank guarantee also, as Ireland's exposure was out of all proportion to other countries.

At a subsequent meeting Goodman changed his tune and claimed that he had consulted the best legal advisers in Ireland and in Britain. His advice was that non-Irish products could be covered by the insurance scheme, and that limiting the insurance to Irish beef was possibly contrary to the free-trade principles in the Treaty of Rome. He also insisted—as he had done at the previous meeting—that the Department of Agriculture knew of the source of the beef being exported to Iraq, and as a consequence the state had never been misled. It seems that the department knew that a lot of the beef came out of intervention or from abroad and therefore was of no value to the Irish economy. The department had chosen to remain silent about what it knew. Why?

I was left with no choice but to act in early October 1989 to void certain export credit insurance policies in respect of beef exports to Iraq. No liability would be accepted in respect of these policies. Goodman immediately instigated legal action against me in the High Court. I confirmed publicly that if the legal proceedings were continued with I would contest them vigorously. There were to be many twists and turns in this sorry story, but in 2003 Goodman finally dropped his action against me and it was dismissed, fourteen years after he launched it in a blaze of publicity.

Voiding the insurance cover was not, unfortunately, the end of my dealings with Goodman. When Saddam Hussein invaded Kuwait in

1990 Goodman's business, like many others, faced difficulties in getting paid for business already completed. I was on holiday in the west in August 1990 when Haughey contacted me by phone. It was unusual for him to contact me in this way, and I immediately suspected that a crisis was brewing. 'Goodman is about to go under,' Haughey explained. 'He's under pressure from the banks.'

Over the previous six months I had been working on a major piece of company law. It was a huge bill, making its way slowly through the Oireachtas. One chapter proposed the introduction of the concept of 'examinership' into Ireland for the first time. What I was proposing was somewhat similar to chapter 11 of the us Code, whereby court protection would allow a troubled business time to see if it could continue to operate as a going concern. The examinership proposal, in one of the early chapters of the legislation, had already got to the committee stage before the summer recess; but Haughey wanted to take the chapter out of the legislation and bring it before the Dáil as a separate bill. As he spoke over the phone about the 'emergency' situation with Goodman companies, I realised he wanted to do this fairly fast.

'When are you proposing to do this?' I asked. 'The day after tomorrow,' he replied.

I was flabbergasted. I had serious concerns about what was being suggested, and also about the time scale. But Haughey was adamant. The Secretary of the Department of the Taoiseach, Pádraig Ó hUiginn, was already working on the task of extracting the examinership legislation. 'It's not a huge undertaking. A bit of drafting,' Haughey remarked.

I had continuing concerns about the direct contact between Haughey and Goodman. It was evident that a lot of background conversations had already taken place before Haughey contacted me. He repeatedly said that thousands of jobs were at risk if we didn't pass the examinership legislation.

The Oireachtas had in the past been recalled for emergency sessions during the recess but always on account of security matters. This was an extraordinary response to the difficulties of a private company. I reluctantly returned to Dublin. The intervention was going to happen, so it was better to keep control of the legislation and monitor the type of amendments accepted.

In my opening speech I set out the financial situation as provided by Goodman's representatives, IBI Corporate Finance.

> As at 17th August, 1990, Goodman International and its subsidiaries (other than Food Industries PLC) owed banks approximately £460 million, which had been available on an unsecured short-term basis. In addition, banks had guaranteed obligations in respect of the performance of Goodman International and its subsidiaries (other than Food Industries PLC) under beef supply contracts in an amount of approximately £200 million. Goodman International and its subsidiaries (other than Food Industries PLC) are owed £180 million by Iraqi entities. This figure includes £11 million of interest due.

An Oireachtas committee had already discussed the substance of the examinership measures in some considerable detail, so the emergency legislation passed in two days. As I explained to the Dáil, the consequences of the process being introduced meant that

> once the examiner is in place he will carry out an initial assessment of the company's affairs, and if he considers from this initial assessment that the company, or part of it, can be saved he will proceed to draw up a rescue plan.

As we voted on the final stage of the bill, Haughey said to me, 'Thanks for breaking away from your holidays.' Goodman immediately moved to place his business into examinership by applying to the High Court.

But the detail that subsequently emerged in court left me even more curious about why Haughey had been so keen to protect Goodman. The number of jobs involved was far less than I had been told. Most of the businesses given protection in the examinership process had nothing to do with the beef industry; about forty of them were property companies. The first I knew of that was when I saw the list in the court proceedings. With the benefit of hindsight, I am inclined to think that the reason Haughey was so frantic to get the bill passed was that he may well have had a personal interest in some of those property companies.

It had been very difficult at first to get the media interested in the beef story, but during this period a few journalists had begun to take an interest in Goodman and his business practices. The problem with export credit was not the only wrongdoing in the beef industry. One reporter, Susan O'Keeffe, made sense of the different strands of the Goodman story, and she brought them together to powerful effect in a Granada 'World in Action' television programme in May 1991.

By way of contrast, RTE came out very badly from the Goodman affair. In February 1989 RTE Radio's agricultural news reported that an Irish meat company was being investigated for fraud, arising from the misrepresentation of the age and quality of beef being sold to Iraq. No company was named, yet the next day RTE issued a long apology, following threats of legal action by Anglo-Irish Beef Processors. The retraction was devastating for the two journalists involved, Joe Murray and Pádraig Mannion, in that it said their original report was 'completely false and without any basis in fact,' and that 'no irregularity of any kind . . . was carried out by the company in question.' The two men were later found guilty of 'unprofessional conduct' by RTE.

What they reported was perfectly true. I knew Murray for many years; we had both lodged at University Hall while students at UCD. He was left with a cloud hanging over him for the rest of his career. He died in May 2011; a year later RTE issued an apology for the wrong done to him. Mannion left Ireland because of what was done to him by RTE.

The national broadcaster was not interested in investigating Goodman. But a British television station, Granada, took a closer interest. Its 'World in Action' programme drew together a host of different strands in the beef industry scandal. The powerful impact of television images and Susan O'Keeffe's dogged pursuit of the story pushed the controversy to a new point. Viewers were told about the tax fraud, the falsification of documents to get EU subsidies, the use of bogus stamps, the falsification of weights, and the switching of meat sent into intervention with an inferior product. There was new evidence about malpractice with export credit insurance. The programme also revealed the close connections between Goodman and Fianna Fáil. But the real significance of 'World in Action' was that for the first time Goodman employees, and in particular a former accountant, gave details of how various alleged frauds and malpractices were carried out.

In the immediate aftermath of the programme in May 1991 Haughey continued to resist an investigation. He was dismissive of opposition deputies who raised the programme's revelations in the Dáil while in private he continued to dig in his heels about setting up a tribunal. But the beef controversy had finally crystallised in circumstances that allowed the Progressive Democrats to insist on an inquiry, and we did. We were not certain, of course, whether our stance would result in an inquiry or in a general election, and that was a risk we had to take. But we were certain that without such an inquiry the truth would have been comprehensively suppressed again and grave damage done to the principle of democratic accountability.

The Government—or, in reality, the Fianna Fáil side of the Government—put a motion before the Dáil on 15 May 1991 reaffirming its confidence in the regulatory and control procedures for the meat industry. The opening Government speaker, Michael O'Kennedy, Minister for Agriculture, defended Goodman and sought to discredit 'World in Action'. He described the programme as anti-Irish and 'cheap, lurid journalism calculated to achieve a sensationalist impact.' But while he was on his feet in the Dáil, Haughey was finally coming to accept the seriousness of the PDS' intentions about an independent inquiry. With the possibility left open that we would not back the Government motion, Haughey sent word to O'Kennedy to confirm his acceptance of a judicial public inquiry. It was a remarkable U-turn, which O'Kennedy confirmed in the final sentence of his contribution by contradicting everything he had said up to then.

A week later a tribunal of inquiry was constituted to inquire into matters described in the resolution as being 'of urgent public importance.' In the Dáil debate establishing the tribunal on 24 May 1991 I warmly welcomed the decision.

> There has been a shadow over the beef-processing industry in this country for some time, arising from a range of allegations which have been made regarding abuses under EC beef support schemes, controversy over credit insurance for beef exports, the apparent dominance of the industry by one group of companies, and the financial collapse of that group last year. Each of these matters has been the subject of concern and discussion in this house and elsewhere. Very serious questions have been raised about the activities of some of the companies involved and the performance of various public authorities in dealing with those activities and companies.

The establishment of a judicial inquiry to investigate very serious allegations of illegal activities, fraud and malpractice in some branches of the beef-processing industry was a watershed in the way that allegations of wrongdoing in business were dealt with by the Government and by the Oireachtas. The decision was about accountability. It was about the way in which Ireland was governed. The minority Fianna Fáil Government that held office between 1987 and 1989 made decisions that at best were reckless, irresponsible and foolish and at worst were illegal.

Haughey and Reynolds were party to all those decisions, from the illegal usurpation of the functions of the IDA to the grossly irresponsible decisions made in respect of export credit insurance. I wished Mr Justice Liam Hamilton, President of the High Court, success in his task as chairman of the tribunal of inquiry.

The tribunal sat for 231 days, from 7 November 1991 to 15 July 1993, and heard evidence from 475 witnesses. Hamilton's report was finally submitted on 29 July 1994 and controversially published a number of days later. But even before then the tribunal had been mired in controversy and contributed to the collapse of the Fianna Fáil-Progressive Democrat coalition. Having become Taoiseach in early 1992, Reynolds was never committed to making his own Government work. From the outset he was intent on ending the coalition.

I gave my evidence in July 1992. It was an opportunity to describe the information in my possession. When asked about the decisions taken by the minority Fianna Fáil Government between 1987 and 1989, and specifically about Reynolds's handling of export credit insurance, I answered accurately in describing the decisions as 'grossly unwise, reckless and foolish.' To have softened my words for political reasons related to the PDs' membership of a coalition with Fianna Fáil would have been wrong.

I do not think any witness was attacked for longer or more vehemently by the state and by two sets of counsel for one organisation. The Attorney-General, Harry Whelehan, saw his role at the tribunal as defending part of the state's interest rather than the public interest. As Fintan O'Toole in his book on the Beef Tribunal observed, 'for the most part, however, the Attorney-General did not even represent the government of the day, made up of Fianna Fáil and the Progressive Democrats, but only the Fianna Fáil part of it.'

My evidence lasted six days, five of which were sustained hostile cross-examination by Dermot Gleeson for Goodman and by counsel for the state, who was openly collaborating with Gleeson.

I exchanged a series of letters with the Attorney-General concerning my cross-examination. I had specific concerns about how counsel for the state had interpreted and calculated figures relating to the potential loss from export credit decisions. That exercise was rather simplistic and was, I believed, undertaken to undermine me and my officials, and was critical of my integrity and competence as a minister. In one of the letters, I wrote:

> You may or may not know, by the way, that no attempt was made by the state's legal team to confirm with officials of my Department the accuracy or otherwise of the proposition put by Mr Hickey [Henry Hickey SC, counsel for the state]. The relevant officials have

been present in Dublin on a full-time basis since the beginning of March last to assist in briefing the legal team.

Whelehan didn't accept any of my points. The facts did not suit him.

The Attorney-General obtained a Supreme Court ruling that it was unconstitutional for the tribunal to ask ministerial witnesses about discussions that had taken place at the Government table. This decision precluded adequate questioning of Fianna Fáil ministers who had served in Haughey's minority Government. In his report, the tribunal chairman admitted that the ruling meant he was 'precluded from inquiring into and reporting on the factors which influenced the government' in reaching decisions about the beef industry.

Having come through this period, I remain strongly of the belief that the Attorney-General, as the Government's legal adviser, should not favour one side over another in a coalition arrangement. Relations, already poor, deteriorated further after I gave my evidence. The level of antagonism directed at Bobby Molloy and myself increased. I felt the Government was over.

I discussed the situation with several senior colleagues. The summer break allowed for a pause, as there were no Government meetings in August. But by the time Reynolds gave his evidence in October it was clear that the Government would not last.

In my evidence, and in the statement I submitted beforehand at the tribunal's request, I sought to quantify the amount of Goodman's claim. I was cross-examined about this by counsel for the state on grounds that were wholly unsound and betrayed a radical misunder-standing on the part of those instructing state counsel of the Goodman statement of claim and associated documents. This dispute, however, did not seem to be of any great significance, as all concerned knew that the potential liability of the state was, to use the report's term, 'very substantial'.

Reynolds, however, when he came to give his evidence, of his own volition and without being asked any question about it, stated that my evidence on this point had been not merely false but knowingly false. When he was pressed by my counsel it was found that he was not suggesting that my figure was wrongly or carelessly computed, or that a mere mistake had been made, but that I had told a deliberate lie. It should be borne in mind that all evidence before the tribunal was given on oath.

This scandalous allegation was, of course, fully exploded by the tribunal's report. The chairman pointed to a degree of ambiguity in the statement of claim and found firmly that the cumulative amount of the claims mentioned in that document is capable of totalling £159 million, exclusive of general damages.

It should be added, in fairness to Reynolds, that it became clear in cross-examination that he had no personal understanding of the statement of claim or of the manner in which the potential liability could be computed. It appeared that he made his gratuitous allegation of perjury against me on the strength of a spin-doctor's notion that he himself could not understand, or did not take the trouble to under-stand. I have no doubt that this was done quite simply for the purpose of setting up a public-relations smokescreen to divert attention from the significance of the tribunal's proceedings, even though he knew it would have profound consequences. It was done cold-bloodedly and without even an understanding of the way in which its truth, or otherwise, could be worked out. This allegation of perjury—for that is what it was—was being made against a minister in his own Government and the leader of the other party in that Government. His behaviour was reckless, and was the proximate cause of the collapse of the Fianna Fáil-Progressive Democrat coalition.

———

When the tribunal's report was finally published, in August 1994, what emerged was a sorry tale of gross incompetence in public office, of secrecy and deception, including deception of Dáil Éireann, of tax evasion professionally organised on a gigantic scale, of simple theft, of scandalous misuse of EU schemes of great importance to Ireland, of inability to recover taxes of which the exchequer was cheated by reason of an amnesty sponsored by Fianna Fáil, and of conspiracy by privileged and well-placed persons.

Having read the report, I was of the view that in any other western democracy a head of government so resoundingly convicted of incapacity would have had the grace to resign. But a complex and detailed report was misrepresented and distorted by Reynolds and his advisers. His response to some of the damning findings was once more to construct a smokescreen. In a briefing circulated by his press secretary on the night the report was officially published, 2 August 1994, it was asserted that 'the Chairman found that all decisions were made in the national interest.' The tribunal found no such thing. It was something of a calculated untruth. What the tribunal concluded was that Reynolds had acted according to his own subjective view of the national interest—radically different from what the national interest actually required.

The 'national interest' would also appear to require that before exposing the state to a potential liability of well over £100 million a more detailed investigation or analysis of the benefits to the economy of such decisions—which involved allocating a large percentage of export credit insurance available for all exports around the world to one particular destination, at such risk to the exchequer if default in payment were made—should have been carried out.

Such an investigation, if made, would in all probability have disclosed that a large portion of the beef to be exported was intended to be obtained outside the jurisdiction, and that an even larger proportion had been or was intended to be purchased from intervention stock, and therefore that the benefits to the Irish economy arising from such exports 'were illusory rather than real.' That was the finding of the tribunal. One would never have thought this when listening to Reynolds's response to the report.

This finding not merely supported the first portion of my allegations but constituted an utterly damning indictment of Reynolds in his activities as Minister for Industry and Commerce. In its plain terms, the content of the tribunal report made nonsense of Reynolds's claim to have been vindicated on the grounds that he acted in the national interest, for it found that he did not take the simple and obvious step of investigating the source of the beef to be covered.

The report justified dramatically my statement to the tribunal that Reynolds's conduct on the export credit insurance scheme—for which he had ministerial responsibility—was 'reckless, irresponsible and unwise.' In respect of the first enormous grant of cover in September 1987 the report concluded that Reynolds was aware of the application before his department received it. The tribunal found no satisfactory evidence to establish the circumstances in which he was informed of the application before it was received in the department, or of the necessity to have it dealt with at such speed, or why it was necessary to have the matter decided with such a degree of urgency that the Department of Finance and the Department of Agriculture and Food did not have an opportunity to express their observations on the matter in the memorandum for the Government.

Neither Reynolds nor Haughey, who dealt with the matter in the Government, nor Goodman or his senior executives had any recollection of who informed Reynolds that the application would be made. The tribunal quoted the observation of the Department of Finance on this proposal in a damning sentence: 'In essence the Minister for Industry and Commerce's proposals are too much of a gamble with the Exchequer's resources.' These observations were not included in the Government memorandum—allegedly because of time constraints.

In the light of the evidence given to the tribunal it was hard to see how Reynolds was able to conclude that all decisions were taken in strict adherence to the guidelines of the export credit scheme. The tribunal noted that the Minister for Industry and Commerce was legally entitled to decide on the availability of export credit insurance for any particular destination, and on its allocation; but making this decision required a detailed investigation or analysis of the benefits to the economy of the minister's decisions of a type that Reynolds wholly failed to carry out or have carried out. Such an investigation would have revealed the true position about the composition of the exports, and that the allocations made for the exports in question 'would not justify the risk involved in granting Export Credit Insurance in the amounts granted.'

To this damning indictment Reynolds had only one answer: that he did not know the true position. The inquiry found that he should have known. To this extent the report salvaged Reynolds's integrity, at the expense of his capacity and his competence. At best it can be claimed that the tribunal found that he had acted in accordance with his personal, mistaken view of the national interest; but by any objective yardstick the tribunal's findings clearly showed that his decisions were wrong, were taken against the evidence and the expert advice available to him, and created the potential for a major financial catastrophe for this state.

I never believed that it was credible for Reynolds and his apologists to claim that they were not informed that intervention beef was being used. The evidence in the tribunal's report brought a number of important facts to light. For example, on 2 July 1987 (which was very early indeed in the whole saga and apparently before any new export credit insurance policies were issued), Anglo-Irish Beef Processors International Ltd submitted a memorandum to the Department of Finance seeking an amendment of section 84A of the Corporation Profits Tax Act (1976) to facilitate more advantageous section 84 borrowing by them. The memorandum set out why it wanted the amendment made. This relatively short memorandum refers no less than three times to the fact that they were exporting beef purchased from intervention stock, and that this was why they needed the amendment. Having considered this memorandum, the tribunal concluded that, 'as it was the practice of Anglo-Irish to purchase beef from intervention for the purpose of export, the amendment was sought.'

Other ministers were made aware that intervention beef was being used in export contracts that were the subject of insurance. The Minister of State at the Department of Agriculture and Food, Joe Walsh, received a draft letter from Goodman on 28 July 1987. He forwarded the letter to the Department of the Taoiseach, seeking the same amendment to section 84 as that referred to in the memorandum to the Department of Finance on 2 July.

He received another letter, dated 16 November 1987, from Goodman International referring to the same amendment and stating that the suggested wording was submitted through Walsh to the Department of the Taoiseach on 28 July. This single episode alone is evidence that Haughey, and several ministers, including MacSharry, Reynolds and Walsh, as well as senior officials in their respective departments, were all informed of the fact that intervention beef was being used by the Goodman Group for export. They were told this on numerous occasions between 2 July 1987 and 21 March 1989.

Reynolds and his recent apologists made great play of the fact that he was not aware that foreign beef or intervention beef was being used to a large extent in export contracts to Iraq. They stated explicitly that if Reynolds had known this fact he would not have given cover for the extensive amounts that he did. It seemed to be conceded that knowingly covering foreign or intervention beef would be extremely negligent and reckless, because a huge risk to the taxpayer would be involved, and there would be no benefit to the Irish economy. However, the tribunal evidence showed that Reynolds was personally informed that intervention beef was being used in the export contracts to Iraq, and that it was covered by export credit insurance.

From a series of confidential telexes in December 1987 between the private secretary to the Minister for Industry and Commerce and the Irish Ambassador in Baghdad there can be no doubt that Reynolds was personally informed of the true position regarding exports to Iraq of intervention beef and what was and was not covered by insurance at that time. Interestingly, a telex seeking urgent information was sent by Reynolds's office to the ambassador on 11 December 1987. The previous evening a social function reported as 'lavish' was held in the Burlington Hotel in Dublin, described in the newspapers as 'the Boss's Ball'. I understood this to mean a Cairde Fáil dinner for Haughey as the president of Fianna Fáil. The *Irish Independent* on Saturday 12 December 1987 reported: 'A vision in sequinned aquamarine, Albert and Kathleen cut quite a dash on the dance floor. And they had Ireland's most important "Baron" as their guest. Larry Goodman, beef baron extraordinaire even ventured onto the floor for a couple of twirls.' No doubt in between the twirls Goodman had ample opportunity to tell Reynolds his requirements. After the ball was over, Reynolds was on the ball next morning and sent yet another telex.

What this episode shows is that Reynolds had been personally informed in December 1987 that Irish companies were supplying intervention beef to Iraq, and that they had the benefit of export credit insurance. Over the following eleven months he issued further very substantial cover for similar beef exports to Iraq.

In my Dáil speech on the tribunal report on 1 September 1994 I asked, as Reynolds had information about the use of intervention beef from December 1987, what benefits there were to the Irish economy in giving extensive insurance on very favourable terms to an exporter who at the relevant time was found to have used foreign beef for 38 per cent of his exports and intervention beef for 84 per cent of the remainder, giving a total between foreign and intervention beef of about 94 per cent of the shipments. What Reynolds never explained was how giving insurance cover to beef, nearly all of which came out of either a foreign country or intervention, was of any value to the Irish economy.

Critics of the tribunal report pointed to omissions in its scope and judgement. In one important respect the report was a huge disappointment: it contained relatively few findings and even fewer recommendations. As Pat Rabbitte noted in the Dáil debate on the report, the chapter on export credit insurance showed beyond any doubt that Reynolds was guilty of breathtaking political misbehaviour, but there was no explicit finding to this effect in the report. The evidence presented to the tribunal was far more important than the report.

I was disappointed that the chairman did not explore the nature of the relationships between Haughey and Goodman and between Reynolds and Goodman. There were several unusual assertions, not least the view that there was no evidence that either Haughey or Reynolds in the 1987–9 period were 'personally close' to Goodman, or that Goodman 'had any political associations with either of them or the party that they represented.' The words 'at the time' may be significant, as there was evidence that Goodman was a guest at Reynolds's daughter's wedding in December 1990; there was also the Cairde Fáil dinner in December 1987. Interestingly, Reynolds swore on four occasions that Goodman was 'never, ever a guest of mine at a Cairde Fáil dinner.' There were also political donations. The public were left to draw their own conclusions.

The straightforward choice confronting the tribunal was to condemn Reynolds for corruption or for incompetence. Because it chose the latter verdict, he claimed vindication.

Reynolds, Haughey and presumably some other members of that minority Government made decisions that were arbitrary, reckless and sometimes unlawful. That much was found against them. Reynolds played a central role in one of the worst episodes of misgovernment this country has witnessed. When asked at the tribunal if he had read the particular departmental memorandum, Reynolds asked how many pages were in it. On being told that it consisted of twenty-one pages of reasoned and detailed advice, he said in a famous phrase that he would not have read such a document, because he was 'a one-page man'. This is surely the nadir of ministerial stewardship.

———

So, who was responsible for this whole affair? Whereas Mr Justice Hamilton did not make sufficient findings, in my view, in his report, it was the responsibility of members of the Oireachtas, who established the tribunal, to draw inferences and make judgements on the facts in the evidence and in the report, and to render accountable those whose conduct called them to account. The job of politicians was to vindicate the principles of democratic accountability, which the report of the Beef Tribunal showed was systematically trampled on by those who abused their position of trust. If there was any real accountability in Irish public life, the people who engaged in such misconduct in public office would have resigned or would have been removed.

The journalist who played a major part in revealing the abuses was prosecuted for contempt; the conspirators, the beneficiaries, were largely untouched. When the report was published, Haughey had retired from public life, while Reynolds largely escaped censure, although it was one of the elements that fractured his coalition Government with the Labour Party, which collapsed a few months later. Goodman ultimately survived the scandal: he regained control of his business after the examinership process and went on to appear in the 'rich lists' produced by various newspapers.

Two decades later, however, in late 2012 the controversy over horse meat being passed off as beef brought back to public attention a whole host of practices central to the earlier controversy. Once more Goodman and his companies were centrally involved; and once more those who benefited from malpractice walked free. Some small fry were forced to carry the can; the beneficiaries were untouched. That is the Department of Agriculture's way.

Legal proceedings initiated against the state in 1989 following my decision as Minister for Industry and Commerce to cancel export credit insurance on beef sales to Iraq were withdrawn by Goodman in 2003. The company had claimed approximately €100 million, in addition to costs and damages, arising from my decision to void policies where non-Irish beef had been included. I was very satisfied with the outcome, even if it was fourteen years late. Such is the way the rich can use the law and the legal system to their advantage. Justice does not enter the equation.

Chapter 11 ᕬ

'DELIGHTED TO MAKE MY EXIT'

Once the 1992 general election was over and a new Government had been formed, my thoughts turned to my own future. The prospect of retirement from party leadership was looming. I had been in the Dáil since 1968 and had been PD leader since December 1985. The period in office from 1989 to 1992 had been highly pressurised, with the scandals engulfing Haughey and later dealing with the behaviour of Reynolds. At that time the support structure for ministers, and for someone like myself who was also party leader, was not great. There was a considerable volume of work.

This was in complete contrast to the situation that developed when the Labour Party formed a coalition Government with Fianna Fáil after the 1992 election. Dick Spring had a plethora of advisers, and he even had a formal support structure—the Office of An Tánaiste—in Government Buildings.

I watched now from the opposition benches as the Beef Tribunal continued to make slow progress. From what was revealed in Dublin Castle—and much of this was known beforehand—there was no doubt that the activities of certain private enterprises were heavily underwritten by public funds. The process of exposure was slow, but over time some, though not all, of these dubious practices and relationships became public.

In the end it took Mr Justice Hamilton three years to deliver his report, and the outcome was very unsatisfactory. The conclusions were vague and often inconclusive; sometimes there were no conclusions at all. Remarkably, given the evidence uncovered, the whole area of contributions to parties and to individuals was not explored. Even though the gross favouritism shown to Goodman was manifest from the evidence, Hamilton avoided that sensitive matter. A few weeks after his report appeared he was appointed Chief Justice by the Government headed by Reynolds.

I have no doubt that during this period I was targeted for my work in exposing wrongdoing in the beef industry. There was a drip-feed of stories throughout 1993 that had the single objective of damaging my reputation. The media were used by some people intent on settling scores. The situation was made worse when newspapers got their hands on PD files that had been dumped in a skip outside the party's head office.

Despite these sideshows, being back in opposition was a relief in many respects after the intensity of government from 1989 to 1992. But even as my batteries were being recharged I was still leaning towards retiring from leading the party. By the summer of 1993 I finally made up my mind about my future in politics. It was time to step back. There was no pressure—internal or external, political or personal—forcing me to go; but by choosing the timing of my retirement as leader I knew I would leave on my own terms. Neither did I want to be prevailed upon to stay. I wasn't sure what I would do next, but I was very clear in my own mind by June 1993. It was also important for the PDs to have an identity beyond me as its first leader.

My resignation as leader was announced on 5 October 1993. I had a preference for Mary Harney to succeed me; I told her I would support her for the leadership, and I was glad when she won. She defeated Pat Cox in a vote of the parliamentary party. Much was later made of the fact that Cox was in Helsinki when my resignation was announced, but there was no attempt to give an advantage to anyone. The day before I went public with the news I confided in Stephen O'Byrnes and some of our members in Limerick East.

More problematic for the party was the fact that only a small group of people had a vote in the leadership contest: our ten deputies. It might have been better in the long run if the party's rules had allowed for a wider electorate. This would have saved some of the rancour, although I have no doubt that the outcome would have been the same, irrespective of what party constituency voted for my successor.

As it was, Harney won by eight votes to two. Cox unfortunately couldn't accept the result: the leadership had apparently been all or nothing for him. He had previously given a public undertaking not to contest the next European Parliament election, to concentrate on national politics from the Dáil seat he had won in Cork. Party policy did not allow a dual mandate. He had repeated this commitment to Harney when she became leader.

In Cox's absence I agreed, very reluctantly, to stand as the PD candidate in the Munster EU constituency in the 1994 elections. Agreeing to contest was a mistake, and that was irrespective of the result. I really was not hugely interested, and I didn't relish the prospect of travelling constantly to attend meetings in Brussels and Strasbourg. I was happier to remain in Leinster House for my final years in politics; but Mary Harney pressed me to stand, and it was important for her as a new leader, and for the party, that the Munster seat won in 1989 by Cox should be retained.

As it turned out, I wouldn't have to worry about Europe: Cox decided to change his mind and to leave national politics, and in early May 1994 he announced his intention of contesting the Munster constituency as an independent candidate. It was extraordinary that a man who only a few months previously had been a candidate for the PD leadership should now turn his back on the party and on his long-time colleagues. It was not a very pleasant time, and I found myself not just fighting an election for a job that I was not keen to do but, after Cox's bombshell, fighting in the most difficult circumstances.

Cox's decision was all the more bizarre in that he had actually spoken in my favour at the PD selection convention in early March 1994, and now, less than eight weeks later, he was walking away from the party he helped found to run as an independent. He was ambitious for himself, and in that narrow sense he made the correct decision, as he went on to become President of the European Parliament. But I still feel it was a pity that he didn't remain in the Dáil, where I think his talents would have led to more lasting benefits for the country.

The fall-out from the leadership election was very hard on Harney. In addition to Cox's behaviour the PDS also lost Martin Cullen, who, in an act of blatant opportunism, left the party to join Fianna Fáil to advance his own career. It was terribly unfair to the party, and to Harney. She had had the worst possible start.

When I stood down as party leader my plan was to leave politics at the following general election and, with the European Parliament no longer on my agenda, that remained my plan. As it turned out, I didn't get out of Leinster House until 2002. Within the party I was under huge pressure to contest the 1997 general election. Harney prevailed on me to run. There was a sense of loyalty to Harney and to the PDS in my contesting again for the Dáil.

When Harney and I spoke about running it was in the context of the Dáil lasting for three years or so. Neither of us envisaged that the Dáil elected in 1997 would last for almost every day of its five-year term. By the time the 2002 general election was called I was relieved to finally make my exit. I had in many ways stayed too long, although I enjoyed chairing the Oireachtas Joint Committee on Foreign Affairs in my final term as a Dáil deputy. Irish foreign policy was under-developed. We assured ourselves that anything of a military or security nature had nothing to do with us. We saw our EU membership as a cash cow. We regarded the squeezing out of Europe of an extra penny or two on a gallon of milk or a few pence in the intervention price of beef as a triumph of our foreign policy. In short, we wanted all the benefits of club membership without having to pay more than a nominal subscription to the club, financially or otherwise.

But the world was changing. The collapse of the Soviet Union and the communist regimes in central and eastern Europe required a European response. The European Union required a common foreign and security policy. Greater maturity was required in Ireland. The situation in the former Yugoslavia proved this argument. The innocent in Bosnia were left abandoned and betrayed by the West while tyranny, genocide and ethnic cleansing proceeded. The foreign policy of a meaningful international bloc like the EU is of limited value if in the last resort—as Kosovo demonstrated—it is unable in appropriate cases to apply meaningful sanctions. Even the most skilful diplomacy will occasionally come up against brick walls. At one meeting of the Committee on Foreign Affairs the Secretary-General of the Department of Foreign Affairs reminded us of Bismarck's dictum: 'Diplomacy without arms is like music without instruments.'

Like Hitler and other tyrants before him, Milošević was stopped in the last resort only by force. In such cases force becomes an integral part of foreign policy. Ireland has had a proud tradition of blue-bereted, lightly armed international peacekeeping involvement; but the former Yugoslavia undoubtedly confirmed the realities of contemporary international relations that Ireland had to face up to. An isolationist reluctance to be involved in the less palatable aspects of international diplomacy was, I concluded, a thing of the past. Seeking the emotional and political protection of the United States in a crisis is no longer good enough. The UN is a worthy body, but it is hamstrung by its own virtually unamendable charter. Why should the protection of the oppressed be dependent on the unanimous agreement of the five permanent members of the Security Council? The Chinese treatment of the Tibetans makes me reluctant to rely on the UN as the essential vindicator of human rights on the planet.

We are clearly instinctively a pro-Western democracy. But our feelings are leavened by a curious combination of Anglophobia and antagonism to aspects of the foreign policy of the United States. The love-hate relationship between Ireland and the United States is a wonder to behold. At times we clasp them to our bosom as if we were the 51st state; one of the inescapable duties of the Taoiseach is to turn up at the White House on St Patrick's Day with a crystal bowl of shamrock and a green tie. But when it comes to American foreign policy we baulk. When NATO, which is an integral part of US foreign policy, is mentioned, many in Ireland recoil and do not want to know. When Bill Clinton, during his two-term presidency, was making a major contribution to the Irish peace process there were many here going on with the usual claptrap about NATO aggression and American imperialism.

When NATO began its operations against Milošević in March 1999 we had an awkward response from the Fianna Fáil-PD Government.

David Andrews, who was Minister for Foreign Affairs, said that Ireland was 'between a rock and a hard place.' There was the predictable response from the usual left-wing bleaters in the Dáil and beyond. The Government was left floundering. I believed that the NATO action against Milošević was inevitable and obviously justified.

The discomfort for some in Ireland was I think heightened by the prominent part played by Britain in the attacks on Milošević and in the liberation of Kosovo. While Anglophobia was a declining phenomenon—and dealt a further blow by the visit to Ireland of Queen Elizabeth II in 2011—it was by no means dead in 1999. A residual suspicion of Britain carried over into opposition to NATO. I tired of hearing the constant mantra of Ireland's 'traditional neutrality' without any acceptance of the realities of the world in which we live. I found it increasingly difficult to ascertain who we were supposed to be neutral between. In Ireland, being neutral seems to mean being anti-American.

With the possible exception of occasional references to the possibility of threats to our 'traditional neutrality', debate on Europe concentrated almost solely on economic matters. These issues are obviously important, but the Irish preoccupation with them has meant that little attention has been paid to wider questions about the general direction in which Europe is developing. In the discussion over several EU treaties we had somewhat unbalanced debates in which all sorts of wild claims and allegations were made. In some quarters there was an attempt to create an atmosphere approaching hysteria. But in each case the treaty was ultimately ratified, and no more was heard until the next treaty came along. The dark forebodings were proved to be groundless.

The Europe we joined in 1973 made worthwhile strides in economic co-operation. Political co-operation in matters internal to the European Union improved greatly. Where we continued to fall down was in the development of a common foreign and security policy. The great weakness is our collective inability to cope on an agreed basis with serious external insecurity. This was the case with the conflict in the Balkans. As Europeans we were rescued from our common paralysis both in Bosnia and Kosovo by the United States. I find it hard to tolerate, either as a European or as an Irish citizen, that we render ourselves impotent where foreign and security policy arises. Irish people are essentially internationalists. By baulking at meaningful co-operation with others we removed ourselves from involvement, from time to time, in dealing with tyrants. Normal considerations of trade and diplomatic friendship must be set aside against the scale of human rights abuses in our time in such countries as Palestine, Bosnia, Rwanda, Tibet, Burma, East Timor and Syria. We need to speak the full truth about human rights abuses and act on that truth.

———

When I left the Dáil in 2002 I agreed to chair Irish Aid's Advisory Committee, which continued my involvement in many areas that had been the remit of the Committee on Foreign Affairs. Then, almost a year after my retirement from the Dáil, I was appointed as Ireland's representative to the European Bank for Reconstruction and Development in April 2003. The EBRD had been established in 1991 and, arising out of one of the infamous deals that Margaret Thatcher extracted from her European counterparts, London was chosen as its headquarters. As all our children were by now grown up, there was nothing keeping Pat and me in Ireland, and we moved full-time to London.

The experience was fascinating. We lived in an apartment at Finsbury Square, near the financial district. I was able to walk to work every day. It was a good quality of life.

The position of director was for a three-year term. I was at first somewhat uncertain before I arrived in London, because I had no banking experience. But the EBRD is not like a normal bank: its task is to fund projects in post-Soviet states in central and eastern Europe and in parts of central Asia. The beneficiary countries include the likes of Poland, Belarus, Azerbaijan, Kyrgyzstan and Uzbekistan. The theory was that they would require help in building properly functioning market economies. Indeed it was the specific remit of the bank to assist the transition to democracy and market economies.

The ambition looks rather naïve now, with the benefit of hindsight, for few of the non-European countries are any kind of an advertisement for the goals originally stated. In fairness, I have to say that they were generous goals, even if the subsequent experience has proved disappointing.

The role of director involved assessing investment projects proposed by the EBRD's staff. The bank provided financing for infrastructure and other projects that assisted in private-sector development. Investments ranged in value from €5 million to €250 million. I travelled quite a bit to countries in the Balkans and in the Baltic region. I saw the job of director as asking questions of the executive staff. Some of them didn't like being queried, but I was thanked for my role when my term came to an end.

In theory, the Irish-nominated director of the EBRD reports to the Department of Finance. But I was mostly left to make decisions in accordance with my own judgement. A lot of the issues have nothing to do with Ireland, which is not a major contributor because of each member-state's contribution level having been set in 1991. Directors from other countries were not so fortunate: they would frequently get calls from their home governments with instructions on what to do about certain projects.

As an international institution backed by such countries as the United States, Germany, France and Britain, the EBRD had a very positive reputation, and people were obviously keen to be supported by it. One Russian oligarch applied for investment support for a project worth several hundred million euros. I reviewed the paperwork and, having done a little research, saw that this man's net personal worth, accumulated in the period after the collapse of the Soviet Union, was actually far greater than the EBRD's assets. 'We shouldn't really be lending this guy money,' I said to my colleagues: 'he's only using us to buy a good reputation for himself.' I could see he wanted to have EBRD on his company's CV. My colleagues knew I was right, but many of them couldn't say so. Their countries couldn't afford to fall out with Russia, where this oligarch was very well connected. He didn't get funding in my time, although I think he did get something later.

One of the biggest projects under discussion in my time with the EBRD was a 1,750-kilometre pipeline to take crude oil from the Caspian Sea to the Mediterranean. Investment in the Baku–Tbilisi–Ceyhan (BTC) pipeline was put at $3.6 billion. The oil was in the Azeri section of the Caspian Sea. We also invested in oil extraction facilities at Sakhalin Island, a large Pacific island in eastern Russia. This was the only known breeding-ground for the western grey whale, and for a time the EBRD directors, including myself, became experts on this animal as pressure was placed on Shell and other exploration companies to ensure its preservation.

I quickly discovered that bankers loved property; they saw it was an easy way to make money. The returns were good. But I expressed concern at proposals to invest in luxury houses of 7,000 square feet in Russia. There was a stalemate on the issue.

The most frequent references to Ireland during my term were when officials and ministers from countries in central and eastern Europe would approach me about Ryanair. There was huge interest in getting Ryanair to fly into their countries, and they all wanted to know if I could put them in touch with Michael O'Leary. Against this background it was therefore personally gratifying when I was in London at the EBRD, remembering the battles of the 1980s, to hear the enthusiastic response to the Ryanair success from right across Europe.

———

When my term as a director at the EBRD ended in 2006 Pat and I returned to live in Ireland. By that point the Progressive Democrats had been in government for nine unbroken years. The party had made a tremendous contribution to the economic development of the country after 1997. But there were new pressures within the Government, and also within the party. There was a view in the PDS that Harney should move out of the Enterprise and Employment brief. I understood the argument that it was important to show that the PDS were about more than just the economy; but I was strongly against Harney moving to the Department of Health. I thought Transport would have been a more appropriate department.

When she volunteered for Health, Bertie Ahern must have been delighted. There were very few takers for the job. The department was in a terrible mess. The health service is all about spending money. It was the same in the Department of Justice, where Michael McDowell was confronted with finding money for immigration, gardaí, prison officers and so on. With the two PD ministers in high-spending departments, the party's core message was diluted.

At that point the PDs had been in government for almost a continuous decade. It was probably time to reinvent the party and its message, but that was impossible while continuing in government. The lesson from the PDs is that smaller parties should not be in government for too long. It is a difficult decision to make, but successive terms in office damage a smaller party. Maintaining difference from the larger party in government is never easy, and that becomes even more difficult over time.

For the PDs the 2007 general election result was, in part, evidence of this situation. Going back into government in 2007, for a third successive term but in a weakened state, only put the party's future in jeopardy. The PDs needed to adapt their message to the economic boom. That is never easy while in government. And when in government it is never easy to voluntarily and strategically decide to pull out, before the electorate makes that decision for you. The PD message after 2002 should have been about reining in public spending and getting value for every euro spent. But that became hugely difficult when the two PD ministers headed departments that demanded more money. Money was being lavishly spent all over the place. The PDs had always been defined by the economy, by economic policy. That was the message for the voters; and, with hindsight, the party should have stayed principally concentrated on the economy.

The history of the PDs shows that the party was at its strongest electorally when we campaigned as an independent party. In 1987, 1992 and 2002 the party declined to sign up to pre-election pacts with either Fianna Fáil or Fine Gael, and in each of those three contests it had a very good return. In 1989 with Fine Gael and 1997 with Fianna Fáil, transfer and policy arrangements only blurred the voters' perception of what the PDs stood for. The 2007 general election was an exception, when the party was damaged by its association in coalition with Bertie Ahern.

By September 2006 Michael McDowell had replaced Mary Harney as PD leader. I believe Harney was an outstanding national politician and, in my view, the outstanding woman politician since the foundation of the state. Throughout his career in public life McDowell too made an enormous contribution, not just to the PDs but also to Irish politics. He was hugely able and had a tremendous influence on the PDs' economic policies. We all contributed to the formulation of policy but McDowell was the best at articulating the party's positions. But for all his ability McDowell was always a bit of a maverick. He had an unpredictable nature, at times a great team player but at others a loner.

He took over from Mary Harney at a difficult time. The revelations about Ahern and ethics were just emerging into the public arena. From the initial evidence it was obvious that Ahern had been up to no good. Perhaps the PDs should have left the Government immediately, but the party opted to accept Ahern's explanation. His evidence at the Mahon Tribunal would undermine that explanation and revive memories of the behaviour of Haughey and his supporters in the late 1980s. By the time Ahern gave his tribunal evidence the PDs had been torn asunder. The May 2007 general election was a disaster for the party. By teatime on the day of the count it was clear that many senior party figures, including Liz O'Donnell and Michael McDowell, would lose their seats. My daughter Fiona was also in trouble in Dún Laoghaire.

I watched on television when Michael McDowell resigned as party leader. I was almost sick when I heard him announce his resignation. He walked out of politics while party candidates were still fighting for seats. I just couldn't believe what he did. He was foolish enough to allow himself to be provoked by a crowd of Provos. They were delighted that he had lost his seat. He should have walked on and said nothing.

I had very good personal and professional relations with McDowell, though sometimes he reacted in ways that wouldn't have been expected. One of those occasions was unfortunately on that election night. I knew the party was finished as I watched the television coverage from the count centre in the RDS. When McDowell resigned, that was the end of the PDS.

It was a very sad ending. The pity is that in the post-2011 period it became clear that the country needed a party with the basic principles of the PDS. There is still very much an opening. But one of the barriers to setting up a new party is money.

The rules on financing political parties are a crippling impediment. They are a response to the corruption revelations in the 1990s, but the legislative and regulatory reaction went overboard. We now have an anti-democratic situation. New parties face an uphill task. It may be very difficult to overcome.

———

Looking back over my political career, I recognise that I didn't always follow a conventional path. I was most content when Jack Lynch was leader of Fianna Fáil. I did my best to make a contribution in whatever role I served, from backbench TD to Government minister to party leader. I had all kinds of ambitions as Minister for Justice to introduce endless reforms, which I was profoundly interested in at that time. But most of the resources of the department, and certainly all my time as minister, were devoted to security matters. I felt like a fireman trying to put out fires rather than being constructive—although if some of those fires had been allowed to burn the consequences would have been horrendous.

One of the lasting personal consequences of my time as Minister for Justice was the hostility it created towards me from the press and from some political colleagues. The criticism was unrelenting and vicious. It was only when I was appointed Minister for Industry and Commerce in 1977 that I had my first real opportunity to pursue positive and constructive policies, and remain away from continuous criticism. But many relationships had been soured by that time and remained so permanently.

I have no regrets that I did not become Taoiseach. In the Fianna Fáil of the eighties I would not have survived long anyway. There is a need in public life for people to say uncomfortable words and to ask awkward questions. To have remained silent would not have served the public interest. There is nothing wrong in saying that any achievement I had was in preventing certain things from happening that otherwise would have happened.

Throughout it all, Pat put up with the absences and the threats. I could never have achieved whatever I did without her wholehearted support and devotion.

INDEX